PARTISAN POLITICS IN THE GLOBAL ECONOMY

Geoffrey Garrett challenges the conventional wisdom about the domestic effects of the globalization of markets in the industrial democracies: the erosion of national autonomy and the demise of leftist alternatives to the free market. He demonstrates that globalization has, in important respects, strengthened the relationship between the political power of the left and organized labor, on the one hand, and economic policies that reduce market-generated inequalities of risk and wealth, on the other. Moreover, macroeconomic outcomes in the era of global markets have been as good or better in strong-left-labor regimes ("social democratic corporatism") as in other industrial countries. Pessimistic visions of the inexorable dominance of capital over labor or radical autarkic and nationalist backlashes against markets are significantly overstated. Electoral politics have not been dwarfed by market dynamics as social forces and globalized markets have not rendered immutable the efficiency–equality trade-off. The findings in this book should hearten advocates of social democracy throughout the world.

Geoffrey Garrett is Professor of Political Science at Yale University. He has published over thirty articles on numerous aspects of the political economy of the industrialized democracies in scholarly journals, including the *American Political Science Review, International Organization, World Politics, Comparative Political Studies, International Journal of Law and Economics*, and the *Journal of Politics*. In addition to the domestic consequences of globalization, his current research focuses on the institutional structure of the European Union, the impact of labor market institutions, constitutional structures and central banking arrangements on economic policy and macroeconomic performance, and the political economy of federalism.

CAMBRIDGE STUDIES IN COMPARATIVE POLITICS

General Editor

PETER LANGE   Duke University

Associate Editors

ROBERT H. BATES   Harvard University
ELLEN COMISSO   University of California, San Diego
PETER HALL   Harvard University
JOEL MIGDAL   University of Washington
HELEN MILNER   Columbia University
RONALD ROGOWSKI   University of California, Los Angeles
SIDNEY TARROW   Cornell University

OTHER BOOKS IN THE SERIES

PARTISAN POLITICS IN THE GLOBAL ECONOMY

GEOFFREY GARRETT

CAMBRIDGE
UNIVERSITY PRESS

PUBLISHED BY THE PRESS SYNDICATE OF THE UNIVERSITY OF CAMBRIDGE
The Pitt Building, Trumpington Street, Cambridge, United Kingdom

CAMBRIDGE UNIVERSITY PRESS
The Edinburgh Building, Cambridge CB2 2RU, UK   http: //www.cup.cam.ac.uk
40 West 20th Street, New York, NY 10011-4211, USA   http: //www.cup.org
10 Stamford Road, Oakleigh, Melbourne 3166, Australia

First published 1998
Reprinted 1999

Printed in the United States of America

Typeset in Garamond #3 10·5/12 point

A catalogue record for this book is available from the British Library

Garrett, Geoffrey, 1958–
Partisan politics in the global economy / Geoffrey Garrett.
   p. cm. – (Cambridge studies in comparative politics)
Includes bibliographical references and index.
1. Economic history – 1971–1990. 2. Economic history – 1990–
3. Free enterprise. 4. Economic security. 5. Economic policy.
6. Socialism. 7. Corporate state.   1. Title. II. Series.
HC59.G347 1998   97–16731
338.9 – DC21   CIP

ISBN 0 521 44154 4 hardback
ISBN 0 521 44690 2 paperback

For Sally

CONTENTS

TABLES AND FIGURES

TABLES

FIGURES

PREFACE

This book has taken me altogether too long to write. I started thinking about partisan politics and the economy fifteen years ago, when it was being established by political scientists and sociologists that social democratic corporatist countries had weathered the economic storms of the 1970s better than the other industrial democracies, with lower inflation and lower unemployment rates. But just as this argument was beginning to gain broader acceptance, the world seemed to change. The conventional wisdom about the 1980s and 1990s is that social democratic corporatism has become a luxury that cannot be afforded in the new epoch of global markets. The left and organized labor can only remain viable if they accept that competing in global markets necessitates growing material inequality and "market friendly" government. Thus, the logic of the market has come to dominate the power conferred on the less well off at the ballot box, and the political economy models based on them.

The following pages are the product of my struggles with the challenges posed by globalization and the viability of social democratic responses to it. I am far less pessimistic about the future than are most people. I contend that social democratic corporatism came through the 1980s more or less unscathed by the forces of market integration and that one should be reticent to conclude differently about the 1990s because of the highly idiosyncratic nature of the decade in Europe. The left and organized labor today no doubt confront important problems, but these are by and large not the product of globalization. Moreover, I think there are solutions to these problems that do not violate the fundamental objective of social democracy: to reduce material inequality without undermining economic efficiency.

The foundations of this book were built while I was a graduate student at Duke University. The initial empirical work was done while I was teaching at University College, Oxford. The original draft of the book manuscript was written after I joined the Department of Political Science at Stanford University. I worked on subsequent iterations during fellowships at the Wissenschaftszentrum, Berlin; the Center for Advanced Study in the Behavioral Sciences, Stanford; the Hoover Institution, Stanford; and the Public Policy Program and the Research School of the Social Sciences, the Australian National University, Canberra. The final version of the manuscript was completed at the Wharton School of the University of Pennsylvania. I would like to thank all of these institutions for providing wonderful environments in which to live and work. Additional financial support for which I am very grateful was provided by the Center for International Studies, Duke University; the Institute for International Studies, Stanford University; the National Science Foundation through its grant to the Center for Advanced Study in Behavioral Sciences; and the Reginald H. Jones Center at the Wharton School.

Over the years, my thinking about the political economy of capitalist democracy has been greatly influenced by many people. I would like to acknowledge the insights of the following people: John Aldrich, Nigel Boyle, Francis Castles, John Ferejohn, Jeffrey Frankel, John Freeman, Judith Goldstein, Stephan Haggard, Alexander Hicks, Robert Inman, Mark Kesselman, Stephen Kobrin, Bruce Kogut, Paul Pierson, Douglas Rivers, Dani Rodrik, Thomas Romer, Bo Rothstein, John Stephens, Robert Wade, and John Zysman. I gratefully acknowledge the invaluable research assistance of Cuneyt Ates, Alexander Shevelenko, Clifford Carrubba, Brian Gaines, and Lisa Taber. Herbert Gilbert was a wonderful copy editor.

I have used numerous published data sources in the book, but I would like especially to thank three people who gave me access to data sets before they had been published. Thomas Cusack graciously shared his political economy database with me, and I would also like to thank Tom for working with me on facets of the argument presented in this book. Andrew Rose allowed me to use his data on government restrictions on capital movements. Duane Swank gave me access to his extensive databases on the political economy of the OFCD and has also been a kindred spirit for much of my research. I would like to thank Deborah Mitchell and Christopher Way as well. Both have been wonderful collaborators on issues in the book. Larry Bartels suggested a way to present the results of my interaction regression equations, which I had not thought of. I would particularly like to thank Michael Alvarez, Jonas Pontusson, James Robinson, and George Tsebelis for reading "close-to-final" drafts (and for giving me excellent suggestions for yet more revisions).

I have had the privilege of working in two research communities that have profoundly influenced this book. The first comprises people working on the politics of labor and business in the industrial countries, most notably Miriam Golden, Peter Hall, Torben Iversen, David Soskice, Peter Swenson, and Michael Wallerstein. The second group comprises political economists working on the domestic effects of international economic integration – particularly Barry Eichengreen, Jeffrey Frieden, Robert Keohane, Helen Milner, and Ronald Rogowski.

My greatest academic debt is to Peter Lange. Peter introduced me to the world of political economy. We have collaborated for more than a decade on the relations between the market and political institutions. Peter has shepherded me through this project from first-year graduate teacher to book editor. Above all, Peter has always been a wonderful friend.

Sally Gibbons agreed to become my wife in the chaotic period when I was trying to finish a "next-to-last" iteration of the manuscript. Sally's superb editorial skills have greatly improved my prose and the clarity of my arguments in the first and last chapters. But these contributions are dwarfed by the importance to me of her love and of our life together. It is my greatest pleasure to dedicate this book to her.

INTRODUCTION

Throughout the world today, politics lags behind economics, like a horse and buggy haplessly trailing a sports car. While politicians go through the motions of national elections – offering chimerical programs and slogans – world markets, the Internet and the furious pace of trade involve people in a global game in which elected representatives figure as little more than bit players. Hence the prevailing sense, in America and Europe, that politicians and ideologies are either uninteresting or irrelevant
> —ROGER COHEN, "GLOBAL FORCES BATTER POLITICS," *THE NEW YORK TIMES WEEK IN REVIEW*, NOVEMBER 17, 1996, PAGE 1.

This book challenges the conventional wisdom about the effects of globalization on domestic politics in the industrial democracies. There is a glut of research claiming that the international integration of markets in goods, services, and above all capital has eroded national autonomy and, in particular, all but vitiated social democratic alternatives to the free market. In contrast, I argue that the relationship between the political power of the left and economic policies that reduce market-generated inequalities has not been weakened by globalization; indeed, it has been strengthened in important respects. Furthermore, macroeconomic outcomes in the era of global markets have been as good or better in countries where powerful left-wing parties are allied with broad and centrally organized labor movements ("social democratic corporatism") as they have where the left and labor are weaker.

These findings have broader implications for the relationship between democracy and capitalism in the contemporary period. People who propose dire scenarios based on visions either of the inexorable dominance of capital over labor or of radical autarkic and nationalist backlashes against markets overlook the ongoing history of social democratic corporatism. There is more than one path to competing successfully in the global economy. The impact of electoral politics has not been dwarfed by market dynamics. Globalized markets have not rendered immutable the efficiency–equality trade-off. These lessons from the industrial democracies should hearten advocates of social democracy throughout the world.

The conventional wisdom about the globalization of markets claims that the ever-increasing capacity of firms and investors to move production and capital around the world has precipitated a sea change away from the halcyon days of the postwar mixed economy.[1] In this new environment of deep trade interdependence, multinational production regimes and global capital markets, government attempts to intervene in the economy are thought to be doomed to fail if they extend beyond minimal "market friendly" measures.[2] The lesson for all governments is supposedly clear: The imperatives of the market impose heavy constraints on the bounds of democratic choice. Good government is market friendly government, and this effectively rules out most of the "welfare state" policies that the left labored long and hard to establish in the forty years following the Depression.

From this perspective, the age-old debate about the relative power of the capitalist economy and the democratic polity as social forces has been definitively settled in capital's favor. From the Depression until the 1970s, it was widely argued that government could (and should) intervene in the economy to reduce inequality without adversely affecting the macroeconomy. In the contemporary era of global markets, however, the trade-off between efficiency and welfare is considered to be harsh and direct. Even left-wing governments that would like to use the policy instruments of the state to redistribute wealth and risk in favor of the less fortunate have no choice but to bow to the demands of the market.

My portrayal of the globalization thesis is anything but a straw man. Consider the following gloomy predictions from recent and influential scholarly research on the future of social democracy. Paulette Kurzer (1993: 252) concludes:

[T]his book does not hold great promise for social democracy. . . . [L]eft-wing parties will continue to seek election and occasionally win power. However, these parties have little in common with their predecessors in terms of articulating progressive options and pursuing programs different from the conservative, or establishment view. . . . In the past decade, growth has been sluggish, and investments have stagnated. Unemployment and declining wages marked the 1980s. Governments could combat such situations by spending money on public programs, increasing public employment, or raising social transfer payments, but no governments can afford to do this today.

Fritz Scharpf's (1991: 274–275) bottom line is very similar:

> Unlike the situation in the first three postwar decades, there is now no economically plausible Keynesian strategy that would permit the full realization of social democratic goals within a national context without violating the functional imperatives of the capitalist economy. Full employment, rising real wages, larger welfare transfers, and more and better public services can no longer all be had simultaneously. . . . For the foreseeable future . . . social democracy has a chance to influence economic policy only if it explicitly accepts the full harshness of world economic conditions and hence the constraints on domestic policy options.

The globalization thesis can, of course, be taken much further than claims about the demise of social democracy. Some have pointed to the rise of xenophobic nationalism as a profoundly destabilizing consequence of globalization. For example, Ethan Kapstein (1996: 37) argues that there are disturbing similarities between the 1990s and the 1930s:

> While the world stands at a critical time in postwar history, it has a group of leaders who appear unwilling, like their predecessors in the 1930s, to provide the international leadership to meet economic dislocations. . . . Like the German elite in Weimar, they dismiss mounting worker dissatisfaction, fringe political movements, and the plight of the unemployed and working poor as marginal concerns compared with the unquestioned importance of a sound currency and balanced budget. Leaders need to recognize the policy failures of the last 20 years and respond accordingly. If they do not, there are others waiting in the wings who will, perhaps on less pleasant terms.

Others argue that the nation-state itself, irrespective of how it is governed, is a dinosaur that is very poorly adapted to the global economy. Management theorist Kenichi Ohmae's (1995: 79) description of the anachronistic and embattled nation state provides a vivid portrayal of this view:

> [T]he glue holding traditional nation states together, at least in economic terms, has begun to dissolve. Buffeted by sudden changes in industry dynamics, available information, consumer preferences, and flows of capital; burdened by demands for the civil minimum and for open-ended industrial subsidies in the name of the national interest; and hog-tied by political systems that prove ever-less responsive to new challenges, these political aggregations no longer make compelling sense as discrete, meaningful units on an up-to-date map of economic activity.

In this book, I challenge the reasoning and conclusions that underpin all of these studies and many others like them.[3] I do not wish to argue that analysts have exaggerated the extent to which goods, services, and capital markets are internationally integrated today. Others have made this case, but it is not necessary for my argument.[4] Rather, I argue that existing studies have significantly underestimated the effects of domestic political conditions both on the way governments react to globalization and on their impact on the national economy. Posed in its starkest terms, my argument is that there remains a leftist alternative to free market capitalism in the era of global markets based on classic "big government" and corporatist principles that is viable both politically (in terms of winning elections) and economically (by promoting strong macroeconomic performance).

The first element of this argument concerns domestic political dynamics. Proponents of the globalization thesis focus almost exclusively on the increased "exit" threats of mobile asset holders. Despite and because of the reality of this phenomenon, market integration has also increased demands on government ("voice") to mitigate the insecurities, instabilities and inequalities it has generated. As Robert Keohane and Joseph Nye (1977) argued twenty years ago, globalization heightens the vulnerability of countries to the international economy – in terms of both the portion of society subject to global competition and the speed with which changes in market conditions are transmitted across borders. Even the OECD (1996: 7–11) is well aware of this relationship:

> Reduced wage and employment security has extended to sectors and population segments that have been historically considered "safe", such as public sector employees and executive and managerial workers. In all countries the nature of employment is changing, with an increasing share of total employment accounted for by part-time work and temporary contracts . . . the share of involuntary part-time employment has been increasing in almost all countries.

These conditions have proved fertile ground for left-wing parties and for economic policies that ameliorate market-generated inequality and risk. Some conservative parties – notably in the Anglo-American countries – have chosen not to cultivate voters who benefit from government efforts to mitigate the dislocations of globalization. But most left-of-center parties have concentrated their efforts on this constituency.[5]

The consequences of government efforts to compensate short-term market losers, however, are not necessarily benign. Indeed, most people would argue that they are bad for competitiveness and can only result in greater capital flight. Dani Rodrik (1997) makes this argument eloquently. He contends that the twin domestic consequences of globalization – increased exit options for mobile asset holders ("footloose capital") and increased voice among the less mobile (most citizens) for policies that cushion market forces – may be on a collision course that will do great harm to all. According to Rodrik (1997: 6–7):

> [T]he cumulative consequence of (globalization) will be the solidifying of a new set of class divisions – between those who prosper in the globalized economy and those who do not; between those who share its values and those who would rather not; and between those who can diversify away its risks and those who cannot. This is not a pleasing prospect even for the

individuals on the winning side of the divide with little empathy for the
other side. Social disintegration is not a spectator sport – those on the
sidelines also get splashed with mud from the field. Ultimately, the deep-
ening of social fissures can harm all.

The second element of my argument is that social democratic corporatism
provides a way to avoid this collision course. Rodrik's argument makes explicit
the common perception that government policies reducing inequality and social
risk are antithetical to the interests of mobile asset holders. This view contends
that whenever footloose capital sees powerful left-wing parties, strong labor market institutions, and interventionist big government, it will exercise its exit
options. Not only will this make it increasingly difficult for government to tax
business to fund its spending objective, but capital flight will also deal a body
blow to economic performance.

There are numerous reasons to be skeptical of this argument. One, ultimately
limited, reason follows from "new growth" theory. In recent years, many economists have argued that the ambit of market friendly government should be
broadened to include policies that produce growth-enhancing collective goods
undersupplied by the market. The clearest example of such goods is public education and training, but the label can also be applied to physical infrastructure.
These collective goods are not only beneficial to citizens in terms of jobs and
improving future life chances; they are also attractive to capital in terms of increasing investment returns. There are nonetheless clear limits to the types of
government policies sanctioned by new growth theory. Most government spending, for example, is considered unproductive.[6]

Indeed, it would be very hard to make the case that income transfer programs
or in-kind benefits for the unemployed, the sick, or the old are "good for growth"
in a direct sense. But this is precisely the argument I wish to make by taking a
broad view of the positive externalities of big government. I contend that the
types of redistributive economic policies associated with strong left-wing parties
are compatible with strong economic performance in the global economy, provided labor market institutions are sufficiently "encompassing" (Olson 1982) to
facilitate collective action among the bulk of the workforce.[7]

Social democratic corporatist regimes are based on a virtuous circle in which
government policies that cushion market dislocations are exchanged for the regulation of the national labor market by the leaders of encompassing trade union
movements. The products of this virtuous circle include predictable patterns of
wage setting that restrain real wage growth in accordance with productivity and
competitiveness constraints, highly skilled and productive workers, cooperation
between labor and business in the work place, and low levels of social strife more
generally. These economic "goods" are attractive even to mobile asset holders in
the volatile global economy, offsetting the disincentives to investment generated
by big government and high labor costs highlighted by neoclassical economics.

I thus contend that there is no good reason to believe that in the global economy, capital flight will be the knee-jerk response of mobile asset holders to social democratic corporatism.

This doesn't mean, of course, that contemporary social democratic corporatism doesn't face important challenges. For example, the graying of society in the context of generous public health and pension entitlements to retirees and the power of public sector trade unions are both significant problems that must be confronted. But there are solutions to these problems that do not violate the fundamental tenets of social democracy. More importantly for my purposes, these challenges have very little to do with globalization. Rather, they are better thought of as inherent products of the success of the social democratic project in the postwar period.

My primary claim is that globalization and national autonomy are not mutually exclusive options. The benefits of globalization can be reaped without undermining the economic sovereignty of nations, and without reducing the ability of citizens to choose how to distribute the benefits – and the costs – of the market. The experience of the social democratic corporatist countries should provide succor, not spawn regret, among advocates of social democracy as an equitable and efficient means for reconciling markets and democracy.

1.1   THE ARGUMENT

The dominant view about the domestic effects of globalization accords a *deus ex machina* quality to market forces. If business occupies (in Charles Lindblom's (1977) famous terms) a "privileged position" in all capitalist economies, its position is even stronger where markets are global but politics is national. Capital can simply choose to exit the national economy if government pursues policies that business people disapprove of. The rubric of bad economic policies is presumed to cover all market "distortions," including government spending on goods and services that could be provided more efficiently by the market, and taxes to pay for them that treat different income sources unequally.

The notion that mobile asset holders in the industrial democracies today have credible exit threats is indisputable. Many firms have production regimes that cross national boundaries, and strategic alliances are increasingly common. The growth of international portfolio investment in equity, bond, and currency markets has been explosive in the past twenty years. Do these developments represent the death knell of social democracy? The conventional wisdom makes two implicit assumptions about the political economy of capitalist democracy. First, the state of the macroeconomy is considered the primary – if not the sole – determinant of a government's prospects for reelection. Second, government interventions in the economy beyond explicitly capital friendly measures precipitate downward spirals in economic performance. When combined with capital's exit options, these two assumptions lead to the conclusion that social democracy is incompatible with global markets.

I argue in Chapter 2 that both of these assumptions are inappropriate. There is ample evidence that macroeconomic outcomes significantly influence elections. But presiding over an expanding pie is not the only path to electoral success. Political parties can also attract support by distributing the social pie in ways that favor certain groups over others. Indeed, the short-term nature of democratic politics creates a bias in favor of distributional strategies: Governments cannot afford to do what is good for the economy in the long run if this immediately hurts their core electoral constituencies (Garrett and Lange 1995).

The most important distributional cleavage in the industrial democracies has long been between those who support the market allocation of wealth and risk – the natural constituency of right-wing parties – and those who favor government efforts to alter market outcomes – the left's core base of support. The welfare state – broadly construed to include not only income transfer programs such as unemployment insurance and public pensions but also the provision of social services such as education and health – is the basic policy instrument for redistribution. Left-wing and centrist Christian democratic parties have long been more willing to expand the welfare state than their counterparts on the right. Some have claimed that the electoral appeal of the welfare state has declined apace with the shrinking of the manufacturing working class (Piven 1991; Kitschelt 1994). But even in the Anglo-American democracies, popular support for the welfare state grew at the same time as the traditional working class shrank (Pierson 1994, 1996). Broader cross-national surveys of public opinion also show that public support for the welfare state continues to be very strong in most countries (Ploug 1996).

The key to understanding the popularity of welfare programs in the global economy is recognizing that although market integration may benefit all segments of society in the longer run through the more efficient allocation of production and investment, the short-term effects of globalization are very different. Indeed, perhaps the most important immediate effect of globalization is to increase social dislocations and economic insecurity, as the distribution of incomes and jobs across firms and industries becomes increasingly unstable. The result is that increasing numbers of people have to spend evermore time and money trying to make their future more secure. Whatever the portion of the labor force that is directly affected by market dislocations, perceptions of growing economic insecurity will always be considerably more widespread. In the contemporary period, this constituency obviously extends well beyond the traditional manufacturing working class.

Given this nexus between globalization and economic insecurity, it is not surprising that government policies that cushion market dislocations by redistributing wealth and risk are at least as popular today as they have ever been. This does not mean that parties across the political spectrum will choose to expand the welfare state; ideological concerns will also play a role. Nonetheless, globalization has provided new and fertile ground for the social democratic agenda (and for more populist and xenophobic appeals for economic closure).

Critics might accept this part of my argument but dismiss it as irrelevant, claiming that the political incentives to pursue interventionist economic policies are overwhelmed by the macroeconomic costs of doing so in the global economy. If such policies only lead to disinvestment and recession, even voters who benefit in the short term from a large public economy will ultimately abandon governments that preside over its expansion. From this perspective, it is only a question of when, not whether, the left bows to the power of the market.

Careful analysis of the evidence about the macroeconomic consequences of big government, however, prompts more caution and less dogmatism. Joel Slemrod (1995) concludes in an exhaustive review of the empirical literature, for example, that there is no overall nor consistent relationship between the size of government and rates of economic growth. In a similar study on unemployment, Charles Bean (1994) argues that there is no clear link between government-generated rigidities in labor markets and rising unemployment in the industrial countries since the early 1980s.[8]

The underlying message of these studies is that although it is easy to point to specific costs of discrete interventionist policies, big government seems to produce positive externalities that are overlooked by its critics. These externalities may take two forms. The first is quite specific and relates to new growth theory. Many economists now believe that government investments in infrastructure – from bridges and roads to research and development to education and training – are beneficial to the economy Thus, government spending on human and physical capital is unlikely to provoke capital flight in global markets.

The second type of externality generated by big government is more general. It is also central to claims about the economic efficacy of social democratic corporatism. Where powerful left parties are allied with encompassing labor movements, policies that redistribute market allocations of wealth and risk are unlikely to provoke capital flight among mobile asset holders.[9]

Consider the following hypothetical example of a left-wing government's decision to increase the duration of unemployment benefits. Even economists who argue that appropriately constructed unemployment insurance schemes are desirable look dimly on increasing the duration of benefits.[10] The wages acceptable to those in employment, and especially those organized into trade unions, increase with declines in the material costs of unemployment. The government must borrow money or raise taxes to fund its new scheme. Thus, increasing the duration of benefits must slow output growth and job creation.

The flaw in this logic is that it ignores the impact of labor market institutions on the behavior of workers. I argue that where national labor market institutions are sufficiently encompassing to overcome labor's collective action problem, the benefits of leftist policies that mitigate the distributional asymmetries inherent in the market allocation of resources and risk offset the costs highlighted by the neoclassical perspective. In contrast, interventionist economic policies are likely to have deleterious macroeconomic consequences where labor movements are not encompassing, precisely because isolated groups of workers can be expected to take advantage of reduced market constraints to push up their wages.

In the scenario outlined above, the government's enhanced unemployment insurance policy helps all those at risk in the labor market. The direct effect of this policy reform is that the threat of unemployment is now less disciplining on the labor market, which could be detrimental to overall economic performance. Those currently in work could push up their wages, reducing demand for the currently unemployed. The result of this "insider–outsider" problem would be higher inflation and higher unemployment (Saint-Paul 1996).

The leaders of encompassing labor movements, however, care about the welfare of the whole labor force, and they have the institutional clout to ensure that the behavior of certain groups of workers does not reduce the welfare of others. In my example, labor leaders have both the incentive and the capacity to mitigate the insider–outsider problem. They appreciate that the best path to increasing total employment at the highest possible level of disposable incomes (both wages and work-related benefits) is to constrain wage growth among those currently employed in accordance with productivity improvements. In so doing, labor as a whole can reap the benefits of the government's policy without incurring the costs that it might otherwise generate.

This argument can be made more general. Indeed, it is at the core of the vast literature on social democratic corporatism.[11] All government programs that alter the market allocation of wealth and risk in favor of labor should prompt the leaders of encompassing organizations to "internalize" the costs of decentralized militancy for the economy as a whole. In addition to upward pressures on wages, these externalities comprise all types of inefficiency and instability associated with groups of workers who have the organizational capacity to voice effectively their grievances. These range from the threat of strikes to unwillingness to cooperate with management at the workplace to more general social agitation.

The combination of left government and encompassing labor market institutions reduces these sources of inefficiency and instability. In turn, the strategic decisions of mobile asset holders will be affected not only by the direct costs of social democratic corporatism – a bigger public economy and higher total labor costs – but also by the benefits – higher productivity and economic, political, and social stability. A price must be paid for these desirable outcomes, but the return is considerable. There is thus no good a priori reason to think that mobile asset holders will choose to exit from social democratic corporatist regimes.

Let me now summarize the structure of the argument. I have suggested that the "class compromise" of capitalist democracy – in which asset holders accept redistributive government policies and governments accept the primacy of market mechanisms – is at least as important in the global economy as it has ever been.[12] Globalization increases the potential long-run social benefits of markets, but it also heightens political opposition to them in the short-run. Governments face the daunting task of reconciling these two forces. Where the left is allied with encompassing labor markets, it is possible to reap the benefits of market integration without increasing the risk of damaging popular backlashes in the form of economic, political and social instability. Farsighted capital can be expected to understand the upside of social democratic corporatism and hence to forego the temptation to use the threat or reality of exit.

The general orientation of this book is not new. Indeed, many will recognize its resemblance to Peter Katzenstein's (1985) depiction of the small European democracies and to John Gerard Ruggie's (1983) notion of "embedded liberalism", both of which draw inspiration from Karl Polanyi (1944). My work extends these analyses in at least two ways.

First, existing research on the viability of interventionist government and social democratic corporatism is concerned almost exclusively with the domestic effects of exposure to trade. In contrast, I examine the consequences of capital mobility as well as trade. This is critical given that the globalization of finance is the defining characteristic of the contemporary world economy and the primary motivation for the recent wave of work proclaiming the demise of social democracy. Indeed, Ruggie (1995) argues that the globalization of finance poses a grave threat to embedded liberalism.

Second, in this book I use the best available data and the most appropriate econometric techniques to test the empirical merits of my arguments about the relationships among globalization and domestic politics, policy, and performance. For too long, work by political scientists and sociologists on the viability of political economic regimes not based on neoclassical economics principles has been more or less ignored by professional economists and policy makers. If one reason for this neglect has been differences in methodology, I hope this book will help bridge the divides between the different social science disciplines.

1.2   THE EVIDENCE

The empirical core of this book can be distilled into three basic propositions about the interrelationships among globalization, partisan politics, and the economy that track the progression of the theoretical argument:

- Globalization has generated new political constituencies for left-of-center parties among the increasing ranks of the economically insecure that offset the shrinking of the manufacturing working class. As a result, enduring cross-national differences in the balance of power between left and right remain. So, too, do marked differences in labor market institutions.

- Globalization has increased the political incentives for left-wing parties to pursue economic policies that redistribute wealth and risk in favor of those adversely affected in the short term by market dislocations, especially in countries where organized labor is also strong. Thus, the historical relationship between left-labor power and big government has not weakened with market integration.

- Globalization has increased the importance of economic, political and social stability to the investment decisions of mobile asset holders. Because the combination of powerful left-wing parties and encompassing labor market institutions promotes stability in the wage-setting process and in society more generally, macroeconomic performance under social democratic corporatism has been as good as – if not better than – that under any other constellation of political power and labor market institutions.

The remainder of this chapter summarizes the evidence using simple descriptive statistics and bivariate correlations for fourteen industrial democracies – Austria, Belgium, Canada, Denmark, Finland, France, Germany, Italy, Japan, the Netherlands, Norway, Sweden, the United Kingdom, and the United States – over the period from 1966 until 1990. More thorough empirical tests based on multivariate panel regressions are undertaken in Chapters 3, 4, and 5.[13] Chapter 6 brings the empirical record up to the middle of the 1990s, but data limitations mean that the analysis in that chapter is more rudimentary than those for the preceding twenty-five years.

THE POWER OF THE LEFT AND ORGANIZED LABOR

Chapter 3 documents the increasing integration of markets among the advanced industrial economies and analyzes its impact on the partisan balance of political power and the organizational structure of national labor market institutions. Exposure to trade and capital mobility increased more or less consistently from the mid 1960s to 1990, but this did not precipitate any clear shift in the balance of political power to the right. Nor did globalization lead to a weakening across the board of the structural power of labor market institutions. Indeed, the marked historical differences among countries in terms of left-labor power were largely unaffected by globalization.

Table 1.1 presents summary data for the political power of left-wing parties in the 1980s and relative to the preceding fifteen years. Power is measured in terms both of participation in cabinet governments and of seats in the lower house of national legislatures. Because the composition of governments can

Table 1.1. *The Political Power of Left-Wing Parties*[a]

Country[b]	Percentage of cabinet portfolios		Percentage of legislative seats[c]	
	Average (1980–1990)	Change[d]	Average (1980–1990)	Change
Sweden	75	-2	52	1
Austria	74	4	50	1
France	57	57	54	25
Norway	49	-7	48	-1
Finland	45	-4	41	-7
Denmark	25	-38	46	1
Italy	24	13	44	2
Belgium	19	-7	33	2
Germany	19	-45	45	1
Netherlands	8	-9	37	1
Canada	0	0	12	4
Japan	0	0	31	-2
United Kingdom	0	-69	36	-15
United States	0	0	0	0
Average	28	-8	38	1

[a]Definitions of left parties based on Castles and Mair [1984]
[b]Ranked by cabinet portfolios 1980–1990
[c]The lower house in bicameral legislatures
[d]1980–1990 minus 1966–1979
Source: Swank [1995]

change dramatically without corresponding movements in the composition of legislatures, the cabinet measure is likely to be much more volatile than the legislative indicator.

There are few surprises in the rank orderings for the 1980s. The strongest left-wing parties were found in the Nordic countries and Austria. In all of these countries except Denmark (where the social democrats lost control of government), left parties continued to hold more than 40 percent of cabinet portfolios – more than enough to have a powerful voice in government. In contrast, Mitterrand's electoral successes moved France (a country in which left-wing parties had historically been weak) into the upper echelons of social democratic power in the 1980s. Turning to the bottom of the league table, social democratic parties were completely excluded from government in Canada, Japan, the United Kingdom, and the United States.[14] Only in the case of Thatcher's Britain was this a departure from the previous period. Finally, three countries in the middle of the table – Belgium, Italy, and the Netherlands – occupied broadly similar positions throughout the 1966–1990 period.

The fact that the direction of change was to the right in three of the four cases in which the balance of government power shifted dramatically in the 1980s might explain why it is so often argued that the political power of the left has decreased with globalization. But it would be an exaggeration to characterize this as a "pervasive" trend. Moreover, the data on leftist representation in national legislatures provide less support for the conventional view. In the 1980s, left parties held more than 40 percent of legislative seats in eight of the fourteen countries in this study, including both Denmark and Germany where coalition dynamics greatly reduced the left's governmental power. Only in Canada and the United States did left-wing parties hold less than 30 percent of legislative seats. Furthermore, the United Kingdom was the sole case in which the left's legislative position weakened substantially from the 1970s to the 1980s.

Thus, only recent British political history is consistent with the view that market integration inevitably must swing the balance of political power to the right. Of course, this case is counterbalanced by the Mitterrand era in France where the left's rise to power was equally dramatic. It is not my intention to analyze the sources of political change in these countries nor cases where the balance of power was more stable. Rather, I simply suggest that it would require a vivid imagination to argue that market integration undermined the political power of the left. The general picture in the industrial democracies has been one of great stability in individual countries and marked differences across them.

Turning to the power of organized labor, most empirical work tries to measure two facets of encompassment: the portion of the workforce that is governed by labor market institutions and the concentration of authority within them. The simplest measure for the scope of labor market institutions is union density (the proportion of unionized employees in the workforce). The number of separate unions that organize workers is a basic indicator of the concentration of authority (Golden 1993). The higher is union density and the smaller the number of unions, the greater the propensity for collective action in national labor market institutions.

These basic indicators of encompassment are reported in Table 1.2. Because the number of unions is only available at five-year intervals beginning in 1970, I have used this year and 1990 to assess the effects of globalization. The attributes of national labor market institutions are presented according to the rank order of the standardized sum of the portion of cabinet portfolios and legislative seats held by left parties in the 1980s because my theoretical argument centers on the coherence of political and organizational conditions. Two things stand out about the data.

First, two decades of rapid market integration did not result in a significant diminution of the structural bases of union power. Average union density in the

Table 1.2. *The Encompassment of Labor Market Institutions*

Country[a]	Trade union membership[b]		Number of unions[c]	
	1990	Change[d]	1990	Change
Sweden	83	17	23	-6
Austria	46	-15	15	-1
France	10	-9	-	-
Norway	54	-2	29	-6
Finland	72	20	24	-7
Denmark	74	14	30	-15
Italy	34	1	20	-4
Germany	31	-2	16	0
Belgium	55	14	18	-1
Netherlands	23	-15	17	-3
United Kingdom	38	-7	76	-74
Japan	25	-8	81	-18
Canada	32	3	90	-20
United States	15	-13	91	-31
Average	42	-1	41	-14
Correlation with left power 1980–1990	.48		-.78	

[a]Ranked by the standardized sum of left power in cabinet
   governments and legislatures, 1980–1990
[b]Union membership/total labor force (%), Visser [1991]
[c]Number of unions affiliated with largest confederation [Golden and
   Wallerstein 1995]
[d]1990 minus 1970

fourteen countries only declined by one percentage point over the twenty years from 1970, whereas the average number of unions in the largest labor confederation shrank by fourteen (reducing the institutional obstacles to collective action). These numbers conceal considerable variations, however, in the trajectories of labor market institutions in different countries.

Union membership increased significantly from 1970 to 1990 in four countries where unemployment benefits are effectively distributed by trade unions – Belgium, Denmark, Finland, and Sweden. The most interesting case where union membership declined appreciably is Austria, long considered a bastion of corporatism. The impact of declining membership on the effective influence of labor market institutions in Austria, however, should not be overstated. This is because collective bargaining agreements are legally extended to virtually the entire Austrian labor force (Traxler 1994). Turning to the number of unions, although there was a pervasive trend toward consolidation in all countries, this was most apparent in countries with weak left parties in the 1980s (most notably the U.K.). Although this no doubt reflects an anti-union offensive, smaller numbers of unions nevertheless make it easier for labor leaders to organize effectively their members.

The second important point illustrated by the data in Table 1.2 is that left power was still strongly correlated with higher union density and with fewer trade unions. Countries at the top of the table thus generally constituted the regimes closest to the "social democratic corporatist" ideal type in the 1980s. The clear exception was France where organized labor was very weak and decentralized. Countries at the bottom of the table, in contrast, were the closest approximations of the "market liberalism" category – dominant center-right parties with very weak labor market institutions. The countries in the middle – and those whose placement on the left power and encompassment scales differed substantially – had more "incoherent" political economies.

Drawing lines among these categories is obviously a subjective matter. Nonetheless, it is clear that Austria and Sweden were the most social democratic corporatist regimes in the 1980s.[15] Analysts have traditionally also included Denmark, Finland, and Norway in the category, and Table 1.2 suggests that this was still appropriate in 1990. At the other extreme, the Anglo-American countries were the regimes closest to the market liberalism ideal type. In my definition, Japan must also be included in this category.[16] This leaves Belgium, France, Germany, Italy, and the Netherlands as more incoherent political economies in the 1980s. The French case is the most clear-cut example of an incoherent regime given the radical disjuncture between François Mitterrand's political power and the weakness of organized labor in France. Few would quibble with the inclusion of Belgium, Italy, and the Netherlands in this category as well. The placement of Germany is more difficult, but the dominance of Helmut Kohl's government after 1982 renders Germany incoherent in my framework.

Taken as a whole, the data in Tables 1.1 and 1.2 belie the widely accepted notion that the political power of left-wing parties and the structural strength of national labor market institutions were both undermined by globalization in the 1980s. Although conditions in the international economy changed dramatically, clear cross-national differences in domestic political economic regimes proved highly resilient. But this fact only prompts a further set of questions. Surely, most people would argue, the political success of the left in the 1980s came increasingly to depend on the abandonment of redistributive government, and the power of labor market institutions had dire consequences for the macroeconomy.

THE POLICY DISTINCTIVENESS OF SOCIAL DEMOCRATIC CORPORATISM

Chapter 4 shows that the historical relationship between left-labor power and big government strengthened with the globalization of markets. This is wholly consistent with my argument that the political incentives for left-wing parties to redistribute wealth and social risk have increased with growing feelings of economic insecurity in the global economy. Table 1.3 reports summary data on fiscal policy and correlates them with a composite index developed in Chapter 3 of left-labor power for the whole period 1966–1990.[17]

Left-labor power and the size of the public economy have long covaried (Cameron 1978). This relationship still held in the 1980s, although there were some important outliers such as Finland and France. For my purposes, however, it is more important that the pace of growth in public expenditures from the 1970s to the 1980s was faster the greater was left-labor power. Although Ronald Reagan and Margaret Thatcher did their best to resist pressures for public sector expansion, spending rose dramatically in other countries, led by Denmark and Sweden among the traditional social democratic corporatist regimes.

Contrary to common suppositions, the positive relationship between accumulated left-labor power over the twenty-five years up to 1990 and the size of budget deficits in the 1980s was very weak. Left-labor power had a stronger impact on the growth of budget deficits from the 1970s to the 1980s. Deficits increased across the board, partly in response to the depth of the international recession in the early 1980s. But increasing deficits were also the product of citizen demands on governments to increase spending without commensurate tax hikes. This tension was more pronounced in strong left-labor cases. One important consequence of the growing relationship between left-labor power and deficits was higher interest rates which necessarily impose a drag on the macroeconomy. I argue in Chapter 4, however, that the interest rates premiums on public debt in social democratic corporatist regimes in the global economy were not particularly large in substantive terms.[18]

The data on income tax progressivity are interesting. There was no relationship between left-labor power and the gap between the highest and lowest rates of personal taxation in the 1980s. The picture with respect to changes from the mid 1970s to the late 1980s, however, is quite different. While taxes in all countries became less progressive in the 1980s, the greatest flattening of income taxation occurred in countries with strong right wing parties and weak labor movements, most notably in the Anglo-American democracies. In marked contrast, there was very little change in the gap between the highest and lowest marginal rate in the exemplars of social democratic corporatism – Austria and Sweden. Right wing governments – led by those of Thatcher and Reagan – dramatically reduced the progressivity of what had been the most progressive systems of income taxation in the world. Governments in social democratic cor-

Table 1.3. *Left-Labor Power and Fiscal Policy*

Country[a]	Government spending (%GDP)[b]		Budget deficit (%GDP)[c]		Gap between highest and lowest rates of income taxation[d]		Effective highest marginal rate of corporate taxation[e]	
	1980–1990	Change[f]	1980–1990	Change	mid 70s– late 80s	Change[g]	1981–1990	Change[h]
Austria	48.9	9.2	7.1	4.8	43	-4	-	-
Sweden	62.4	15.1	9.8	5.7	51.5	-3	49.6	-8
Finland	39.9	6.1	3.9	3.6	-	-	-	-
Denmark	58.3	16.4	10.0	8.4	23	0	45.0	0
Norway	50.9	6.5	3.5	1.6	22.5	-17	50.8	0
Italy	48.5	11.2	12.8	4.4	51	-22	44.4	10.1
Germany	46.0	4.9	8.3	2.3	34	0	55.4	-6
Belgium	53.8	12.6	8.2	5.8	44.5	3	39.4	2
Netherlands	57.1	10.2	11.0	4.7	54	4	34.0	-1
United Kingdom	44.3	4.1	6.8	0.7	36.5	-23	41.5	-18
Japan	32.9	9.6	3.9	2.2	-	-	41.8	-4.5
Canada	44.6	8.2	10.0	5.8	25	-26	40.0	-2.2
United States	36.6	3.6	7.3	2.3	36	-40	36.8	-2
France	49.5	10.3	5.6	3.3	53	-4	43.3	-3
Average	48.1	9.1	7.7	4.0	40	-11	43.5	-2.7
Correlation with left-labor power	0.51	0.33	0.13	0.34	.01	.45	.60	.20[i]

[a]Rank order based on average scores for the left-labor power index, 1966–1990
[b]Total government spending (current disbursements) OECD, *Historical Statistics* (various)
[c]Budget deficit (current disbursements minus taxation revenues), OECD, *Historical Statistics* (various)
[d]Heclo, Heidenheimer and Adams [1990: 21–1212] and OECD, *The Tax/Benefit Position of Production Workers* (various)
[e]The highest rate of corporate taxation less investment incentives. Cummins, Hassett and Hubbard [1995: tables 1 and 2]
[f]1980–1990 minus 1966–1979
[g]Late 1980s minus mid 1970s
[h]1990 minus 1981
[i]Based on average scores for the left-labor power index, 1980–1990

poratist regimes, in contrast, have always relied more on spending programs rather than on different income tax rates to redistribute wealth.

Corporate taxation is perhaps the most likely place one would expect to see the globalization effects envisaged by neoclassical economics – manifest in dramatic cuts in rates to mitigate the prospect of widespread capital flight, especially among strong left-labor regimes. However, the relationship between left-labor power and the highest effective rates of corporate taxation (that is, the top marginal rate less investment incentives) was very strong in the 1980s, stronger even than was the case for government spending. Moreover, with the important exception of Sweden, all the reductions in corporate tax rates from the 1970s to the 1980s occurred at the lower end of the left-labor power spectrum. Chapter 4 shows that corporate tax revenues in the 1980s were no greater in countries with strong left-wing parties and labor market institutions – suggesting that other forms of tax concessions to firms were prevalent in social democratic corporatist regimes. Nonetheless, the figures on the highest marginal rates of corporate taxation stand in marked contrast to the conventional wisdom about the effects of globalization.

In sum, the effects of globalization on economic policy were precisely the reverse of the conventional wisdom. It is commonly thought that big government, countercyclical fiscal policies and progressive tax systems were central to social democratic corporatism in the relatively closed economies of the 1960s and 1970s, but that these policies were rendered infeasible by globalization. In contrast, I show that these policy strategies became increasingly distinctive features of social democratic corporatism in the 1980s.

Nonetheless, Chapter 4 does demonstrate that there has always been an interest rate premium attached to left-labor power and that the size of this premium increased with globalization. Proponents of the globalization perspective might wish to seize on this finding as support for the proposition that social democratic corporatism is maladapted to the era of global markets. If this were true, however, the costs of the leftist alternative to market capitalism should have been evident in the form of deteriorating macroeconomic performance.

THE MACROECONOMIC CONSEQUENCES OF SOCIAL DEMOCRATIC CORPORATISM

Chapter 5 shows that the growing policy distinctiveness of social democratic corporatism in the global economy did not adversely affect the real economy in the period up until 1990. Indeed, growth was faster and unemployment rates were lower in cases where strong left parties were allied with encompassing labor movements than they were under any other constellation of political and organizational conditions (including liberal market regimes where strong right-wing parties were combined with weak labor market institutions). In contrast, rates of inflation increased with left-labor power. Different people no doubt will place different weights on real aggregates versus price stability as economic objectives. Irrespective of this choice, my analysis shows that the macroeconomic consequences of social democratic corporatism in the global economy were far better than the dire predictions of most analysts.

Table 1.4 presents summary performance data for the 1980s and for changes from the 1966–1979 period. My argument about the politics of economic performance is that outcomes should be better in coherent political economies – either cases of strong left-wing parties and encompassing labor market institu-

Table 1.4. *Social Democratic Corporatism and Economic Performance*

	Economic growth		Unemployment[a]		Inflation	
	1980–1990	Change[b]	1980–1990	Change	1980–1990	Change
Social democratic corporatism[c]						
Austria	2.4	-1.9	3.2	1.6	3.8	-1.4
Denmark	1.5	-1.5	8.3	3.8	6.5	-2.0
Finland	3.3	-0.6	4.8	1.5	7.2	-1.7
Norway	2.7	-2.2	3.0	1.6	8.0	0.9
Sweden	1.9	-0.9	2.2	0.6	8.2	1.0
Average	2.4	-1.4	4.3	1.8	6.7	-0.6
Incoherent[d]						
Belgium	2.0	-1.8	10.9	5.9	4.8	-1.3
Germany	2.1	-1.4	7.6	5.2	2.9	-1.3
Italy	2.1	-2.1	10.3	4.1	10.8	1.3
Netherlands	1.6	-1.8	9.6	6.4	2.9	-3.6
Average	1.9	-1.8	9.6	5.4	5.3	-1.2
Market liberalism[e]						
Canada	2.6	-1.9	9.2	3.2	6.4	0.0
France	1.9	-2.5	9.0	6.3	7.0	-0.5
Japan	4.2	-2.8	2.5	0.9	2.5	-5.4
United Kingdom	2.0	-0.4	9.5	5.9	7.6	-2.6
United States	2.6	-0.6	7.1	1.6	5.5	-0.6
Average	2.7	-1.6	7.5	3.6	5.8	-1.8

[a]OECD standardized definition
[b]1980–1990 minus 1966–1970
[c]Countries that ranked in the top five on the left-labor power index for the period 1966–1990
[d]Countries that ranked in the middle four on the left-labor power index for the period 1966–1990
[e]Countries that ranked in the bottom five on the left-labor power index for the period 1966–1990

tions or cases where the political left and organized labor are both much weaker – than in less coherent settings.

The economic growth results were consistent with my expectations about the effects of regime coherence. Average growth rates in the 1980s were higher for the social democratic corporatism and market liberalism categories than for the incoherent countries. Furthermore, although growth slowed across the industrial democracies from the 1970s to the 1980s, the slowdown was less pronounced in the coherent regimes. There was, however, considerable variation in growth performance within these broad categories. Growth in the 1980s was slower in Denmark than in any other country, but growth was unusually rapid in Finland. Japan was still the fastest growing economy among the fourteen countries in the 1980s, although it had come back to the pack considerably from the 1960s and 1970s.

The most noticeable facet of the unemployment results is the clearly superior performance of social democratic corporatism. Five countries were able to maintain average unemployment rates below 5 percent in the 1980s; apart from Japan, these were all social democratic corporatist regimes. The only historically strong left-labor case with poor performance was Denmark, where conservative governments (rendering the political economy more incoherent) allowed unemployment to increase substantially in the 1980s.

The pattern of cross-national variations in inflation rates was very different from that for real aggregates. Inflation rates were higher in the social democratic corporatist countries in the 1980s – and declined less quickly from the 1970s – than in either of the other two categories. The only good inflation performer at the top of the left-labor power table was Austria. With the conspicuous exception of Italy, inflation rates were very low in the incoherent cases, but it should be remembered that this was coupled with very high unemployment rates. The poor inflation performance of the social democratic corporatist regimes is at odds with my theoretical argument and with earlier work (Alvarez, Garrett and Lange 1991, Cameron 1984). In Chapter 5, I contend that the inflation bias of social democratic corporatism in the global economy results from the fact that it is easier to generate real wage restraint and labor quiescence in conditions of moderate nominal wage increases (Akerlof 1996), especially where reducing interoccupational wage differentials is an explicit goal of the labor movement (Iversen 1996b).

To sum up, whereas the growth results are completely consistent with my argument about the beneficial consequences of regime coherence, the social democratic corporatist countries were clearly different from the other countries in the analysis with respect to inflation and unemployment. Unemployment rates were lowest in cases where strong left-wing parties were allied with encompassing labor market institutions, but this was offset by inflation rates that were higher than under market liberalism or in more incoherent regimes. Critics might wish to highlight the inflation findings as evidence of the economic costs of social democratic corporatism. But even they would have to accept that the strong performance of these regimes with respect to real aggregates casts serious doubt on the more general notion that the interventionist policies associated with social democratic corporatism have been rendered infeasible by globalization.

THE 1990s

There is one potential criticism of my analysis of the effects of globalization on domestic politics: The constraining effects of market integration on social democratic corporatism finally came home to roost after 1990. There are three simple pieces of evidence that can be adduced to support this proposition. First, residual capital controls were eliminated in the early 1990s in three corporatist countries that decided to join the European Union – Austria, Finland, and Sweden. Second, unemployment rose dramatically in two of these countries from 1990 to 1995 – Finland and Sweden. Finally, these governments responded to their unemployment problems by reducing the generosity of welfare benefits.

Chapter 6 presents a rudimentary analysis of the political economy of capitalist democracy in the first half of the 1990s using descriptive statistics and bivariate correlations similar to those I have presented in this section. My analysis makes three basic points. First, the policy distinctiveness of social democratic corporatism with respect to the size of the public sector actually increased in the first half of the 1990s, perhaps as a result of even greater demands on government to ameliorate market dislocations.

Second, it would be wrong to conclude from rising unemployment in Finland and Sweden that social democratic corporatism became economically infeasible in the 1990s. I argue that the economies of both countries suffered from a unique concatenation of forces associated with the end of the Cold War. The European economies all went into recession in the aftermath of the cataclysmic events of 1989. Perhaps most importantly, the high German interest rates that followed German unification put a brake on economic activity throughout the continent – especially for countries whose currencies were pegged to the deutsche mark (DM). These costs fell particularly heavily on Finland and Sweden because they decided to fix their exchange rates to the DM at precisely the worst time. The jury must surely still be out on whether the historically strong unemployment performance of the corporatist countries will never again be recaptured.

Finally, Chapter 6 acknowledges that contemporary social democratic corporatism does face serious challenges. However, I argue that these have little to do with globalization. The crisis of the social democratic welfare state is a demographic crisis, not the product of market integration. Expanding public sector employment has also made it harder for corporatist labor movements to tailor wage demands to competitiveness constraints. These are real problems, and I propose some solutions that do not compromise the fundamental principles of social democracy. Nonetheless, I wish to reiterate that the forces of globalization do not figure prominently in the real challenges facing the corporatist regimes.

1.3 VARIATIONS IN GLOBALIZATION

Most work on the effects of globalization makes the tacit assumption that the process of international integration has been consistent across different types of markets and different countries. So, too, do my analyses in the preceding section. In one sense, this is reasonable because the recent trend in most markets and in most countries has been toward ever more integration. Nonetheless, thinking about globalization as a homogeneous process masks clear and important differences in the extent of market integration, both across countries and across markets. In this study, I analyze the integration of different national markets into the global economy with respect both to exposure to trade and to capital mobility. Whereas existing quantitative studies focus exclusively on the facet of market integration that is easiest to measure – trade – the central dynamic highlighted in more qualitative accounts of the domestic consequences of globalization is the freedom of mobile asset holders to move money across borders.

There have always been marked differences among the industrial democracies with respect to dependence on foreign trade. As David Cameron (1978) pointed out almost twenty years ago, countries with strong left-wing parties and labor market institutions historically have been bigger traders. This is borne out in the data for the 1980s presented in Table 1.5. Although Belgium and the Netherlands in the middle of the left-labor power distribution stood out as the most trade dependent countries, there was still quite a strong correlation between left-labor power and the contribution of exports and imports to gross domestic product (GDP). Trade was more important in all of the social democratic corporatist regimes at the top of the table than in any of the liberal market regimes, with Japan and the United States standing out as by far the least trade dependent countries in the industrial world. Moreover, although trade grew in importance from the 1970s to the 1980s in all countries with the exception of Norway, the pace of trade expansion tended to be somewhat faster at higher levels of left-labor power.

Turning to capital mobility, the proliferation of global capital flows in recent years has been well documented. Economists, however, argue that they are poor indicators of the actual integration of financial markets.[19] The measure of capital mobility used in this book is increasingly common in cross-national research. It is derived from the International Monetary Fund's (IMF) monitoring of the extent of government restrictions on cross-border capital flows.[20]

The data on government restrictions on capital mobility reported on the right-hand side of Table 1.5 are the opposite of those for exposure to trade. Although the average number of capital controls in the fourteen countries halved from the 1966–1979 period to the 1980s, there were large cross-national variations in capital mobility. Half of the countries had no government restrictions on cross–border financial flows throughout the 1980s, but none of these was a

Table 1.5. *Left-Labor Power and Globalization*

Country[a]	Exports+imports/GDP (%)[b]		Government restrictions on cross border capital movements[c]	
	Average (1980–1990)	Change (1980–1990) Minus (1966–1979)	Average (1980–1990)	Change (1980–1990) Minus (1966–1979)
Austria	75	16	1.0	-0.6
Sweden	64	14	1.0	-0.6
Finland	57	8	2.8	0.1
Denmark	67	8	0.8	-0.9
Norway	83	-4	1.0	-0.6
Italy	43	6	0.8	-0.3
Germany	61	16	0.0	0.0
Belgium	133	44	0.0	-0.6
Netherlands	110	19	0.0	-1.4
United Kingdom	53	6	0.0	-1.1
Japan	27	4	0.0	-1.4
Canada	52	8	0.0	0.0
United States	19	6	0.0	0.0
France	45	12	1.0	0.2
Average	64	12	0.6	-0.5
Correlation with left-labor power	0.39	0.10	0.50	-0.11

[a]Rank order based on average scores for the left-labor power index, 1966–1990
[b]OECD, *Historical Statistics* (various)
[c]IMF, *Annual Report on Exchange Arrangements and Exchange Restrictions* (various)

social democratic corporatist regime. Finland stood out as the country with the greatest controls on capital flows, but significant restrictions remained in Austria, Denmark, Norway, and Sweden as well.[21] As a result, the correlation between left-labor power and capital controls was positive and stronger than that for trade. In the 1980s, social democratic corporatist countries were big traders that significantly restricted international financial flows. Moreover, the last column of the table shows that the correlation between left-labor power and capital controls weakened, but only marginally, from the 1970s to the 1980s.

The simple point to be drawn from these data is that one cannot accurately delineate the impact of market integration on the political economy of the industrial democracies by assuming that globalization has been a process that has affected all markets and all countries equally. This observation has a crucial impact on the methodological choices I have made in this book. One cannot accurately measure the impact of globalization on the domestic relationships between politics, policy and performance without carefully tracking the manifestations of market integration in different countries.

Thus, although the type of analysis presented in the previous section is easy to undertake and easy to interpret, one should be very wary about accepting its results because it is wrong to assume that globalization affected all countries equally in the 1980s. Instead, more sophisticated multivariate statistical techniques must be used to delineate the interactive effects of market integration and domestic political conditions on economic policies and outcomes in different countries. I present the results of such analyses in Chapters 4 and 5. Fortunately, these show that the basic patterns of relationships outlined in this chapter continue to hold even when subjected to more rigorous empirical scrutiny.

Most importantly, my analyses show that the effects of increasing capital mobility on the relationships among social democratic corporatism, economic policies, and macroeconomic outcomes have been very similar to those of greater exposure to trade. Pace Cameron (1978) and Katzenstein (1985), corporatist countries responded to higher levels of trade by expanding the public economy, with beneficial consequences for the real economy. One might have thought these relationships would be very different under conditions of greater capital mobility. But my analysis shows that they are not. Corporatist governments have responded to the integration of financial markets just as they historically have reacted to trade exposure – with bigger government – and without undermining their growth and unemployment performance.

CONCLUSION

This book shows that the basic patterns of partisan politics that obtained in the halcyon days of capitalist democracy from the end of World War II until the mid 1970s continue to characterize the advanced industrial countries today. Those who argue that national autonomy in the economic sphere – and social democratic alternatives to the free market in particular – are outmoded relics of a different age greatly exaggerate the constraining effects of market integration. They also dramatically underestimate the impact of domestic political conditions both on the range of policy choices that may be politically popular and on the consequences of these policies for the macroeconomy. This should be heartening for anyone who believes that clear choices for citizens between different policy agendas is a hallmark of effective democracy.

I do not wish to suggest, however, that social democratic corporatism is the only path to political and economic success in the era of global markets. Rather, there are clear trade-offs to be made. The balance sheet is very familiar. Social democratic corporatism is characterized by higher levels of government spending, more progressive systems of taxation, higher rates of economic growth, and lower rates of unemployment. However, these regimes tend to suffer from bigger deficits, higher interest rates, and higher inflation. In contrast, countries with powerful right-wing parties and much weaker labor unions have smaller and less progressive public economies, smaller deficits, lower interest rates, and lower rates of inflation. But they also grow more slowly and have higher rates of unemployment.

Evaluating the relative merits of the different regimes should be left to public deliberations. Even in the global economy, and despite the fanfare to the contrary, citizens still have a real choice to make about how to govern the market, ultimately based on one's view of the fairness of market allocations of resources. This divide has always been the sine qua non of democratic politics. It remains so today.

2

POLITICS, POLICY, AND PERFORMANCE

This chapter establishes the theoretical foundations of my argument about the effects of domestic political and organizational conditions on economic policy and macroeconomic performance in the global economy. The first three sections of the chapter develop a closed economy understanding of the political economy of capitalist democracy that can be used as a baseline against which to compare the case where countries are deeply integrated into global markets. Section 2.1 argues that governments of the left and right can be expected to pursue partisan economic policies consistently – based, respectively, on the reform or acceptance of market allocations of wealth and social risk – only when these are consistent with strong macroeconomic outcomes.

Section 2.2 reviews the corporatism literature on the macroeconomic effects of labor market institutions. The basic insight of this literature is that labor markets will function effectively – in terms of gearing economywide wage developments to maximizing overall levels of employment – where the workforce is either atomized (free labor markets) or highly organized and coordinated (encompassing labor market institutions). In contrast, wage push is expected to curtail employment and economic activity where individual trade unions are strong but their behavior is not coordinated by powerful central labor confederations.

Section 2.3 analyzes the interaction between partisan political competition and labor market institutions in a closed economy context. The central feature of this model is that the economic viability of left- and right-wing policies is contingent upon the organizational characteristics of national labor market institutions. I argue that economic policy should be more consistently partisan and macroeconomic performance should be stronger the more "coherent" conditions are in the politics and the labor market. There are two ideal types of coherent arrangements. On the one hand, "social democratic corporatism" is constituted by the combination of strong left-wing parties and encompassing trade union movements that can coordinate the behavior of the bulk of the labor force. The other coherent combination is where powerful right parties confront much weaker labor market institutions – "market liberalism." The less closely cases conform to these ideal types (the more "incoherent" are political economic regimes), the less consistently partisan economic policies will be and the poorer macroeconomic outcomes will be.

The remaining two sections of the chapter examine the impact of globalization on the closed economy model. Section 2.4 assesses the merits of three arguments made by scholars who contend that the international integration of markets has undermined the social democratic corporatist alternative to market liberalism. First, the electoral heartland of the left is viewed to have shrunk with the movement of low-wage/low value-added manufacturing jobs to less-developed countries. Second, the decline of the manufacturing working class and the concomitant rise of the service economy are seen to have lessened the ability of "labor" to act collectively.

Finally, the ability of governments to manipulate markets is widely considered to have been significantly reduced because even though politics remains national, markets are increasingly global. The credible exit threats of mobile asset holders are considered to give them a de facto veto over government policies of which they disapprove. Thus, even if there remain political incentives for left-wing governments to redistribute wealth and social risk and even if their allies in encompassing labor market institutions can still effectively organize the bulk of the labor force, the specter of capital flight has all but vitiated the social democratic corporatist alternative to market liberalism.

Section 2.5 develops an open economy model that takes into account these purported changes in the political economy of capitalist democracy. I argue that globalization has not undermined social democratic corporatism. The political foundation of this regime remains the redistribution of wealth and risk in favor of those adversely affected by market forces. Moreover, the effective implementation of the left's partisan policies continues to rest on the support of encompassing labor market institutions. Nonetheless, the operation of social democratic corporatism in the global economy is different from its closed economy counterpart.

The core political constituencies of the left are no longer dominated (if they ever were in practice) by the manufacturing working class. But this does not necessarily bode ill for the political foundations of social democracy. With greater market integration, the portion of the economy exposed to international competition has grown to comprise more of the service sector, and the left can still curry support among these "economically insecure" voters by ameliorating the short-term dislocations associated with rapidly changing international market conditions. Moreover, public sector employment has grown rapidly in many countries in the past two decades, and these employees are natural supporters of social democratic parties.

In the global economy, it is harder to use the countercyclical monetary policies of classical Keynesianism used to ameliorate market dislocations. But globalization is not particularly constraining on fiscal policy. In particular, one should expect the left to concentrate increasingly on expanding the public economy in a way that is balanced by tax increases as the primary means for redistributing wealth. The closed economy argument must also be modified with respect to the role played by labor market institutions. The primary challenge for labor leaders today is to mitigate the tensions between the interests of workers in industries exposed to international trade and those who are not. This can be achieved, however, where labor market institutions are encompassing. In this case, labor leaders can be expected to continue to engage in a mutually beneficial exchange with left-wing governments – based on tailoring economywide wage developments to the competitiveness of the exposed sector.

2.1 POLITICAL COMPETITION AND ECONOMIC POLICY

There are two contending conceptions of the behavior of political parties in democratic polities. One is that parties are fundamentally policy seeking: They fight elections in order to pursue the policies they prefer. The other perspective is that parties are office seeking. In Anthony Downs's [1957: 28] famous terms, parties "formulate policies in order to win elections, rather than win elections in order to formulate policies." The reality is surely inbetween these two extremes. Politicians undoubtedly have substantive policy objectives, but it would be unreasonable to characterize most politicians in stable democracies as blind ideologues. A more sophisticated conception of the behavior of political parties in government is to consider their priorities to be lexically ordered. Irrespective of the importance governments attach to policy objectives, they must give primacy to the goal of reelection. Where the pursuit of partisan objectives does not prejudice their electoral prospects, governments can be expected to enact policies that further these goals. If, however, there is a clash between the two, governments are likely to move away from their partisan-preferred strategies in an attempt to improve their prospects for reelection.[1]

The operative issue is thus determining the conditions under which the pursuit of partisan policies is conducive to reelection. It has long been a staple of empirical research that the left benefits electorally by intervening in the market allocation of resources and risk in ways that favor workers and the poor, whereas the right gains by being more accepting of market forces.[2] There is an equally long game theoretic tradition, however, that questions whether parties ever benefit by deviating from the preferences of the median voter.[3] This line of reasoning can be extended to proportional representation systems by arguing that the dynamics of coalition bargaining generate strong pressures for compromise, consensus, and policy convergence (Jackman 1986).

But the convergence logic of the median-voter theorem has its critics within the game theoretic community. The power of party activists, the prospect of abstention among voters with strong partisan preferences, and deterring the entry of new parties have all been argued to generate centrifugal pressures in two-party systems (Alesina and Rosenthal 1994; Baron 1994; Brody and Page 1973; Palfrey 1984; Przeworski and Sprague 1986). Others suggest that coalition bargaining in multiparty systems will also often lead to distinctively partisan governments and policies (Austen-Smith and Banks 1988; Baron 1991).

There is also considerable debate as to whether governments can manipulate the economy in partisan fashion. Douglas Hibbs's (1977, 1987) influential analyses of the "political Phillips curve" assume there is a trade-off between inflation and unemployment that politicians can exploit. Left governments accept greater increases in inflation for a given decrease in unemployment than will their more conservative counterparts – because this will redistribute wealth and social risk in favor of their core electoral constituencies among workers and the poor. With the rise of rational expectations economics, the notion of an exploitable Phillips curve has repeatedly been questioned. Nonetheless, Alberto Alesina has shown that even within this framework, governments can influence the mix of inflation and unemployment for significant periods of time after elections (Alesina 1989; Alesina and Roubini 1992).

What conclusions should be drawn from this vast and disparate literature on the economic consequences of political competition? The most prudent path is to argue that the balance of political power between the left and right matters, in terms of both the policies that governments pursue and how these affect the economic aggregates, but that one should not exaggerate these effects.

There is, however, a problem with even this cautious rendering of the political competition approach to the interaction between democracy and the market. Its fundamental assumption is that voting decisions – and, in turn, government behavior – are primarily, if not solely, motivated by distributional issues. This is unrealistic. It has rarely, if ever, been the case that the core constituencies of the left (much less those of the right) have been large enough on their own to justify party strategies based solely on furthering their interests (Przeworski and Sprague 1986). There is a wealth of empirical evidence from numerous countries and at both the individual and aggregate levels demonstrating that voters – regardless of their distributional preferences – reward governments that preside over a relatively prosperous macroeconomy and punish those under whom the economy worsens.[4] Aggregate economic performance (most notably, rates of per capita economic growth) is not a zero-sum distributional issue, but rather something of which all citizens want more. Thus, governments can significantly improve their prospects for reelection, irrespective of the push and pull of distributional politics, by presiding over a buoyant macroeconomy.

We can thus conceive of the electoral game in capitalist democracy as having two dimensions. Distributional politics matter, but governments that disregard the macroeconomic consequences of their policies will suffer at the polls. Obviously, governments are more likely to pursue partisan policies if they are also consistent with reelectable levels of macroeconomic performance. But there is a lot hidden behind this proposition.

Charles Lindblom (1977) argued long ago that the "privileged position of business" in capitalist democracies creates powerful pressures for governments interested in macroeconomic performance to pursue very similar economic strategies – overwhelming incentives to pursue redistributive policies. His reasoning was straightforward. In capitalist economies, the generation of societal wealth lies fundamentally in the hands of private entrepreneurs. Because all governments seek to stimulate aggregate economic performance for electoral reasons, they have little choice but to pursue strategies that will induce capitalists to invest in the national economy. In turn, the best way for governments to promote investment is to minimize their interventions in the economy.

The logical extension of this argument is that capitalism, even when there are strong distributional pressures to mitigate market forces, drives out leftist parties and leftist policies. This conclusion would seem even more compelling in the global economy. In Lindblom's framework, capitalists have two options: They can reinvest their profits in the home economy or they can consume them. Market integration gives productive capital a third option: exiting the national economy in search of higher rates of return abroad. The easier it is for asset holders to exit, the greater the need for governments to pursue policies that encourage these actors to reinvest in the national economy. Again, so the argument goes, this means radically cutting back government interventions in the economy.[5]

If this line of argument were correct, there would be little point in exploring further the dynamics of capitalist democracy. Mobile asset holders would stand in judgment over all governments, and they would frown on those that constrain the free play of market forces. The penalty – the flight of productive financial and industrial capital – would be so severe that no government would contemplate intervening in the market irrespective of the distributional consequences of so doing.

The rest of this chapter argues theoretically that this conclusion is unwarranted (the following chapters assay its empirical limitations). I make two basic points. First, there have always been political incentives for governments to intervene in the economy to alter market allocations of wealth and risk (that is, there has always been considerable demand for left-wing parties and policies), and these incentives have not been eroded by globalization. This is because market integration has an important political effect that is often overlooked: Market integration increases the portion of the population vulnerable to market dislocations.[6]

In turn, there are good reasons to suggest that democracy generates a bias in favor of distributional politics (Garrett and Lange 1995). The holding of elections at regular and short intervals means that governments cannot be concerned about policy reforms that will improve macroeconomic outcomes in the long run if the short-term distributional consequences are dire. For example, left governments will be reticent to reduce the size of the welfare state even in circumstances where this might stimulate investment and growth. Cutting back the welfare state will do immediate harm to the core constituencies of the left. If the macroeconomic benefits of undertaking this reform take some time to materialize — critically, if they are not evident by the time of the next election — the government is unlikely to pursue this strategy.

Second, I also argue that under certain circumstances, interventionist government is good for the macroeconomy and will prompt neither disinvestment (the closed economy case) nor capital flight (under conditions of global markets). Specifically, the combination of left-wing government and power labor market institutions that can coordinate the behavior of most of the labor force generates a highly productive and stable economic, political, and social environment that is attractive to investors — even those with ready exit options.

To make this point, I begin by discussing the impact of labor market institutions on the macroeconomy. I then develop frameworks to understand the interactive effects of the left–right balance of political power and organizational characteristics of national labor market institutions, first in the context of a closed economy, and then with respect to an integrated global economy.

2.2 LABOR MARKET INSTITUTIONS AND ECONOMIC PERFORMANCE

Economists, political scientists, and sociologists have spent considerable time analyzing the impact of labor market institutions on the economy. Early work in political science and sociology posited that the greater the organizational power of labor, the lower both inflation and unemployment rates would be.[7] The logic underpinning this assertion is that the more the labor market is organized, the greater the incentives for union leaders to be concerned with the health of the national economy and the more likely they be would to restrain overall wage growth.

Mancur Olson (1982) presented a theoretically coherent rendering of this argument. He argued that the negative externalities usually associated with labor power — wage-push inflation and lower aggregate levels of economic activity and employment — can be mitigated in cases where labor market institutions are "encompassing." Where most of the labor market is organized into trade unions and authority is highly concentrated in peak union confederations, labor leaders will internalize the externalities of decentralized wage militancy. This is because the leaders of encompassing labor market institutions will forego the temptation to push up wages in the short term because they know that this will only lead to higher inflation, which in turn will constrain economic growth and ultimately reduce the wages and employment prospects of all workers.

There is, of course, a serious limitation to this argument about encompassing organizations that early proponents of "corporatism" did not take seriously. For Olson, encompassing organizations are an exception to the basic rule of neoclassical economics that labor markets function more efficiently the weaker trade unions are. Atomized workers cannot collude to obtain wages above market-clearing levels. Thus, in the absence of trade unions there would be no externalities (in the form of wage militancy) to internalize.

The neoclassical view about the costs of trade unionism and the corporatist perspective on the benefits of encompassing labor market institutions were reconciled by Lars Calmfors and John Driffill (1988). Their "hump-shaped" hypothesis distinguishes three scenarios, based on the level at which most wage contracts are made – in individual firms, at the industry level, or nationally.[8] Calmfors and Driffill argue that economic performance will be good where wage setting is predominantly at the firm level. Small and isolated groups of workers cannot alter the market determination of wages because individual firms cannot pass on higher costs to consumers in competitive markets.

Calmfors and Driffill then argue that where wages are primarily set at the industrial level (that is, where labor market institutions are stronger on most indicators), wage-push inflation will result – irrespective of the deleterious consequences of this behavior for overall levels of employment and economic activity. In this case, union leaders can use their organizational power to push up wages without fear of losing their jobs because their employers (who act as monopolists in their industry) can pass on the costs of wage increases to consumers. Their behavior, however, will increase inflation in the rest of the economy, constraining aggregate economic activity and employment.

Finally, Calmfors and Driffill contend that wage militancy will be mitigated by national wage-bargaining arrangements. National leaders have strong incentives to internalize the externalities associated with labor power. They understand that economywide wage restraint today will improve the material well-being of all workers in the longer run. In this case, macroeconomic performance will be just as good as where wages are set predominantly at the firm level.

The Calmfors-Driffill hypothesis, however, can be criticized for concentrating too much on the level at which wage bargains are struck. In a recent study, Miriam Golden (1993) argues convincingly that the internal structure of labor movements – and specifically the ability of central union leaders to coordinate the behavior of large sections of the workforce – is a more important determinant of macroeconomic outcomes than the level of wage bargaining per se. The reason for this is that if centralized wage agreements are to be effective, they must be adhered to at lower bargaining levels. But there are powerful incentives for groups of workers and their employers to free ride on central agreements with higher local wage settlements ("wage drift").

The concentration of union authority in peak confederations whose constituents comprise the bulk of the workforce mitigates wage drift in two ways. On the one hand, the leaders of encompassing organizations have strong incentives to coordinate economywide wage restraint so as to maximize both employment and wages for the labor force as a whole. On the other hand, the leaders of encompassing organizations may informally sanction constituents who do not abide by such agreements (sometimes with the help of employer associations). One should thus expect that, in equilibrium, the presence of national wage agreements will covary with the encompassment of labor market institutions. Central wage setting may be imposed in cases where underlying structural conditions are inappropriate. But in such cases, the effectiveness of national agreements will inevitably be undermined by wage drift.

The consequences for economic performance of variations in the coverage of labor market institutions and the concentration of authority within them can be mapped directly from the hump-shaped hypothesis. First, macroeconomic outcomes will be good in cases that approximate free labor markets, where isolated groups of workers do not have the organizational clout to bid up wages above market-clearing levels. Second, in cases where individual unions are strong but where authority in the labor movement as a whole is not concentrated in a single peak confederation, labor faces a severe collective action problem. Maximizing wages while keeping all of its members in jobs is the objective of every individual union. If all unions pursue this strategy, however, nominal wage increases will be eroded by higher economywide inflation, which in turn will slow economic growth and increase aggregate unemployment. But there is no incentive for any individual union to care about these externalities. However, where most of the workforce is organized into trade unions or covered by collective bargaining agreements and their behavior is coordinated by a powerful central confederation, outcomes should be just as good as in the free labor market case – because union leaders will internalize the externalities of wage increases.

2.3 THE CLOSED ECONOMY MODEL

Two basic propositions can be derived from the previous sections. First, democratic political competition generates incentives for parties of the left and right to redistribute wealth and social risk in favor of their core political constituencies, but this is much easier to do where partisan policies do not adversely affect macroeconomic outcomes. Second, two different types of national labor market institutions are conducive to strong macroeconomic performance – those in which trade unions are too weak to subvert the operation of market forces and those in which organized labor movements are sufficiently encompassing to internalize the externalities of wage militancy.

In a series of papers with Michael Alvarez and Peter Lange, I have developed an approach that synthesizes these two propositions by arguing that the strategic behaviors of governments and actors in the labor market are mutually contingent (Alvarez, Garrett and Lange 1991; Garrett and Lange 1986; Lange and Garrett 1985). Because labor market institutions affect the macroeconomy, one should expect that governments will take into account labor market reactions to different types of economic policies. Similarly, because economic policies affect the allocation of wealth and risk, the behavior of labor market actors will be affected by likely government policy responses to different levels of militancy.[9]

This section presents an understanding of government–labor interactions in the context of a "closed economy" (on which my prior work was implicitly based). The closed economy has four characteristics. First, exposure to trade is relatively low and there are substantial barriers to cross-border capital flows. Second, governments can effectively manipulate aggregate demand using both fiscal and monetary policy. Third, the core political constituencies of the left and the right are easily defined in terms of the capital–labor divide. Finally, the interests of workers are relatively homogeneous.

Let us begin by considering the behavior of a government dominated by left parties under the three different types of labor market institutions outlined in the previous section – encompassing, strong but uncoordinated, and weak (the upper panel of Figure 2.1). In the closed economy context, left governments can use countercyclical fiscal and monetary policies to maintain high levels of employment. Moreover, left governments can be expected to supplement market incomes for the less well-off using the tax-transfer system – through direct income transfers to the unemployed, the old, and the young; the public provision of social services such as health, education, and day care; industrial policies propping up jobs in declining sectors; and progressive systems of taxation. This cluster of policies is often described as the "Keynesian welfare state" (Krieger 1986).

When governments pursue Keynesian welfare state policies, there are strong incentives for the leaders of encompassing labor market institutions to use their authority to restrain overall wage growth. They know that the government's policies create slack in the labor market that unionized workers could use to their advantage by pushing up wages. However, labor leaders also understand that such behavior would ultimately be self-defeating. Wage-push inflation would not only push up interest rates and retard economic and employment growth; it would also put pressure on the government to lessen its Keynesian welfare state orientation.

The result of this interaction between left-wing governments and encompassing labor market institutions should thus be stable partisan policies coupled

Labor market institutions

Balance of political power		Weak	Strong but uncoordinated	Encompassing
Left	Political economic regime:	Incoherent	Incoherent	Social democratic corporatism (SDC)
	Economic policies:	Move toward ML	Oscillate between SDC and ML	Keynesian welfare state
	Behavior of organized labor:	Market-dominated	Militant	Wage regulation (generic collective action problems)
	Macroeconomic performance:	Moderate	Poor	Good
Right	Political economic regime:	Market liberalism (ML)	Incoherent	Incoherent
	Economic policies:	Pro-cyclical, small government	Oscillate between ML and SDC	Move toward SDC
	Behavior of organized labor:	Market-dominated	Militant	Skeptical wage regulation
	Macroeconomic performance:	Good	Poor	Moderate

Figure 2.1 *Politics, policy and performance in closed economies*

with strong macroeconomic performance on all dimensions – high rates of growth and low rates of inflation and unemployment. The upper-right cell of Figure 2.1 thus reflects the closed economy dynamics of "social democratic corporatism."

Things are likely to be very different, however, when left governments are confronted with labor movements characterized by strong individual trade unions whose behavior is not subject to the centralized authority of a peak confederation (the upper-middle cell of Figure 2.1). This is an incoherent combination of political power and labor organization because the government will not be consistently able to pursue Keynesian welfare state policies without adversely affecting the macroeconomy. Organized labor is faced with a pervasive collective action problem that it cannot solve institutionally. Keynesian welfare state policies would only heighten this problem because they reduce the disciplining effects of market forces on the workforce. Nonetheless, the government will be sorely tempted to persist with partisan policies for considerable periods of time in virtue of their distributional effects. Moreover, the incentives to act in this manner will be increased by the existence of strong individual trade unions that can lobby effectively in the political arena.[10]

Thus, the most likely scenario where left-wing governments confront decentralized labor market institutions is one of policy instability and poor economic performance. The government has incentives to pursue Keynesian welfare state policies on entering office, but labor militancy will undermine their macroeconomic effectiveness. Even if the government tried to impose market disciplines on wage setting, however, this would not improve economic performance because individually strong unions will react by being more militant. Thus, left governments (and right ones as well) are in a real bind when confronted by decentralized labor market institutions. The most likely results are instability in economic policies in the context of deteriorating macroeconomic outcomes.

The final left government scenario is where labor market institutions are very weak (the upper-left cell of Figure 2.1). Distributional incentives remain to pursue the Keynesian welfare state, but the government cannot expect that these policies will improve macroeconomic performance. The inevitable consequence of policies that reduce market disciplines in this context is greater wage militancy (as a result of reducing market disciplines on wage bargains in individual workplaces). Thus, the political economic regime is still incoherent because the government's partisan-preferred policies are incompatible with good macroeconomic performance.

There is, however, a significant difference between the cases of weak and decentralized labor market institutions. In the latter case, moving to more market-oriented policies will not help economic performance because individual unions can effectively veto them through wage militancy. This is not the case where labor is essentially unorganized. The deck is clearly stacked against the Keynesian welfare state where labor market institutions are very weak. Even governments dominated by left-wing parties can be expected over time to move toward more free market-oriented policies, in an effort to improve macroeconomic outcomes. Whether this strategy will ultimately prove electorally successful is not certain, however, since a heavy price must be paid for a buoyant macroeconomy – the abandonment of partisan redistribution. Nonetheless, left-wing governments have incentives to experiment with this strategy where their allies in the labor market are very weak.

Now consider the interactions between governments dominated by right-wing parties and the different types of labor market institutions (the bottom panel of Figure 2.1). The mirror image of social democratic corporatism is the case where right-wing governments face very weak labor market institutions that cannot alter the market allocation of wages and employment ("market liberalism," the lower-left cell). In this situation, the government is free to pursue its partisan agenda in favor of the wealthy and capital through fiscal and monetary policies that do not change during downturns in the business cycle, by cutting the level of government spending and taxation and by eschewing industrial policies that distort the market allocation of capital.

Where individual unions are strong but their behavior is not centrally co-ordinated, right-wing governments face the same problems as their counterparts on the left (the lower-middle cell of Figure 2.1). The wage push that is usually associated with strong but uncoordinated labor market institutions cannot be mitigated by classical economic policies nor by the Keynesian welfare state. As a result, the course of policy under right-wing governments that face decentralized labor market institutions will likely be quite unstable, and macroeconomic performance will deteriorate – as was the case for the left-uncoordinated cell.

The final scenario is that in which a government dominated by right-wing parties confronts an encompassing set of labor market institutions (the lower-right cell of Figure 2.1). Organized labor can be expected to counter economic policies designed to heighten market discipline with coordinated labor militancy (that is, the regime remains incoherent). On the other hand, the leaders of encompassing labor market institutions have the capacity to regulate economywide wage growth, but they will act in this fashion only if they are confident that the government will pursue policies that are favorable to workers. Thus, there are macroeconomic benefits to moving away from neoclassical economic policies and toward the Keynesian welfare state, and one should expect right-wing governments grudgingly and over time to do so. Of course, labor leaders will always be skeptical about the commitment of right-wing governments to the Keynesian welfare state, and hence outcomes are unlikely to be as strong as would be the case where left-wing parties are dominant.

In sum, the closed economy model generates three important predictions. First, governments can be expected to pursue consistently partisan policies only in coherent political economies (where either the left is allied with encompassing labor market institutions or the right confronts very weak trade unions) because these are the only instances in which partisan policies are likely to have desirable macroeconomic consequences. Second, policy instability and poor performance will characterize strong but uncoordinated labor market institutions under both left- and right-wing governments. This is because individual trade unions are strong enough to resist government efforts to impose market disciplines on them but the labor movement as a whole is not sufficiently coordinated to respond to beneficial government policies by restraining economywide wage growth. Finally, slow but steady movement away from partisan policies – accompanied by improving macroeconomic outcomes – is likely to be common in starkly incoherent regimes where there is a clear mismatch between the government's redistributive agenda and labor market institutions (the left-weak and right-encompassing cases).

2.4   THE CHALLENGE OF GLOBALIZATION

The analysis presented in the preceding section is subject to a potentially damaging criticism. The "closed economy" model may have been a reasonable representation of the political economy of capitalist democracy in the 1950s and 1960s, and perhaps even the 1970s. But it does not fit well with the realities of global markets in the past fifteen years. In particular, most analysts conclude that the viability of social democratic corporatism has been undermined by globalization and that today market liberalism is the only stable viable strategy available in the industrial democracies.[11] There are three important strands to this critique.

First, some assert that the structure of societal preferences has changed in ways that have significantly lessened the electoral appeal of traditional leftist policies (Kitschelt 1994; Piven 1991). Second, others claim that globalization has fragmented the "working class" into conflicting groups that are divided according to their positions in the international division of labor – making economywide wage regulation extremely difficult for even the most encompassing labor market institutions (Moene and Wallerstein 1992, 1995; Pontusson and Swenson 1996; Swenson 1991a). Finally, still others contend that globalization has made it virtually impossible for left-wing governments to pursue economic policies that depart in any substantive way from free market principles (Cerny 1990; Iversen 1996a; Kurzer 1993; Moses 1994; Scharpf 1991).

The remainder of this chapter develops a different argument stressing the viability of social democratic corporatism in the global economy. I begin by reassessing the three propositions that form the core of the conventional doom-and-gloom view about the effects of market integration on leftist alternatives to free market capitalism.

POLITICAL DEMANDS FOR SOCIAL DEMOCRACY

Consider first the claim that the electoral environment in the capitalist democracies is no longer conducive to traditional social democracy (that is, using gov-

ernment policy to redistribute wealth and social risk). Kitschelt (1994) focuses
on two factors: the shrinking of the manufacturing working class and the rise of
postmaterialist issues (such as the environment, feminism, and human rights)
that cut across the left–right economic divide. A key weakness in this argument
is that the working class has never been large enough for left parties to win office
simply on the basis of its support (Przeworski and Sprague 1986). To be successful, social democratic parties have always had to attract other constituencies.
The weight attached to voters from outside the manufacturing working class
undoubtedly has increased in recent years. But the real question for left parties
is whether this entails abandoning their agenda for the redistribution of wealth
and risk. There is good reason to think this is not the case.

The potential constituencies of leftist redistributive policies extend to all
voters who suffer in the short term from market dislocations. This category has
never been confined to the manufacturing sector. In the past, for example, farmers
were often strong supporters of left parties. Although this coalition is no longer
viable, there is no reason to believe that the portion of the electorate that would
support economic policies ameliorating market dislocations has decreased.

Most importantly, globalization has increased the portion of national economies that are exposed to international competition, and this in turn has been
associated with growing income inequality and even more broadly based feelings
of economic insecurity in the industrial democracies (Rodrik 1997; Wood 1994).
Demands for traditional leftist policies may thus have increased with market
integration, particularly given the lengthy periods of stagnation and rising unemployment that have characterized the Western economies since the second oil
shock. Moreover, the portion of total employment in the public sector has risen
throughout the industrial democracies in the past twenty years – in some cases,
quite dramatically. Because left parties tend to support expansion of the public
economy, government employees would seem to be natural supporters of traditional social democracy.[12]

How big is the left's potential support base among those who benefit from
policies that cushion the effects of volatile global markets? Even if one makes a
conservative estimate based on those directly benefiting from interventionist government, one could reasonably conclude that the left's natural constituency today
is at least as big as the manufacturing working class ever was. As Peter Flora
(1989: 154) observed: "Including the recipients of (pensions), unemployment
benefits and social assistance – and the persons employed in education, health
and the social services – in many countries today almost half of the electorate
receive(s) transfer or work income from the welfare state."

It is thus not surprising that public opinion surveys in a range of industrial
democracies show that support for the welfare state is at least as strong today as
it has ever been (Ploug 1996). Perhaps most notably, this is even the case in the
Anglo-American democracies where deregulation, liberalization, and privatization were the watchwords of the 1980s (Pierson 1994, 1996).

Of course, none of this evidence about the demand for social democratic policies in the global economy means that left-wing governments will deliver them. Governments are more likely to pursue partisan economic policies where these do not have deleterious consequences for macroeconomic outcomes. The remaining two elements of the thesis that social democratic corporatism is mal-adapted to globalization focus on the issue of aggregate performance.

THE ROLE OF ENCOMPASSING LABOR MARKET INSTITUTIONS

The conventional view about the declining efficacy of social democratic corporatism is straightforward. The ability of even the most encompassing labor market institutions to regulate economywide wage growth has been undermined by rising conflicts among different groups of workers. Left governments thus can't pursue interventionist economic policies because their labor allies cannot speak with one voice. Today, so goes the argument, employees in different firms or industries may share more interests with owners and managers – based on their common position in the international division of labor – than they do with their nominal "class allies."

The potential for sectoral conflict within the ranks of labor in the global economy is clearest between workers in sectors exposed to international competition and those that are effectively insulated from competitive pressures, either by government protection or because their services are more-or-less not tradable. The most important group in the latter category is the public sector, but international competition in other sectors, such as retail, remains very weak.

I do not wish to argue that these intersectoral tensions are not real. Rather, I contend that encompassing labor market institutions can reconcile conflicts between employees in the exposed and sheltered sectors of the economy in ways that are consistent with competing in global markets. My argument is thus that the challenge facing the leaders of encompassing institutions is different in the global economy than it was in the closed economy context. Instead of dealing with a generic collective action problem, labor leaders must now seek to match economywide wage developments to the competitive dynamics of international markets. Nonetheless, this is a goal that is achievable where most of the labor market is organized and authority is highly concentrated within the organized labor movement.[13]

Let us begin by establishing the differences between labor market dynamics in the portion of the economy that is exposed to international competition and those parts that are effectively insulated from it. Wage setting in the tradables sector is disciplined by international supply and demand. Workers will not push up wages beyond world market prices because of the direct and dire consequences of such action for their welfare – they will lose their jobs. Those who are sheltered from international market competition, in contrast, are not so constrained. The case of public sector workers is clearest: They can reasonably assume that the government will prop up public sector employment with little concern for productivity, especially during economic downturns. But wage push in the public sector has deleterious consequences for firms exposed to international competition. Higher domestic inflation will lead to higher interest rates, which will push up exchange rates. In turn, this will lower the competitiveness of the exposed sector.

The primary objective for encompassing labor market institutions in the global economy is to ensure that economywide wage growth does not undermine the competitiveness of the exposed sector. This is not an easy task, but it is one that organized labor has long played in corporatist countries. Indeed, Peter Swenson's (1991b) influential analysis of the emergence of corporatism in the 1930s in Sweden demonstrates that even business leaders supported the centralization of trade union authority. They did so precisely because this was the best method for stopping wage militancy in the (nontraded) construction sector that was weakening the competitive position of exports from the metalworking sector. With the rise of government employment in Scandinavia in the 1960s and 1970s, this objective was reformulated by labor leaders in terms of constraining wage growth in the public sector – the "Aukrust" and "EFO" models (Flanagan 1983).

Thus, as was the case for the political appeal of left-wing parties, one should consume with caution the conventional wisdom that the left's allies among organized labor movements can no long deliver the types of wage regulation that have always been central to social democratic corporatism. Let us consider now the final element of the conventional wisdom about the damaging effects of globalization – the loss of economic policy autonomy.

ECONOMIC POLICY AUTONOMY

There is only one clear instance in which market integration vitiates national policy autonomy. This is the case of monetary policy where there are no barriers to cross-border capital movements and where a country is a member of a fixed exchange rate regime (Mundell 1961). For all currencies (except the anchor in an "n-1" system), efforts to run monetary policies that are more expansionary than those in other members of the regime will fail. Money will flow out of the country until interest rates rise to equal those in other members. In the period under consideration in this book, the situation that most closely approximates this ideal is the "new" European Monetary System (EMS) from 1987 – when the rules on intra-marginal interventions were stiffened – until the currency crises of 1992 and 1993.[14]

Some might want to argue that effective fixed exchange rate regimes have characterized many of the European democracies since the days of the "snake" in the early 1970s. However, the history of the snake and the early years of the EMS is littered with examples of exchange rate depreciations, either within nominally fixed rate regimes (realignments) or as a result of leaving such regimes. These depreciations were invariably the result of choices by national governments that the monetary policies required to maintain a fixed exchange rate could not be justified domestically, either economically or politically. Moreover, until the early 1990s, many EMS members maintained extensive capital controls, giving them considerable monetary autonomy within the fixed rate framework. It has also been argued that the desire of countries to participate in Europe's would-be Economic and Monetary Union has long constrained monetary policy. For example, the Swedish government's "shadowing" of the deutsche mark in the run up to its application to join the European Union is often cited as an important cause in the purported breakdown of social democratic corporatism in that country (Iversen 1996a). Of course, Sweden – along with numerous EMS members – chose to abandon fixed exchange rates when the costs became clear.

All of these arguments about the constraining effects of fixed exchange rates implicitly assume that in conditions of high levels of capital mobility, governments have little choice but to abrogate monetary policy autonomy through external commitments to fixed rate regimes (Moses 1994). It must be stressed, however, that this is a very different view from the framework pioneered by Mundell. He argued that capital mobility does not constrain monetary policy autonomy if the exchange rate floats. Moreover, fixing the exchange rate only makes sense in Mundell's framework under a restrictive set of conditions – basically where a country's economy is so tied to its neighbors' that sharing a common monetary policy will not adversely affect national business cycles. Even in contemporary Europe, few countries meet the "optimum currency area" desiderata (Eichengreen 1992).

Why do so many people seem to believe that governments must pursue fixed exchange rates when capital mobility is high? The technical answer has to do with rational expectations economics. Real interest rates will be lower for countries in credible fixed exchange rate regimes because this will lower prospects for future inflationary policies. In the real world, most attention is focused on the argument that exchange rate movements will always exaggerate changes in real economic "fundamentals" and that the ensuring instability will be bad for investment, trade, and growth (McKinnon 1988). According to this line of argument, it is increasingly difficult for governments to fine-tune depreciations because the markets will interpret looser monetary policy as a signal of a more general laxity in government policy. Speculative attacks in the currency markets will ensue, and it will take a long time for the exchange rate to return to a level that is sustainable in equilibrium. Thus, the bottom line of this argument is that governments can only insulate themselves against the damaging vicissitudes of the currency markets by participating in stable fixed exchange rate regimes.

The empirical record is far from clear, however, with respect to the costs of floating under conditions of high capital mobility. The damaging currency crises in recent years – the breakup of the EMS in 1992 and 1993 and the peso crisis in Mexico in 1994-1995 – concerned commitments to fixed rates, rather than floating ones (Eichengreen, Rose, and Wyplosz 1995). In turn, there is little evidence in the European case that even the currencies that were forced out of the EMS in highly visible public U-turns in government policy – notably sterling and the lira – suffered from "overshooting" in their subsequent depreciations. Indeed, these economies have managed smooth depreciations of their currencies to levels that have stimulated domestic activity without significantly increasing inflation. This has led some prominent economists to contend that reverting to a floating exchange rate regime may be the best policy option for many European countries (Goodhart 1995).[15] Finally, economists have been hard pressed to find significant costs of currency instability in terms of investment and trade (Cushman 1988).

Thus, one should be extremely careful and cautious when basing claims about the constraining effects of globalization on monetary policy. Let us now move on to what is often considered the heart of social democratic economic strategy – the running of budget deficits during recessions to stimulate domestic demand. Even if one assumes that there is a short-run Phillips curve trade-off between inflation and unemployment that left-wing governments can exploit to further their redistributive agenda, two arguments can be made suggesting that the ability to pursue countercyclical fiscal policy is mitigated by integration into international markets. On the one hand, the greater a country's exposure to trade, the less significant are domestic sources of demand for overall levels of national economic activity, and hence the less bang a government will get for each deficit buck.

On the other hand, deficits may act as a signal of fiscal recklessness in a world of integrated capital markets for which offending governments must pay a hefty interest rate premium. The markets know that today's borrowing must be repaid in the future by cuts in spending, higher taxes, or higher inflation. The last is generally thought to be least politically costly for governments (i.e., voters suffer from "fiscal illusion" (Buchanan and Wagner 1977)). Thus, running deficits today may presage inflation tomorrow, and market skepticism will be manifest in the tangible form of interest premiums on national debt.

The empirical record doesn't offer much support for these arguments. Many countries – not only the United States but also a number of small European countries led by Belgium – have been able to live with large deficits in the recent past without paying substantial interest rate premiums. Belgium, for example, has even been able to maintain a stable peg against the DM while accumulating the largest public debt in the OECD. This is because the globalization of financial markets has created a very large and competitive pool of lenders willing to fund government debt, easing the monetary costs of fiscal expansion (Corsetti and Roubini 1995). At some point, of course, higher debt burdens may trigger fears among the financial markets of governments defaulting on their loans – resulting in dramatic reductions in the availability of credit. Unlike Latin America in the 1980s, however, this limit does not yet seem to have been reached in any industrial democracy, not even in Belgium or Italy (Corsetti and Roubini 1991).

Thus, as in the case of monetary policy, it is not clear that globalization stops governments from being able to run deficits that are larger than some international norm. What about the size of government (assuming that public spending is balanced by tax revenues collected)? The conventional wisdom is that globalization puts downward pressure on taxing and government expenditures. The simple reason for this is that mobile asset holders – the managers of multinational corporations and portfolio investors – can credibly threaten to exit the national economy. In turn, many presume that they would always choose exit in the face of a large public economy because government spending is inefficient and because taxes are distortionary. In turn, the credibility of this threat would force governments to cut spending and taxes.

But should we really expect mobile asset holders always to exit unless governments cut spending and taxes, exerting powerful lowest common denominator pressures on the public economy? The answer depends on whether these asset holders believe they can increase their long-run profit stream by moving offshore. I wish to argue that this is often not the case because large public economies may provide numerous benefits for capital.

First, the recent spate of research on the endogenous sources of economic growth shows that government spending can increase productivity and competitiveness by generating collective goods that are undersupplied by the market. This is because the logic of collective action and scale economies renders it more efficient (and more likely) for governments than private actors to generate a wide array of services – ranging from the education and training of the labor force to the provision of basic physical infrastructure – that contribute positively to growth (Aschauer 1990; Barro 1990; Lucas 1988; Romer 1990). Ceteris paribus, mobile asset holders might not like having to pay the taxes to support these spending programs. But there is no a priori reason to expect that the costs to them in the form of higher taxation will outweigh the benefits they receive from the positive externalities of the public provision of human and physical capital. Obviously, this cost–benefit calculation would be tipped more strongly in favor of supporting government expenditures if tax increases were levied less on corporate profits than on other forms of government revenue.

Second, if my argument about the likely behavior of encompassing labor market institutions is correct, one should expect that in these cases there will be significant economic benefits from a broader range of public sector activities – extending well beyond those that fit the desiderata of the new growth theory. The conventional welfare state policies, industrial subsidies, and indeed any policies that mitigate market dislocations increase the incentives for the leaders of encompassing labor market institutions to use their market power to restrain overall wage growth. Wage restraint is clearly in the interests of mobile asset holders. Again, the question is whether these benefits outweigh the costs of higher taxation. But this is an empirical question, not a matter for didactic theorizing.

Finally, numerous economists have argued that government spending contributes to general social stability by reducing income inequality and that this increases investment and growth (Alesina 1995; Perotti 1996; Persson and Tabellini 1994). If this argument is correct, one again should expect capitalists to choose not to exercise their exit options in the face of big government if they believe that public expenditures generate stable investment platforms.

SUMMARY

The basic point of this section is straightforward but very important. The central notion of the globalization perspective that market integration systematically constrains the policy autonomy of national governments, and the left in particular, should not be taken as gospel. With the single exception of monetary policy under full capital mobility and fixed exchange rate regimes, the jury is out with respect to the strength of globalization constraints. In particular, there is no reason to believe that global markets select against big governments matched by high taxes where labor market institutions are encompassing.

Furthermore, the political incentives for left-wing governments to expand the public economy are just as great in the global economy as they have ever been. Although the specific role played by encompassing labor market institutions is different under globalization than in a closed economy, they can still be expected to behave in ways that improve the macroeconomic consequences of leftist policies - by gearing wage settlements to competitiveness considerations.

Thus, the closed economy model must be modified to take into account the distinctive features of the global economy. But its underlying logic of coherent and incoherent combinations of the balance of political power and the organizational attributes of labor market institutions remains the same. The next sections spells out these relationships in the open economy context.

2.5 THE OPEN ECONOMY MODEL

The basic parameters of the open economy model are similar to those in the closed economy context. The electoral incentives for governments dominated by left parties to redistribute wealth and risk in favor of those who are adversely affected by global market dislocations are greater than those for right-wing governments. The nature of labor market institutions, in turn, influences the macroeconomic consequences of partisan policies and hence the likelihood that governments will consistently pursue them. There are two important differences, however, between the closed and open economy models.

The first difference pertains to the types of partisan policies governments will try to pursue. Recall that in the closed economy case, a fundamental policy distinction between the left and the right concerned the propensity to use the tools of Keynesian countercyclical demand management. Notwithstanding the uncertainty concerning just how constraining globalization is on fiscal and monetary policies, it seems prudent to assume that differences between the left and right will not be so apparent with respect to these basic indicators of macroeconomic policy in the global economy. In particular, left governments would prefer, all else being equal, not to have to pay interest rate premiums associated with expansionary macroeconomic policies under conditions of high capital mobility.

In the open economy case, the clearest partisan policy cleavage is likely to concern the size of the public economy. The left will still prefer bigger government, preferably funded by progressive taxation systems, because this combination reduces market-generated inequalities of wealth and risk. Under appropriate circumstances, big government will also increase competitiveness both directly – by increasing the stock of human and physical capital – and indirectly – with measures designed to induce organized labor to restrain wage growth and to promote a stable environment for investment. The preferred open economy strategy of the right, in contrast, is likely to concentrate on reducing the size of government and flattening the tax structure. These policies not only can be expected to increase competitiveness from a neoclassical perspective, but they also have the beneficial consequence for right-wing parties of redistributing wealth to the wealthy and mobile asset holders.

The second difference between the closed and open economy models is the role that labor market institutions play in social democratic corporatist regimes. Recall that in the closed economy context, the task confronting leaders of encompassing organizations was to mitigate free rider problems among groups of workers with similar interests. Labor confronted a classic collective action problem. Generalized wage restraint today would be good for all workers because it would maximize their employment prospects and income stream in the long run. However, small groups of workers have no incentive to contribute to this collective good. The leaders of encompassing institutions do, and they possess the institutional power to generate wage restraint.

The task confronting the leaders of encompassing labor market institutions in the open economy is different. There is now a distinct cleavage between the interests of workers in sectors exposed to international market pressures and those that aren't (most importantly, the public sector). Whereas competitiveness concerns will constrain wage growth in the exposed sector, there is less for public sector workers to fear if they pursue a strategy of wage militancy. This is because governments have an interest in keeping them in work and will pass on the costs to others through deficits, inflation, and higher interest rates. But higher interest rates will lead to higher exchange rates, reducing the competitiveness of the exposed sector.

Thus, a pivotal issue for the viability of social democratic corporatism in the global economy is whether organized labor can ensure that the exposed sector is the wage leader for the economy as a whole. As in the closed economy context, the leaders of encompassing labor market institutions have both powerful incentives to internalize the externalities of public sector wage militancy and the organizational capacity to control it. This is not the case, however, where individual unions (particularly in the public sector) are powerful but their behavior is not coordinated by a peak confederation of labor. Here, powerful public sector unions will bid up their wages regardless of the effects on the competitiveness of the exposed sector.

We can now reformulate the interaction between the balance of political power and labor market institutions in the context of the open economy (see Figure 2.2). Consider first the behavior of governments dominated by left-wing parties. Such governments would prefer to expand the public economy. However, this strategy will only be compatible with good macroeconomic outcomes in cases where labor will respond to policies that lessen market disciplines with economywide wage restraint. This is only possible where labor market institutions are encompassing (the upper-right cell of Figure 2.2). This describes the nature of social democratic corporatism in the global economy.

Where individual unions in the exposed and sheltered sectors of the economy are strong but their behavior is not coordinated by a powerful peak organization, things look much worse for governments dominated by left parties (the upper-middle cell of Figure 2.2). In this case, if the left pursues market-cushioning policies, powerful public sector unions will take advantage of this by pushing up their wages. In turn, this will have deleterious consequences for the competitiveness of the exposed sector, and macroeconomic performance will deteriorate. Thus, one should expect left governments to move away from such policies and toward those designed to heighten market disciplines. But this is unlikely to work well either, because public sector unions still exercise an effective veto over policies they don't like. The result of this highly incoherent regime will thus be policy instability and poor performance.

The upper-left cell in Figure 2.2 also represents an incoherent political economy – where the left's allies in the organized labor movement are very weak. In this situation, the writing is on the wall for the left. Their partisan-preferred policies can only increase the power of workers to bid up their wages in the market – to the detriment of the economy as a whole. If the government is to stand any chance of reelection, it will need to move steadily away from its partisan agenda and toward the policies preferred by its counterparts on the right.

Turning now to the prospects for governments dominated by right-wing parties, there is an open economy analog of "market liberalism," but it is based on a policy regime combining sound money with aggressive microeconomic reforms designed to free up market forces. This regime is only consistent with good macroeconomic performance where labor market institutions are very weak (the

Labor market institutions

Balance of political power		Weak	Strong but uncoordinated	Encompassing
Left	Political economic regime:	incoherent	Incoherent	Social democratic corporatism (SDC)
	Economic policies:	Move towards ML	Oscillate between SDC and ML	Redistributive big government
	Behavior of organized labor:	Market-dominated	Militant public sector	Wage regulation (exposed sector as wage leader)
	Macroeconomic performance:	Moderate	Poor	Good
Right	Political economic regime:	Market liberalism (ML)	Incoherent	Incoherent
	Economic policies:	Monetarism, small government	Oscillate between ML and SDC	Move toward SDC
	Behavior of organized labor:	Market-dominated	Militant public sector	Skeptical wage regulation
	Macroeconomic performance:	Good	Poor	Moderate

Figure 2.2 *Politics, policy and performance in open economies*

lower-left cell of Figure 2.2). In the case of strong sectoral unions, efforts to impose market disciplines are likely to be effectively resisted by individual unions – especially those in the public sector. But as I argued above, changes in policies towards those of social democratic corporatism will be ineffective in this case as well. A cycle of policy instability and poor performance is the most likely outcome (the lower-middle cell of Figure 2.2).

Finally, one should again expect right-wing governments to move toward the policies of social democratic corporatism in cases where labor market institutions are encompassing. This is the only way that the right can try to convince labor leaders that they should use their power to generate economywide wage restraint. Although this strategy will obviously have adverse distributional consequences for the government's core electoral constituencies, the macroeconomic benefits of mimicking the policies of the left are likely to outweigh them.

In sum, this section has adapted the closed economy framework to the realities of the global economy. There is no gainsaying the differences in the political economy of an open economy: with respect to the composition of the electorate, the sectoral makeup of the economy, and the range of effective government policies. Nonetheless, these differences do not alter the basic structure of domestic political economic dynamics. As a result, there is a viable social democratic corporatist alternative to market liberalism in the global economy. The importance of regime coherence, however, should also be emphasized. In both the closed and open economy frameworks, the conditions under which governments can simultaneously redistribute wealth to their core constituencies and preside over a buoyant macroeconomy are limited to those where the balance of political power is coherent with the structure of labor market institutions. In these cases, I expect partisan politics to be alive and well in the global economy.

CONCLUSION

This chapter has developed a theoretical understanding of the likely course of government policy and economic performance under different constellations of market integration and under different combinations of the balance of political power and labor market institutions. I have argued that policies will be distinctively partisan and economic outcomes will be good in more coherent political economies – where politically powerful left-wing parties are allied with encompassing labor market institutions and where right-wing dominance is coupled with very weak institutions in the labor market. The more open the economy, the more this partisan distinctiveness will be apparent with respect to the size of the public economy, rather than with the propensity of governments to engage in countercyclical demand management.

I have also distinguished between two types of incoherent regimes (i.e., where governments cannot be expected continuously and successfully to pursue partisan policies). On the one hand, policy instability and poor performance are likely to be the norm for both left and right governments where unions are individually strong but their behavior is not coordinated by powerful peak associations of labor. This is because unions are strong enough to veto policies they don't like (i.e., those preferred by the right) but not well enough coordinated to respond with widespread wage restraint to policies that favor them (those of the left).

The other type of incoherent political economy is where there is a radical mismatch between the types of policies the government would like to pursue for distributional reasons and those that will promote macroeconomic performance under prevailing conditions in the labor market. In this case, I hypothesize that governments over time will come to accept some of the distributional costs of moving away from partisan policies in an effort to preside over reelectable levels of economic performance. They may not be able to succeed in this endeavor, but the governments' prospects are nonetheless brighter than they would be if governments were to stick to their partisan guns.

Having presented the theoretical argument, I now wish to move on to empirical tests. I begin this task in the next chapter by presenting data on trends in the industrial economies between 1966 and 1990 with respect to market integration, the balance of political power, and labor market institutions. Chapters 4 and 5 then assess the impact of these changes on economic policies and economic performance over the same period.

3

MARKET INTEGRATION
AND DOMESTIC POLITICS

This chapter begins my empirical analysis of partisan politics in the global economy. I present data on the major independent variables in the study for fourteen countries over the period 1966–1990. The countries are Austria, Belgium, Canada, Denmark, Finland, France, Germany, Italy, Japan, the Netherlands, Norway, Sweden, the United Kingdom, and the United States. I examine developments with respect to two basic facets of globalization – trade and capital mobility – and two sets of domestic variables – the partisan balance of political power and the structural attributes of national labor market institutions.

My primary objective is to highlight two empirical weaknesses in the conventional wisdom about globalization and domestic politics in the industrial democracies. First, in contrast with the common perception that the globalization process is seamless and pervasive, I demonstrate that there are substantial cross-national differences in the integration of the industrial democracies into international markets. Second, with respect to domestic politics, simplistic views about "convergence" belie substantial and enduring cross-national variations in the partisan balance of political power and the structural attributes of labor market institutions. These findings have significant implications for the research strategies that are appropriate for analyzing the interactive effects of globalization and domestic politics on economy policy and performance. Most importantly, it is crucial that the domestic effects of trade and capital mobility are examined separately, rather than assuming they are part of a unified and universal process of globalization.

Section 3.1 begins by discussing how to measure globalization. I settle on two broad and fundamental indicators – exposure to trade as a portion of total economic product and government restrictions on cross-border capital flows. Trade and capital mobility both increased across the western countries during the 1966–1990 period. But this trend conceals enduring cross-national differences between these two facets of globalization. Even in the late 1980s, countries that were bigger traders had financial systems that were more closed than was the case in countries that relied less on exports and imports. This suggests that the contemporary challenges posed by market integration vary across countries. For the traditional big traders, the primary task is to cope with increased capital mobility. Conversely, for countries with historically open financial systems, the recent wave of globalization is primarily about increasing exposure to trade.

Section 3.2 analyzes the balance of political power among the industrial democracies. The data do not support the commonly held view that increased market integration has had dire consequences for left-wing parties. The balance of political power in legislatures between the left and right was very stable from 1966 to 1990. The composition of partisan governments was more volatile, but changes reflected fluctuations in the international business cycle more than increasing market integration. The left came to power in a number of countries following the first oil shock in 1973, only to be replaced by more conservative governments after the second oil crisis at the end of the decade. In turn, left-wing parties returned to power as many of the industrial economies stagnated in the latter 1980s. Notwithstanding these fluctuations, clear cross-national differences in the balance of political power endured throughout the 1970s and 1980s. Most importantly, left-wing parties have always been considerably stronger in Austria and the Nordic countries – Denmark, Finland, Norway, and Sweden – than in France, Japan, the United Kingdom, and the United States.

I examine the organizational attributes of labor market institutions in Section 3.3. The data belie common perceptions of "trade unions in terminal decline." The unionized portion of the labor force was not in free fall across the board in the 1980s. Indeed, although membership declined significantly in some countries (such as Britain, France, and the United States), unionization increased significantly in much of northern Europe where unemployment benefits are tied to union membership. Most of the union growth in these countries was in the public sector, increasing the potential cleavage between union members in jobs that are exposed to international competition and those that are more sheltered from it. Furthermore, there is little evidence that the power of central labor confederations over their members has declined in recent years. Indeed, with reductions in the total number of unions in many countries, labor's capacity for collective action may actually have increased in the 1980s.

Section 3.4 describes patterns of association among the different indicators of globalization and the balance of domestic power. With respect to domestic political economic regimes, there has always been a relatively strong correlation between the political power of the left and the organizational strength of trade unions. Thus, taking the 1966–1990 period as a whole one can clearly distinguish five "social democratic corporatist" regimes – Austria, Denmark, Finland, Norway, and Sweden – from the ranks of "market liberalism" – Canada, France, Japan, the United Kingdom, and the United States. Domestic arrangements in the remaining countries in this study – Belgium, Germany, Italy, and the Netherlands – have tended to be less "coherent."

There has always been a positive correlation between the combined power of the left and organized labor, on the one hand, and exposure to trade, on the other. However, precisely the opposite has been true for capital mobility: Left-labor power has been associated with more restrictions on cross-border capital movements. Even though these relationships weakened in the 1980s, one can safely conclude that the primary challenge posed by globalization for social democratic corporatism is to deal with capital mobility. For the liberal market regimes, it is increasing exposure to trade that represents the most important change associated with international market integration.

3.1 MARKET INTEGRATION

There can be little doubt that the integration of markets among the industrial economies increased between the mid 1960s and 1990, with respect both to trade in goods and services and to international finance.[1] The headline numbers on trade are well known (Milner and Keohane 1996:10–11). The volume of exports and imports grew at almost twice the rate of total economic output in the industrial democracies during the 1970s and 1980s. The growth of intraindustry trade outstripped increases in interindustry trade, heightening competition in similar product markets. World trade has become progressively less dominated by exchanges within the OECD, with the rise of the NICs and the spectacular bursts of transactions with OPEC around the first and second oil crises.

The most basic indicator of trade integration is exports plus imports in goods and services as a portion of GDP. Figure 3.1 displays these data averaged for the fourteen countries studied in this book over the period 1966–1990 (right-hand scale). Trade grew from around 45 percent to over 65 percent of GDP by the mid 1980s, followed by a small downward correction toward the end of the decade. A significant portion of this growth was accounted for by increases in trade with countries outside the OECD. Imports from OPEC accounted for over 15 percent of total imports for the countries in this study between the first and second oil shocks (left-hand scale), but this subsequently declined with falling oil prices (helping to explain the decline in total trade/GDP after 1985). At the same time, imports from the first wave of East Asian and Latin American NICs – Brazil, Hong Kong, Mexico, Singapore, South Korea, and Taiwan – grew steadily throughout the period, to constitute almost 10 percent of total OECD imports by 1990.[2]

Turning to financial integration, the raw figures on the growth of international capital flows are staggering. The Bank of International Settlements estimates that daily turnover in the global foreign exchange market was $US 880 billion in 1992, rising even higher to around $1,200 billion in 1995 (*Financial*

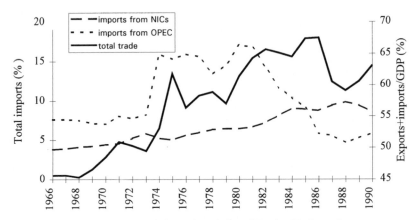

Source: OECD, Historical Statistics and Statistics of Foreign Trade, various,
14-country averages

Figure 3.1 *Trade*

Times 9/20/1995:1). International bank lending grew from around $200 billion
in 1973 to almost $4,000 billion in 1992. Between 1981 and 1992, international
issues of bonds increased ninefold to almost $1,800 billion. Cross-border equity
flows also grew rapidly between 1979 and 1990 to reach over $1,600 billion
(Herring and Litan 1995: 26-27). Annual inflows of foreign direct investment
increased almost tenfold from the latter 1970s, climbing to $185 billion in 1989
(Milner and Keohane 1996:12).

Economists argue, however, that one cannot use mushrooming cross-border
financial flows as evidence that a global (or at least OECD-wide) market for capital
has developed.[3] The reason for this skepticism is that surges in capital flows might
simply reflect volatility in market conditions affecting investment decisions. Conversely, there could be no cross-border financial flows even in a world of complete
capital mobility – if the investment environment were stable and all capital was
already efficiently allocated.

Two indicators have been developed by economists to measure the real extent
of financial market integration. The first was pioneered by Martin Feldstein and
Charles Horioka (1980). It is based on the relationship between savings and
investment. In a world of integrated financial markets, domestic savings would
not constrain domestic investment – because attractive investment opportunities
would pull in capital from abroad. Conversely, if national savings significantly
affect national investment, there must not be a global capital market. The Feld-
stein-Horioka approach has been criticized on various grounds, but its primary
problem from my perspective is that savings-investment correlations only estimate the integration of financial markets at a given point in time for a group of

countries as a whole. This approach thus cannot reveal cross-national differences in the openness of national capital markets.

The second measure of capital mobility favored by economists is the difference between "covered" interest rates among a group of countries. It is intuitive that the cost of capital in different countries should converge if there are no barriers to financial movements among them. However, one cannot rely on raw interest rates (even real rates) because these contain information about other factors influencing the cost of capital, notably the markets' expectations about future inflation and exchange rate movements. Covered rates take out these expectations and hence reveal true cross-national differences in the cost of capital (Frankel 1993; Marston 1995). Unfortunately, this measure can only be constructed for the Group of Seven economies since the early 1970s because forward exchange rate markets are much more recent and much thinner in many of the countries included in this study.

As a result of these problems with more conventional measures of capital mobility, I follow the trend in recent OECD-wide empirical work in international economics by relying on the International Monetary Fund's (IMF) annual monitoring of the extent of government restrictions imposed on cross-border capital flows (Leiderman and Razin 1994; Eichengreen, Rose, and Wyplosz 1995).[4] The categories are restrictions on the capital account, bilateral payments with IMF members, bilateral payments with nonmembers, and foreign deposits. The great virtue of these data for cross-national research is that they provide annual observations for a relatively large number of countries.

Figure 3.2 presents annual averages for the fourteen countries in this study based on the IMF's coding of capital controls (right-hand scale), with estimates for the saving-investment relationship provided to check their validity (left-hand scale).[5] These measures are highly correlated over time, increasing our confidence that the IMF data capture important trends in capital mobility. The story is simple and not surprising. There was a pronounced increase in the integration of financial markets from the late 1960s to the late 1980s.

In sum, there is no gainsaying the dramatic increases in the integration both of capital markets and of goods and services markets among the industrial democracies from the mid 1960s to 1990. Technological changes that have lowered the costs and increased the speed of transportation and, more importantly, communication have increased the opportunity costs of closure throughout the industrial countries. At the same time, the ability of governments to monitor and control international economic activity has declined (Bryant 1987; Goodman and Pauly 1993; Herring and Litan 1995). The result has been what everyone today refers to as the process of "globalization."

Focusing solely on this over-time trend toward more globalized markets, however, conceals two important but frequently overlooked aspects of market integration. Most studies treat globalization as if it were a seamless and ubiquitous phenomenon; trade growth and increased capital mobility are considered

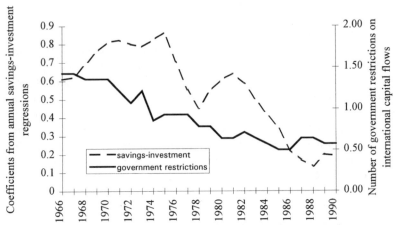

Sources: OECD, Historical Statistics, various. IMF, Annual Report on Exchange Arrangements and Exchange Restrictions. Government restrictions are annual 14-country averages.

Figure 3.2 *Capital mobility*

two halves of the same acorn. As a result, cross-national differences in market integration are assumed away. This is simply not an accurate depiction of globalization in the industrial democracies.[6]

Figure 3.3 depicts the relationship between average exposure to trade and capital mobility for the fourteen countries in this study in the baseline period before the globalization process began in earnest – 1966 to 1973. The first thing to note about this figure is the clear relationship between trade and capital controls in this period. Countries that were more dependent on trade tended to impose more restrictions on cross-border financial movements. The figure also shows that countries occupied very different positions in the two-dimensional market integration space. At one end of the spectrum, the United States stood out as the economy with the most open capital markets. At the same time, United States was less dependent on trade than any other country (followed, but not closely, by France, Italy, and Japan). The Netherlands and Norway anchored the other end of the spectrum as very large traders that imposed significant controls on cross-border capital movements. Capital restrictions were even more stringent in Austria, Denmark, Finland, and Sweden, but these countries were not quite so reliant on trade.

The picture had changed in important respects by the end of the 1980s (see Figure 3.4). For the period 1985–1990 there was no correlation between exposure to trade and capital mobility. This was largely because residual capital controls were removed in many countries during the 1980s. However, there are three clear outliers in the figure – Finland, where extensive capital controls were maintained,

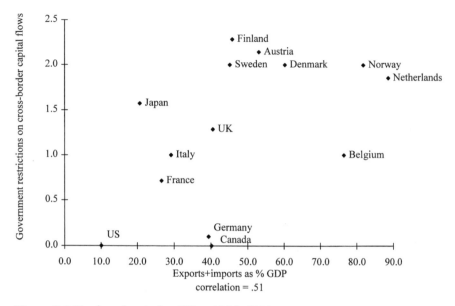

Figure 3.3 *Trade and capital mobility, 1966–1973*

and Belgium and the Netherlands, where total trade exceeded GDP but where all capital controls had been removed by 1985. If these countries were excluded, the inverse relationship between exposure to trade and capital mobility would have still held for the period 1985–1990. Austria, Denmark, Norway, and Sweden were large traders that continued to impose some controls on international financial flows in the late 1980s, whereas Japan joined the United States as a small trader with open capital markets. More generally, one could go further to say that there was a significant difference between the European economies and the other industrial democracies: Trade was more important in Europe but this was accompanied by tighter controls on capital flows.

There are numerous reasons why large traders have been slower to remove capital controls than countries less exposed to trade. One is political, and I return to it many times in this book: Countries where the left and organized labor are powerful tend to be large traders with relatively closed capital markets.[7] From an economist's perspective, however, the answer would have its roots in classical trade theory. Small countries tend to trade heavily to exploit scale economies; their domestic markets are not large enough to support the wide range of goods and services their citizens want to consume. Furthermore, because most of the small countries in our sample are in western Europe, gravity models that stress the importance of geographic proximity to cutting transportation costs give an added reason for the trade dependence of these economies (especially in the context of the European Union's customs union). Turning to the relationship be-

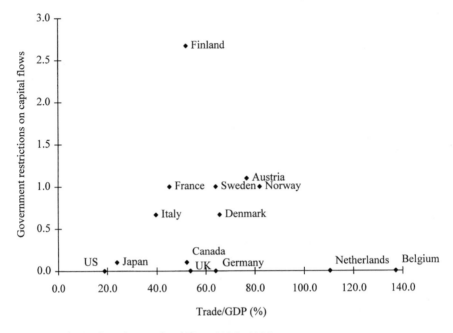

Figure 3.4 *Trade and capital mobility, 1985–1990*

tween trade and capital mobility, one plausible argument is that maintaining a stable balance of payments system is vital to the economic success of small countries. Wild fluctuations in capital inflows or outflows would have significant effects on trade. Capital controls can be used to reduce instability in payments and exchange rates.

For present purposes, however, the causes of cross-national differences in the nature of market integration are less important than their consequences for domestic politics, policy and performance. In this vein, it is clear that the challenges posed by globalization differ considerably across countries. The logical extension of the data trends reported in this section is that capital controls would soon cease to exist in the industrial democracies. Indeed, this is what has happened for the countries in this study. Those nations that still imposed capital controls in 1990 are now members of the European Union (with the exception of Norway, whose citizens rejected accession in 1994). Pursuant to the Maastricht treaty, these countries have been compelled to remove their remaining barriers to capital mobility. Although the trend will no doubt be more gradual, trade will likely increase in importance for the larger economies as the market size needed for firms to reap scale economies continues to grow in many sectors.

In sum, the major development since the 1960s for the smaller economies in western Europe has been a dramatic increase in the freedom of capital to move across national boundaries. Conversely, for the larger economies – and for Japan and the United States above all – the globalization phenomenon has been dominated by heightened exposure to trade. In assessing the impact of market integration on domestic political economies, these differences in the national manifestations of globalization must be kept in mind.

3.2   THE BALANCE OF POLITICAL POWER

The electoral viability of left-wing political parties is commonly thought to have been one important casualty of globalization. Because both trade and capital mobility increased in a more-or-less secular fashion from the mid 1960s to 1990 throughout the industrial democracies, a simple test of this contention is to examine over-time trends in the balance of political power. Figure 3.5 presents the annual fourteen country averages for partisan representation in cabinet governments and in the lower house of national legislatures. The balance of power indicator is derived from the influential expert survey by Francis Castles and Peter Mair (1984) on the placement of parties on a left-right scale.[8] The balance measure weights center, left, and right party groupings by their shares of legislative seats and cabinet portfolios. The balance of power in cabinet governments delineates the direct control of different families of parties over the instruments of economic policy. The legislative measure indicates the broader political constraints under which governments operate. On both variables, higher scores denote a shift to the left in the balance of political power. The data are effectively bounded by mainstream social democratic/labor parties (the British Labour party, the German Social Democratic party, etc. are scored as "2") and conservative parties (the Republican party in the United States, the Liberal Democratic party in Japan, and so forth, are scored as "0"). Centrist parties such as the Free Democratic party in Germany – and by the convention of comparative parties research, the U.S. Democrats – are coded as "1."

The balance of power in legislatures – averaged across the countries in this study – was remarkably stable at the center of the political spectrum throughout the 1966–1990 period. In contrast, the composition of cabinet governments was much more volatile. Left governments became more prevalent in the early 1970s, but the balance of power swung to the right in the late 1970s and early 1980s. The strength of the left subsequently increased again at the end of the decade.

These fluctuations in cabinet government composition cannot plausibly be explained in terms of globalization, because market integration among the advanced industrial democracies as a whole increased more-or-less consistently throughout the 1966–1990 period. Rather, the fate of governments seems to have been tied to the international business cycle. The fact that there were many incumbent right-wing governments when the first OPEC oil shock hit made a swing to the left in the mid and late 1970s quite likely. The converse was true

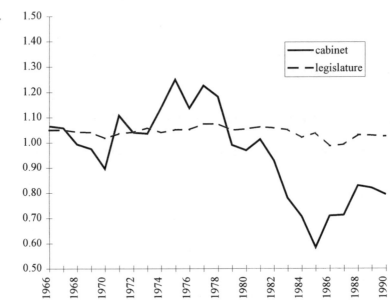

Sources: Mackie and Rose (1991); Keesings Contemporary Archives (various).
14-country averages. Higher scores denote more left power.

Figure 3.5 *Cabinet governments and legislative seats*

for the period following the second oil crisis, when the balance of cabinet power moved to the right. But this also made more probable the left's resurgence in the late 1980s – as economic performance began to decline again in many countries.

Of course, these aggregated data conceal important and enduring variations across countries. Table 3.1 breaks down national balances in political power in legislatures and cabinet governments for the two periods I used in discussing trade and capital mobility – 1966–1973 (the benchmark) and 1985–1990 (the era of global markets). In the benchmark period, there was considerable cross-national variation in the balance of political power in legislatures. Left-wing parties fared best in Austria and the Nordic countries, whereas the right was strongest in France, Japan, and North America. Given that legislative majorities translate into government monopolies, cross-national variance in the balance of power in cabinets was significantly greater than that for legislative seats.

Consistent with the aggregated data, there was very little change in the cross-national distribution of legislative power by the late 1980s. Indeed, the only two cases where there was any significant movement – Canada and the United Kingdom – both employ single-member district, first-past-the-post electoral systems where small changes in the popular vote can have dramatic effects on represen-

Table 3.1. *The Balance of Political Power*

Country	1966–1973			1985–1990		
	Legislative Seats	Cabinet Portfolios	Rank	Legislative Seats	Cabinet Portfolios	Rank
Sweden	1.43	2.00	1	1.39	2.00	1
Austria	1.44	1.57	2	1.38	1.50	2
Finland	1.31	1.59	3	1.14	1.21	5
Norway	1.30	1.06	4	1.16	1.45	4
Italy	1.25	1.15	5	1.37	1.24	3
Germany	0.96	1.52	6	0.98	0.17	10
Belgium	1.01	1.25	7	1.03	0.98	8
Netherlands	1.18	0.90	8	1.11	0.84	7
Denmark	1.09	1.01	9	1.01	0.25	9
United Kingdom	1.04	0.86	10	0.74	0.00	12
Canada	0.71	1.00	11	0.48	0.00	14
Japan	0.78	0.00	12	0.76	0.00	11
United States	0.57	0.29	13	0.60	0.00	13
France	0.49	0.00	14	1.03	1.08	6

The ranks are based on the sum of standardized scores for the legislative and cabinet balance of power terms.

tation in the legislature (especially in the presence of significant third parties, as was the case in both countries in the 1980s). To take a well-known example, the share of the vote won by Thatcher's Conservative party actually declined marginally between the 1979 and 1983 elections, but its majority in the House of Commons increased by a hundred seats because of the massive underrepresentation of the Alliance parties.

Turning to the distribution of cabinet portfolios between 1985 and 1990, there were important shifts to the right in some countries in the balance of power compared with the late 1960s and early 1970s. It would be rash, however, to draw strong conclusions from these data regarding the purported demise of the left. On the one hand, the balance of cabinet power was still tilted to the left in the same northern European countries as it had been in the late 1960s. On the other hand, the major gains for the right between the benchmark period and the late 1980s were made in countries where the left had been weak in legislative terms in the late 1960s (most notably, in North America and the United Kingdom).

Moreover, it must be remembered that the composition of cabinet governments is generally quite unpredictable and volatile. Plurality electoral systems can generate big inter-election swings in government composition on small changes in voting behavior. The dynamics of coalition bargaining in multiparty systems often do not have much to do with the legislative strength of different parties (Laver and Schofield 1990). The balance of cabinet power clearly matters for public policy. It is nonetheless important to take a broader indicator, such as legislative seats, into account when one is measuring the overall balance of left-right power. Focusing solely on swings in cabinet government is often likely to be quite misleading.

Taking the data on the balance of political power as a whole, it would be hard to conclude that the political fortunes of the left declined apace with, and because of, globalization from the mid 1960s to 1990. It must be emphasized, however, that the data presented here only pertain to nominal partisanship, that is, as measured by the political successes of parties with different labels. They say nothing about the impact of the political balance of power on public policy or on the economy. Critics might argue, for example, that the only reason left-wing parties were able to remain politically competitive through the 1980s is that they abandoned their traditional policies and moved ever closer to the market orientation of their conservative counterparts.[9] Alternatively, one might contend that even if left parties continued to pursue partisan policies, these had dire effects on the economy (increasing the probability of partisan convergence in the future). I take up these issues directly in Chapters 4 and 5.

3.3   LABOR MARKET INSTITUTIONS

The second element in the conventional wisdom about the domestic effects of globalization is that market integration has significantly weakened organized labor movements. As was the case for the balance of political power, the best available quantitative data do not support this contention. Figure 3.6 plots changes in the average size and composition of trade unions at five-year intervals from 1970 to 1990.[10] The simplest measure of the strength of organized labor is union density, that is, the number of union members relative to the size of the labor force (Visser 1991). On this measure (left-hand scale), the strength of trade unions increased significantly in the 1970s to reach a peak in 1980, when an average of 47 percent of the labor force was unionized. As is well known, union membership declined in the 1980s. Nonetheless, the magnitude of this decline should not be overstated – 42 percent of the workforce was still in trade unions in 1990. This is far from a "free labor market."

These aggregated numbers conceal some dramatic cross-national variations in trade union membership. Table 3.2 presents data for 1970 and 1990. In the benchmark year, there were five countries in which more than half of the labor force was unionized – Austria, Denmark, Finland, Norway, and Sweden. At the other end of the spectrum, unions were least numerically strong in Canada, France, and the United States, but even in these countries more than one fifth of

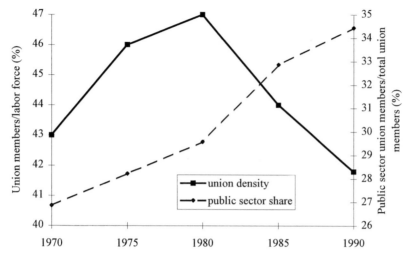

Source: Visser (1991). 14-country averages

Figure 3.6 *The density and composition of trade unions*

the labor market was organized. This is by now a familiar pattern. As was the case for the balance of political power, trade unions were numerically considerably stronger in northern Europe than elsewhere.

Turning to 1990, although average union density across the countries in this study had declined marginally (by one percentage point) from 1970, density increased substantially in some countries but plummeted in others. In three of the countries at the top of the 1970 standings – Denmark, Finland, and Sweden – union membership increased by 14 percentage points or more (as was also the case in Belgium). This growth in membership can be linked to the fact that unemployment benefits are distributed by trade unions in these countries (Western 1995). Among the "strong labor" cases in 1970, it was only Austria that saw a substantial decrease in union membership. This reduction, however, must be qualified because by Austrian law collective bargains struck by trade unions are automatically extended to virtually the entire labor force (Traxler 1994). Density dropped considerably in countries near the bottom of the standings – France, the Netherlands, and the United States.[11] The United Kingdom could also be included in this grouping because union density had reached almost 50 percent of the labor force when Thatcher came to power, but had dropped below 40 percent by 1990.

One cannot, however, base assessments of the strength of national labor market institutions solely on union density. Indeed, most arguments about the declining strength of labor concentrate on the growing divergence in the interests

Table 3.2. *Labor Market Institutions*

	1970					1990				
	Trade union membership		Major confederation			Trade union membership		Major confederation		
Country	Density	Public sector share	Share of total members	Affiliated unions	Rank	Density	Public sector share	Share of total members	Affiliated unions	Rank
Austria	61	22	100	16	1	46	31	100	15	1
Sweden	66	23	66	29	2	83	38	58	23	4
Denmark	60	22	77	45	3	74	35	68	30	2
Norway	56	29	76	35	4	54	44	61	29	8
Germany	33	29	83	16	5	31	30	83	16	3
Belgium	41	27	48	19	6	55	35	57	18	6
Finland	52	26	68	31	7	72	34	56	24	5
Italy	33	17	60	24	8	34	23	47	20	7
United Kingdom	45	29	84	150	9	38	32	85	76	9
Canada	29	20	75	110	10	32	35	59	90	13
Netherlands	38	31	36	20	11	23	43	70	17	11
Japan	35	18	37	63	12	25	17	62	81	10
United States	28	23	62	122	13	15	34	80	91	12
France	22	60	48	52	14	10	51	31	41	14

The data for the public sector share of total membership and unions affiliated to the major confederation were missing for Belgium and France respectively, and were coded at the means for the other countries to minimize their influence on the indices. The labor market institutions ranks were based on standardized scores for the four indicators combined as (density minus public sector share plus major confederation share of total union members minus the number of its affiliates).

of unionized workers, on the one hand, and the decreasing ability of central confederations to resolve these conflicts of interest in ways that do no undermine macroeconomic performance, on the other (Iversen 1996a; Pontusson and Swenson 1996). The data in Figure 3.6 (right-hand scale) demonstrate an important change in the composition of trade unions from 1970 to 1990 – the increasing portion of members coming from the public sector.

Table 3.2 shows that this trend of increasing public sector union power was relatively consistent across the countries in this study. With the exception of France and the Netherlands, the relative power of public sector union members was greatest in the countries with the highest total trade union membership. For example, in Sweden in 1990, more than 80 percent of the labor force was unionized, and almost two in five of these union members were in the public sector. In contrast, union members constituted only one quarter of the Japanese workforce, and less than one in five of these people was a government employee.

Let us now turn to the structural attributes of labor market institutions that might mitigate the potentially damaging consequences of public sector union power. "Encompassment" is a notoriously difficult concept to measure. Analysts have traditionally made qualitative judgments about the concentration of authority in the hands of central labor leaders (Cameron 1984; Schmitter 1981). However, data that have recently been collected by Miriam Golden, Peter Lange, and Michael Wallerstein make possible both cross-national and time-varying quantitative comparisons of the power of labor leaders over their memberships.

Figure 3.7 plots changes from 1970 to 1990 for two measures of union concentration – the percentage of all unionized workers who are members of the largest labor confederation in a country and the number of unions affiliated with that confederation. These data show that there has been neither a clear nor a pervasive reduction in the organizational power of peak labor confederations. The average portion of union members in the largest confederation did decline, but only marginally, during the 1970s and 1980s. In contrast, the average number of unions in the major confederation decreased somewhat – reducing the obstacles to collective action by the labor movement.

Again, these general trends mask important and enduring cross-national variations in the concentration of union authority. On the basis of the Golden and Wallerstein measures, authority has always been most concentrated in the Austrian and German labor movements. At the other end of the spectrum, unions are most decentralized in Canada, France, Japan, the United Kingdom, and the United States – although for different reasons.[12]

Perhaps the most interesting cases in Table 3.2 are Norway and Sweden. These countries have long been considered paradigmatic instances of encompassing labor market institutions, largely as a result of the success of national wage settlements in the 1960s and 1970s. The breakdown of these agreements in the 1980s was a powerful stimulus for more general assertions about the demise of corporatism. It must be noted, however, that using these data rather than the

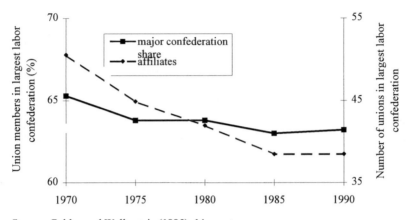

Source: Golden and Wallerstein (1995). 14-country averages

Figure 3.7 *The concentration of authority in labor market institutions*

more qualitative codings often deployed in the literature, labor authority was never as concentrated in Norway or Sweden as in Austria or Germany. Moreover, the share of union members in the largest confederations in both countries declined between 1970 and 1990. Coupled with the increase in the size of public sector unions in these countries, it is not so surprising that national wage-setting deals became harder to maintain the 1980s. In contrast, whereas formal national wage-setting was never as pronounced in Austria or Germany as in Scandinavia, the structural attributes of labor market institutions in the Germanic cases have always been better suited to economywide coordination of wage behavior.

But stepping back from these rather subtle differences between the German and Scandinavian models, the data presented in this section simply do not support the generalized notion of "unions in decline." Labor market institutions were very sticky from 1970 to 1990. Moreover, as was the case for political power, there was a marked difference between the strength of labor market institutions in northern Europe and their weakness in France, Japan, and North America. This trend largely endured through the era of global markets.

Let us now turn to the relationship between the political power of the left and the strength of national labor market institutions. Recall from Chapter 2 that my argument centers on the coherence of the political power and organized labor regimes. I suggested that economic policy should be more consistently partisan and macroeconomic outcomes should be better either where powerful left-wing parties are allied by encompassing labor market institutions (social democratic corporatism) or where right-wing parties are dominant and confront very weak trade union movements (market liberalism) than they are in less coherent regimes.

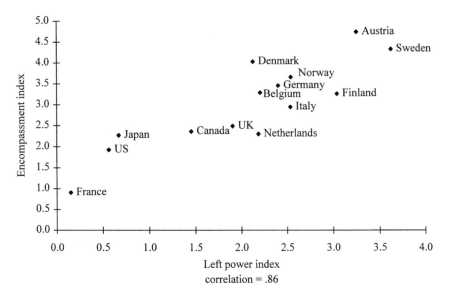

Figure 3.8 *Left power and labor encompassment, 1966–1973*

Figures 3.8 and 3.9 display the relationship between a composite measure for the balance of political power and an index of the encompassment of labor market institutions. The political power measure sums standardized scores for the legislative and cabinet government indicators. The encompassment index is increasing in union density and major confederation share, but decreasing in public sector share and the number of confederation-affiliated unions (i.e., standardized scores for density and major confederation share, minus standardized scores for public sector share and affiliates). These two measures can be aggregated into a single left-labor power index that I use in Chapter 4 by summing the standardized scores for political power and the encompassment of labor market institutions.

In the benchmark 1966–1973 period (see Figure 3.8), there was a very strong positive relationship between the political power of the left and the encompassment of labor market institutions. This is not surprising given the plethora of research on the reasons these two variables go together. Austria and Sweden stood out as the paradigmatic cases of social democratic corporatism, but one could arguably include all the other countries of northern Europe and perhaps even Italy in this category. At the other end of the spectrum, France, Japan, and the United States were closest to the market liberalism ideal type, followed by Canada and the United Kingdom. Clearly, regime coherence was very high in this period.

The correlation between the balance of political power and labor market institutions was considerably weaker in the 1985–1990 period (see Figure 3.9).

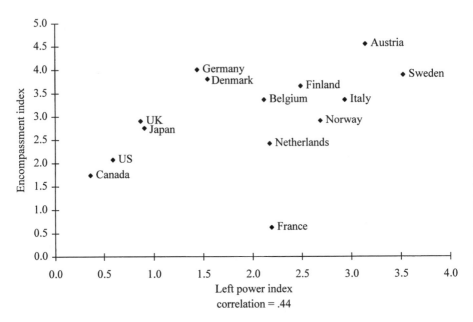

Figure 3.9 *Left power and labor encompassment, 1985–1990*

Nonetheless, there were still clear cases of social democratic corporatism and market liberalism. Austria and Sweden remained the countries with the strongest left-wing parties and labor market institutions, followed by Finland, Italy, and Norway. The North American countries were the paradigms of market liberalism, followed by Japan and the United Kingdom (which became a clear liberal market political economy as a result of Thatcherism (Garrett 1993)). Nonetheless, the fourteen countries as a whole were less tightly clustered around the 45-degree angle than had been the case in the 1966–1973. Three significant "incoherent" outlying cases should be noted.

Even though France was governed by "cohabitation" between Mitterrand and a right-wing majority in the National Assembly for half of the 1985–1990 period, the left was still far more powerful than were French labor market institutions. Conversely, the presence of governments dominated by the right in Denmark and Germany in the context of encompassing labor market institutions rendered these political economies incoherent. One would thus expect that economic policy should have been less consistent and performance poorer in these three cases than in more coherent regimes in the latter 1980s, or indeed than had been the case in Denmark, France, and Germany in the early 1970s.

In sum, this section has presented a battery of data pertaining to different facets of power in politics and the labor market over the period 1966–1990. There is little in the data to support the conventional wisdom about the domestic effects of globalization – namely, that market integration undermined the structural bases of left power and corporatism. The political power of the left and the capacities for collective action among organized labor movements did not decline in any appreciable way across the industrial countries as a whole from the late 1960s to the late 1980s. Moreover, large historical cross-national differences proved highly resilient to the globalization of markets. The coherence of political economic regimes did decline appreciably in some cases in the 1980s. Nonetheless, clear examples of social democratic corporatism and market liberalism remained. It is simply not the case – as the conventional wisdom implicitly claims – that all countries have come to converge in the lower-left quadrant of Figure 3.9.

It is thus now time to move on to the remaining parts of the debate about the domestic effects of globalization. The next two chapters discuss the impact of differences in domestic political economic regimes on economic policies and performance in the industrial democracies under conditions of globalized markets. Again, my modus operandi is to question conventional views about the demise of leftist alternatives to the free market. Before this can be done, however, it is necessary to highlight one final observation about globalization: The nature of market integration differs across domestic regime types.

3.4   THE RELATIONSHIP BETWEEN GLOBALIZATION AND LEFT-LABOR POWER

This section considers the relationship between market integration and the power of the left and organized labor. I show that although the exposure to trade and left-labor power continue to go together, the power of the left and organized labor has always been associated with the imposition of more controls on cross-border capital movements. This has implications both for the challenges posed by globalization in different countries and for the analytic strategies appropriate to delineating the effects of market integration on economic policy and performance.

Figures 3.10 and 3.11 plot the composite left-labor power index (the standardized sum of the balance of political power and labor market institutions indices) against total trade as a portion of GDP for the benchmark period, 1966–1973, and in the era of global markets, 1985–1990. As David Cameron (1978) first noted, countries that are more exposed to trade tend to have both stronger left-wing parties and more powerful organized labor movements. But this relationship is not particularly strong and weakened somewhat between the two periods. Notably, left-labor power was considerably higher in Austria and Sweden than in Belgium and the Netherlands, even though trade was far more important to the Benelux economies.

The weakening of this relationship makes sense given that Cameron's ar-

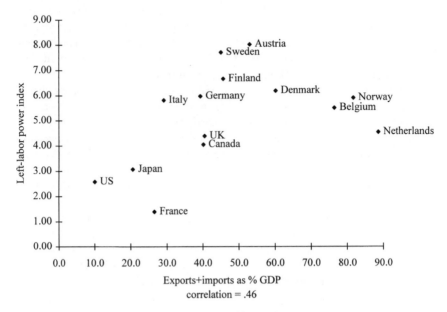

Figure 3.10 *Trade and left-labor power, 1966–1973*

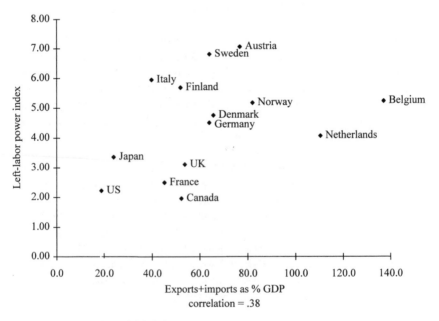

Figure 3.11 *Trade and left-labor power, 1985–1990*

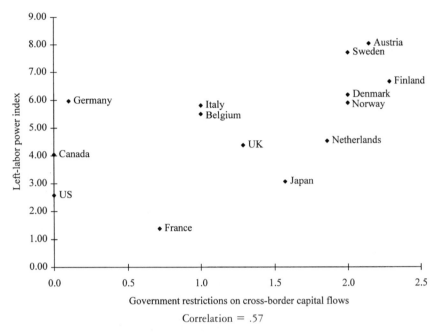

Figure 3.12 *Capital mobility and left-labor power, 1966–1973*

gument is historical. He argued that big traders tended to be late industrializers that concentrated production in a few industries. This was conducive to the organization of workers into unions. In turn, union power was fertile ground for the rise of left-wing parties. All else being equal, one would thus expect this relationship to have weakened the longer the time since industrialization occurred in these countries. But it might also be argued that this trend reflects the constraints of globalization: It has become harder for the left and organized labor to thrive where trade has grown most rapidly. Even if this were true, this effect has not been particularly marked. It is certainly not the case, for example, that in the era of global markets there was an inverse relationship between trade and left-labor power.

Figures 3.12 and 3.13 plot left-labor power against the extent of capital controls in the periods 1966–1973 and 1985–1990, respectively. The basic story told by these figures is that capital mobility has always been and remains inversely correlated to left-labor power. In the first period, there was a clear clustering among the five countries with the strongest left parties and labor market institutions and with the most capital controls. This relationship had weakened marginally by 1985-1990. More countries had removed all of their controls on cross-border capital flows, and only Finland retained heavy restrictions on capital movements. Nonetheless, the basic left-labor power–capital controls association endured.

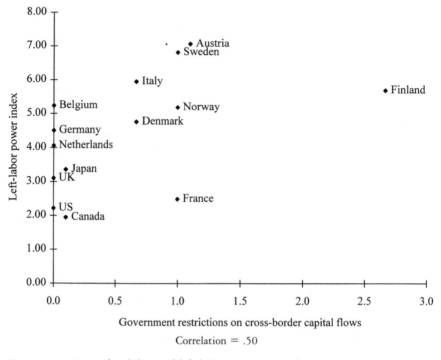

Figure 3.13 *Capital mobility and left-labor power, 1985–1990*

The simple point to be taken from these data is that despite the general trend to more globalization across the board in the industrial policies, it remains the case that regimes dominated by left parties and encompassing labor movements tend to be bigger traders, but also to have more closed financial markets. The converse is true for countries with stronger right-wing parties and weaker labor market institutions.

The most important consequence of this relationship for my purposes pertains to methodology. The common move in the literature on globalization is to assume that it is a one dimensional phenomenon that affects all of the industrialized democracies more or less equally. This assumption is inappropriate. I showed earlier in this chapter that trade and capital mobility tend to be inversely correlated. This section has demonstrated that they also have markedly different associations with left-labor power. Therefore, it is simply not possible to assess the effects of globalization on economic policy and performance or on the relationships between left-labor power and policy and performance without analyzing trade and capital mobility separately. Plotting over-time trends in policies and performance or their correlation with left-labor power is an intuitive and readily understood way to assess the impact of globalization on domestic politics. But it is also very misleading because trade and capital mobility do not go hand in hand. Instead, the appropriate methodologies for analyzing the domestic effects of globalization are multivariate – using both trade and capital mobility variables – and conditional – assessing the effects of left-labor power at different levels of trade and capital mobility.

CONCLUSION

This chapter has highlighted four observations about market integration and domestic politics in the industrial democracies from the mid 1960s to 1990. First, globalization increased continuously and consistently throughout the period, but at any given point in time there always was an inverse relationship between exposure to trade and capital mobility. Second, the political power of the left and the strength of labor market institutions were not in secular decline during this period. Moreover, important cross-national differences in domestic regimes endured. The left and organized labor have always been more powerful in Austria and Scandinavia (social democratic corporatist regimes), whereas the right has been most dominant and labor market institutions have tended to be weakest in France, Japan, and North America (approximating the market liberalism ideal type). Third, whereas the balance of political power and the strength of labor market institutions have always been strongly associated with each other, the overall coherence of domestic arrangements has decreased with the globalization of markets. Finally, the power of the left and organized labor has been greater in countries that are more exposed to trade but where capital is less mobile.

Having established these basic relationships among the key independent variables in this study, it is now time to turn to their consequences for economic policy and performance. This entails estimating multivariate regression equations that delineate the interactive effects of trade, capital mobility, the balance of political power, and the encompassment of labor market institutions. The next chapter presents the economic policy analysis. The investigation of macroeconomic outcomes is undertaken in Chapter 5.

4

ECONOMIC POLICY

Chapter 3 demonstrated that the increasing globalization of markets in the 1966–1990 period did not precipitate a secular decline in the power of the left and organized labor in the industrialized democracies. This says nothing, of course, about the consequences of partisan politics for the economy during this period. Most importantly, it is commonly assumed that nominally "leftist" parties have only been able to remain politically competitive in the era of global markets by abandoning their traditional commitments to interventionist economic policies (Kitschelt 1994). I argued in Chapter 2, however, that the political incentives for left-wing parties to pursue interventionist economic policies should have increased with market integration – to ameliorate the economic dislocations and insecurities associated with globalization.

This chapter tests these contending hypotheses against a range of economic policy indicators for the period 1966 to 1990 – ranging from broad fiscal and monetary policy stances to the major components of government spending and the structure of taxation. I begin with over-time plots and bivariate correlations to give readers a feel for basic trends in the data. The analysis then moves on to more precise econometric tests that isolate the effects of domestic political conditions and market integration on economic policy.

The data and analyses provide strong support for my argument with respect to most facets of fiscal policy, where the relationship between left-labor power and redistributive and interventionist government policy increased – rather than decreased – both with heightened exposure to trade and with greater capital mobility. At the same time, however, my analysis also shows that market integration did exert some constraining influence on the left's policy agenda. Most importantly, it was not possible for governments in strong left-labor cases to increase total tax revenues at the same pace as spending grew. The result was an increasingly strong relationship between left-labor power and larger budget deficits in the global economy. Moreover, financial markets imposed interest rate premiums on left-labor power under conditions of high capital mobility. Nonetheless, the distinctiveness of the policy core of social democratic corporatism – extensive government spending and progressive systems of taxation, both of which redistribute wealth and social risk in favor of workers and the poor – increased with international market integration among the advanced industrial economies.

The chapter is broken down into three sections. Section 4.1 analyzes government spending. Viewed in isolation, market integration did put some downward pressure on the size of the public economy. This was more than outweighed, however, by the positive impact of left-labor power on public sector expansion. Indeed, government spending was greatest of all in countries with powerful left-wing parties and encompassing labor market institutions that were also highly integrated into global markets. Conversely, spending was lowest in cases of high international market integration with strong conservative parties and weak trade unions. Thus, the effects of partisan politics on government spending increased, not decreased, the more integrated a country was into the international economy.

Taxation is examined in Section 4.2. Here the story was more complicated, and I have chosen to divide the analysis into two components – revenues from taxation and the structure of tax systems. Tax revenues were more stable over time than spending. As a result, although the effects of market integration and partisan politics on government revenues were generally similar to those for expenditures, the magnitude of these relationships tended to be smaller and less significant statistically. There is no evidence, however, of any cross-national convergence in tax revenues as a result of globalization.

Turning to the structure of taxation, despite a trend toward flatter systems of personal income taxation across the industrial democracies, the positive relationship between left-labor power and the progressivity of income taxation became stronger with the globalization of markets. Moreover, the propensity of countries with strong left-wing parties and encompassing labor market institutions to impose higher rates of corporate taxation was unaffected by the integration of international markets.

Section 4.3 discusses macroeconomic policy. In contrast with the folklore about the halcyon days of the Keynesian welfare state, left-labor power was not associated with greater reliance on countercyclical demand management in the era of relatively closed markets during the late 1960s and early 1970s. But as market integration subsequently increased, the combined power of the left and organized labor became increasingly associated with bigger budget deficits. The results in Sections 4.1 and 4.2 show that these deficits were caused by an inability of governments to increase tax revenues at the same rate as spending grew. In turn, the evidence on monetary policy shows that governments in strong left-labor regimes had to pay higher interest rates for their borrowing as globalization increased. These interest rate premiums, however, were quite small and cannot on their own justify pessimism about the economic feasibility of social democratic corporatism in the global economy.

4.1 GOVERNMENT SPENDING

Figure 4.1 plots annual changes from 1966 to 1990 in the average size of the public sector and its major components for the countries in this study.[1] Average total government spending grew as a portion of GDP by almost fifteen percentage points from the late 1960s to the mid 1980s and then leveled off at almost 50 percent of domestic output. This pattern was replicated for the two largest components of the budget that together constitute the core of the modern welfare state – direct income transfers (most importantly public pensions and unemployment benefits) and civilian government consumption (in-kind benefits such as the public provision of education and health). Consistent with aging populations and rising unemployment in most countries, the growth of the transfer budget was faster than that for consumption expenditures. Indeed, transfers became the largest component of government spending in the early 1980s, and the gap with consumption spending grew throughout the decade. The remaining two components of the budget were much smaller. Government subsidies to industry tended to grew proportionately with the bigger budget items. In contrast, capital spending declined after the early 1980s – perhaps reflecting the rise of privatization programs in many countries.

These fourteen-country averages conceal cross-national variations in spending patterns. I hypothesized in Chapter 2 that government expenditures should have been higher the more the balance of political power was tilted to the left and the more encompassing labor market institutions were. Moreover, I suggested that this relationship should have strengthened with globalization, because the electoral incentives for the left to redistribute wealth and risk should have grown with the heightened dislocations and economic insecurity generated by market integration.

Because both trade and capital mobility increased in secular fashion during the 1966–1990 period for most of the countries in this study (see Chapter 3), over-time changes in the correlations between government spending and the left-labor power index developed in Chapter 3 can be used to test my argument about the effects of globalization on partisan politics. It should also be remembered that using the aggregate left-labor power index is appropriate for examining the interactive effects of partisan politics and labor market institutions on economic policy. This is because incoherent regimes receive left-labor scores in the middle of the distribution, and I hypothesized that incoherence will be associated with intermediate values on measures of economic policy interventionism (see Chapter 2).

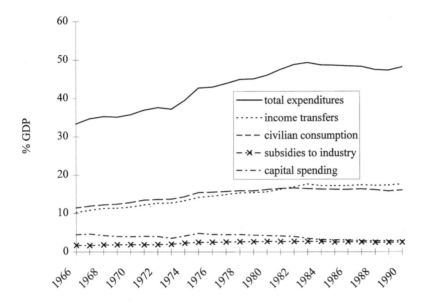

Source: OECD, National Account Statistics (various). 14-country averages

Figure 4.1 *Government spending*

The time-varying correlations presented in Table 4.1 lend considerably more support to my argument than they do to the globalization thesis (Appendixes 4.1 and 4.2 show the data for each country for the periods 1966–1973 and 1985–1990).[2] With respect to total government spending, the correlation with left-labor power increased markedly between the benchmark period (1966–1973) and the years after the first oil shock. The correlations were somewhat weaker in the 1980s, but the relationship between left-labor power and greater government spending was nonetheless considerably stronger in the era of global markets (1985–1990) than was the case in the 1966–1973 period.

Turning to the components of government spending, the income transfer and industrial subsidies correlations provide strong support for my argument. There was little relationship between left-labor power and income transfers up until 1980, reflecting the historical preference of Christian democratic welfare states for cash transfers over the public provision of in-kind benefits (Esping-Andersen 1990). However, the positive correlation between left-labor power and income transfers more than doubled in the 1980s. This pattern was even more marked for industrial subsidies. Civilian consumption was the only component of government spending for which the over-time correlations lent some support to the view that globalization lessened the impact of partisan politics.[3] None-

Table 4.1. *Left-Labor Power and Government Spending*

	Total expenditures	Income transfers	Civilian consumption	Industrial subsidies	Capital expenditures
1966–1973	0.36	0.14	0.67	0.35	0.17
1974–1979	0.56	0.12	0.63	0.62	0.40
1980–1984	0.50	0.30	0.58	0.56	0.24
1985–1990	0.51	0.34	0.48	0.63	0.10

Figures are correlations between the left-labor power index and government spending (as % of GDP) in each of the periods.

theless, the positive correlation even in the last period was almost as strong as that for total government spending – far from a trivial relationship.

At this point it must be emphasized, however, that despite their tractability, these time-varying bivariate correlations suffer from two major limitations with respect to analyzing the interactive effects of globalization and left-labor power on government spending (and all other facets of economic policy as well). First, this type of analysis assumes that the impact of globalization can be assessed simply by monitoring changes in the spending–left-labor power relationship over time. But as Chapter 3 demonstrated, there has always been considerable variation in the extent to which different countries are integrated into global markets. Second, it is well known that government spending is driven far more by the business cycle and demography than by political conditions. This does not necessarily mean that politics and globalization are irrelevant. But it does imply that one must control for these relationships so as to isolate the effects of the variables of primary interest in this study.

In order to analyze more accurately the effects on public expenditures of globalization and left-labor power, I regressed the various indicators of government spending on a battery of business cycle and demographic controls, as well as trade, capital mobility and left-labor power, and interactions among them. The analysis used data from all of the countries and all of the years in the study (i.e., there are $14 \times 25 = 350$ observations). I followed the estimation procedures advocated by Nathaniel Beck and Jonathan Katz (1995a, 1995b) to deal with the methodological problems associated with analyzing panel data of similar dimensions to those in this book: the inclusion of a lagged dependent variable to mitigate serial correlation among the error terms, using panel corrected standard errors to take into account heteroskedastic errors, and controlling for fixed effects by including both country and period dummy variables. The basic structure of the spending equations is:

$$SPEND_{it} = b_1 SPEND_{it-1} + b_2 CAPMOBILITY_{it} + b_3 TRADE_{it} +$$
$$b_4 LLPOWER_{it} + b_5 CAPMOBILITY.LLPOWER_{it} + b_6 TRADE.LLPOWER_{it} \quad (1)$$
$$+ \Sigma(b_j PERIOD_{jt}) + \Sigma(b_k COUNTRY_{ki}) + \Sigma(b_l X_{lit}) + \mu_{it}$$

In this equation, the b's are parameter estimates. SPEND represents total government spending and its components. The subscripts $_i$ and $_t$ denote, respectively, the country and year of the observations. CAPMOBILITY is the number of government restrictions on cross-border financial flows, multiplied by minus one for easier interpretation (that is, higher scores indicate more capital mobility). TRADE is exports plus imports as a percentage of gross domestic product. LLPOWER is the left-labor power index. "." represents a multiplication dot. The $_j$ period dummy variables (1966–1973, 1974–1979, 1980–1984, 1986–1990) are designated by PERIOD (the excluded reference year is 1985). The $_k$ (fourteen) country dummy variables are denoted by COUNTRY (N.B.: the intercept is suppressed). The $_l$ economic and demographic control variables (X) are economic growth, unemployment and the portion of the population over sixty-five years old. μ is an error term.

One might wish to criticize this equation for failing to disentangle the causal relationships between globalization and left-labor power. Recall that there are good reasons to believe that countries that were historically large traders will have strong left-wing parties and labor market institutions today (Cameron 1978). I also showed in Chapter 3 that restrictions on cross-border capital flows were removed more slowly in countries with high scores on left-labor power. This endogeneity on the right-hand side of Equation 1 might bias the estimated regressions and could call for the use of even more complicated systems of equations (such as two-stage least squares). In this case, however, this added complexity is not required.

The reduced form equation I use controls for the historical effects of market integration and political conditions using country dummy variables, whereas the capital mobility, trade, and left-labor power terms isolate their impact on government spending in the period under analysis. For example, one could predict that the parameter estimates for the Netherlands country dummy variable would always be very large in the spending regressions because that country was characterized by high trade and high left-labor power in the period before 1966. But this does not mean that the contemporaneous effects of the variables (i.e., the annual effects in the period 1966–1990) would also be positive. Indeed, the globalization hypothesis proposes exactly the opposite set of relationships: The interaction between market integration and left-labor power should have depressed government spending because social democratic corporatism is maladapted to the global economy. This is not to say that the historical relationships identified by Cameron and others do not hold. Rather, I simply want to point out that my reduced form equations are well equipped to disentangle these historical and contemporaneous effects.

Table 4.2. *The Determinants of Government Spending, 1966–1990*

Independent variables	Total spending	Income transfers	Civilian government consumption	Subsidies to industry	Capital spending
Lagged dependent variable	.81***	.86***	.86***	.79***	.71***
	(.02)	(.03)	(.02)	(.04)	(.08)
GDP growth	-.399***	-.168***	-.138***	-.014*	-.052***
	(.028)	(.014)	(.011)	(.007)	(.017)
Unemployment	.086*	.068***	.008	-.022*	-.038*
	(.045)	(.019)	(.018)	(.011)	(.022)
Old age population	.241**	.134***	.006*	-.017	-.064
	(.104)	(.052)	(.005)	(.027)	(.056)
Capital mobility	-.89***	-.19	-.38***	-.07	-.05
	(.30)	(.15)	(.15)	(.09)	(.18)
Trade	-.0432*	-.0084	-.0163*	-.0082	-.0158
	(.0237)	(.0123)	(.0090)	(.0063)	(.011)
Left-labor power	.082	.068	.134	-.096*	.081
	(.190)	(.093)	(.097)	(.051)	(.124)
Capital mobility*left-labor power	.228***	.066**	.075***	.015	.011
	(.055)	(.027)	(.026)	(.019)	(.034)
Trade*left-labor power	.0077**	.0007	.0015	.0026***	.0002
	(.0036)	(.0019)	(.0015)	(.0009)	(.0020)
Period dummy variables					
1966–1973	-.32	.43*	-.09	.00	-.29
	(.46)	(.24)	(.19)	(.12)	(.25)
1974–1979	.16	.26	.02	.17*	.15
	(.33)	(.17)	(.14)	(.09)	(.19)
1980–1984	-.04	.08	-.14	.17**	-.10
	(.29)	(.15)	(.12)	(.08)	(.15)
1986–1990	-.40	.04	-.11	.14*	-.14
	(.30)	(.15)	(.12)	(.08)	(.15)
Country dummy variables					
Austria	6.17***	1.02	2.38**	.83	2.94**
	(2.29)	(1.19)	(.85)	(.61)	(1.43)
Belgium	7.16***	1.12	2.48**	.68	3.60**
	(2.55)	(1.32)	(1.08)	(.69)	(1.52)
Canada	7.83***	.38	3.25***	1.00**	2.53**
	(1.78)	(.91)	(0.76)	(.48)	(1.03)

The government spending regression equations are reported in Table 4.2. Not surprisingly, all facets of the public economy were very sticky during the period 1966–1990 (the coefficient on the lagged spending term was very large). Annual GDP growth was negatively associated with spending because slow growth in a given year did not result in commensurate spending cuts (Roubini and Sachs 1989). Total spending and income transfers increased both with higher levels of unemployment and with more aged people, but this was compensated for by cuts in other elements of the budget. The period dummy variables were

Table 4.2. *The Determinants of Government Spending, 1966–1990 (continued)*

Independent variables	Total spending	Income transfers	Civilian government consumption	Subsidies to industry	Capital spending
Country dummy variables					
Denmark	7.57***	.34	3.31***	1.17*	2.64**
	(2.25)	(1.18)	(0.98)	(0.62)	(1.23)
Finland	6.81***	.63	2.78***	1.13**	2.71**
	(2.00)	(1.02)	(0.87)	(0.52)	(1.19)
France	7.15***	1.30	2.25***	.98*	2.72**
	(2.00)	(1.06)	(0.85)	(0.54)	(1.19)
Germany	5.67**	.12	2.32**	.92	2.80**
	(2.24)	(1.17)	(0.97)	(0.62)	(1.36)
Italy	6.50***	.48	1.99**	1.15**	2.34*
	(2.03)	(1.06)	(0.88)	(0.55)	(1.21)
Japan	6.02***	.87	1.76***	.73*	2.94***
	(1.52)	(.78)	(0.65)	(0.41)	(1.00)
Netherlands	9.04***	2.48**	2.57***	.69	3.30**
	(2.41)	(1.23)	(0.99)	(.63)	(1.40)
Norway	7.68***	.97	2.84***	1.52**	3.25**
	(2.41)	(1.23)	(1.03)	(0.65)	(1.47)
Sweden	8.13***	.69	3.31***	1.24*	2.78*
	(2.42)	(1.23)	(1.04)	(.64)	(1.46)
United Kingdom	5.66**	-.35	2.43**	1.01	2.83**
	(2.20)	(1.15)	(0.95)	(0.60)	(1.32)
United States	5.29***	-.14	1.97***	.64	1.87**
	(1.56)	(.82)	(0.66)	(.43)	(0.92)
Observations	350	350	350	350	350
Adjusted R-squared	.986	.990	.989	.958	.826
Wald's test for the joint significance of the left-labor power-capital mobility interaction	.00001	.011	.018	.130	.951
Wald's test for the joint significance of the left-labor power-trade interaction	.0001	.115	.015	.012	.039

OLS estimates using panel corrected standard errors; intercept suppressed; *** $p<.01$; ** $.01<p<.05$; * $.05<p<.10$

generally insignificant, with the exception of subsidies to industry. Controlling for all the other variables in the equation, this facet of the public economy was larger after 1973 than in the benchmark period. Finally, most of the country dummy variables were significant in all of the equations except that for income transfers (where spending in the Netherlands was significantly higher than the rest of the equation estimated).

Regression diagnostics reveal that the results were not sensitive to the se-

quential exclusion of individual cases from the analysis. The estimation procedures successfully removed serial correlation and heteroskedasticity among the
error terms. Hence, any remaining effects for market integration and left-labor
power should be taken seriously.

The patterns of coefficients for the market integration–left-labor power interactions (i.e., the independent effects of each term combined with the parameter
estimate for their multiplicative interactions) were strikingly similar for the total
spending equation and for the two largest components of government expenditures, income transfers and civilian consumption. Increasing exposure to trade
and capital mobility, ceteris paribus, tended to depress spending – supporting
the view that market integration generated lowest common denominator pressures on government budgets. On the other hand, left-labor power was associated
with higher levels of government spending, which is evidence that traditional
partisan politics also mattered.

Most importantly, the coefficients for the multiplicative interaction terms
were positive and frequently significant. This indicates that, over and above their
independent effects, the combination of strong left parties and powerful labor
market institutions with high levels of exposure to trade (and even more notice-
ably, with highly mobile capital) resulted in higher levels of spending.[4]

In order to test directly the core empirical question in debate – whether government spending went up or down (and by how much) when left-labor power
and market integration increased simultaneously (moving either between countries or over time) – I made a series of counterfactual estimates of government
spending under different constellations of domestic political conditions and integration into global markets (based on the equations in Table 4.2). This was done
by setting all the other variables in the regression equations to their mean levels
and multiplying these means by their corresponding coefficients, and then by examining the counterfactual impact of various combinations of left-labor power
and globalization (again, multiplying these by their regression coefficients).[5] This
process was only undertaken in those cases where the interaction specification (i.e.,
the coefficients for left-labor power, the indicator of globalization, and their multiplicative interaction) was jointly significant at the .05 level or better.[6]

So as not to exaggerate the substantive effects of these relationships, the
counterfactuals were not based on the tails of the distributions in the sample for
left-labor power and market integration. Rather, I relied on combinations of the
20th and 80th percentile scores in the data set on each relevant variable. For
trade, these scores were respectively 28.4 percent (Italy in 1967) and 85.7 percent
(Norway in 1980) of GDP. For capital mobility, the 20th percentile was the case
of two categories of restrictions on cross-border capital flows (for many countries
in the earlier years); countries with no capital controls (half the sample in the
late 1980s) constituted the 80th percentile. The 20th percentile score on the left-
labor power index was 2.85 (for France in 1988), whereas the 80th percentile
was 7.05 (Finland in 1973).

Counterfactual estimates for the combined effects on government spending of variations in left-labor power and integration into global markets are presented in Figure 4.2. These two-by-two boxes can be interpreted in a number of ways. Moving from left to right shows whether growing trade or capital mobility was associated with higher or lower government spending. Moving up and down indicates whether more left-labor power increased or decreased public sector expenditures.

From the standpoint of my argument, the most important information is contained in the lower-right cell of each box. If my argument is correct, government spending should have been higher in this cell – combining high left-labor power with high exposure to trade or capital mobility – than in any other. I would also expect the gap between the lower-right and upper-right cells to be greater than that for the cells in the left-hand column. This would imply that the effects of partisan politics were greater in the global economy than in cases where markets were less integrated.

The top panel of Figure 4.2 contains the two boxes with counterfactual estimates of total government spending under different combinations of left-labor power and market integration. These strongly support my argument about the effects of globalization on partisan politics. Government spending was always greater when left-labor power was "high" (the 80th percentile) than when it was "low" (the 20th percentile), irrespective of the level of market integration. Where left-labor power was low, government spending decreased if one moved from low to high levels of market integration. But the converse was true at high levels of left-labor power.

The counterfactual estimates of government spending were highest of all in the lower-right cells, and the gap between the low and high left-labor power cells was larger in the high trade and capital mobility cases than in the cells with low market integration. This is precisely the opposite of the convergence thesis and exactly as my argument predicts. Partisan politics had more impact on government spending where countries were highly integrated into the international economy than in more closed contexts.

The size of these effects was far from trivial. For example, moving from the 20th to the 80th percentile on the left-labor power index at high levels of trade and capital mobility is estimated to have increased total government spending by more than two percentage points of GDP. Given the stickiness of spending over time and the impact of the business cycle and demographics on spending patterns, these partisan differences would have loomed large in the real world.

Furthermore, the regression equations on which these counterfactuals are based use a technique that significantly reduces the estimated effects of globalization and left-labor power on government spending. Recall that all the equations include a lagged dependent variable to remove serial correlation among the error terms. This could also have been done using an AR(1) transformation adapted to the panel context (Garrett and Mitchell 1996; Huber, Ragin, and Stephens 1993).

Figure 4.2. Counterfactual estimates of government spending (% GDP)

A. Total government spending

	Trade			Capital mobility	
	Low	High		Low	High
Left–labor power Low	43.1	41.9		42.8	42.3
High	43.5	44.2		43.1	44.5

B. Income transfers

	Low	High
Left–labor power Low	14.7	14.7
High	14.6	15.1

C. Civilian consumption

	Low	High		Low	High
Left–labor power Low	15.0	14.3		14.9	14.5
High	15.5	15.1		15.2	15.5

D. Subsidies to industry

	Trade	
	Low	High
Left–labor power Low	2.3	2.2
High	2.1	2.7

E. Capital spending

	Low	High
Left–labor power Low	3.9	3.0
High	3.8	3.0

The counterfactuals were calculated on the basis of the public spending regression equations reported in Table 4.2. Only interaction specifications that were jointly significant at the .05 level or better were included in the analysis. Low (high) levels of trade and capital mobility refer to the 20th (80th) percentile scores in the sample. Low (high) levels of left–labor power refer to the 20th (80th) percentile scores on left–labor power index. All other variables were set at their means.

Figure 4.2 *Counterfactual estimates of government spending (% GDP)*

If a generalized least squares procedure had been used, the size of the estimated effects in Figure 4.2 would have been two to three times larger than those reported in Table 4.2. I chose not to follow this strategy, however, because I agree with Nathaniel Beck and Jonathan Katz that introducing a lagged dependent variable is a better way to model explicitly the dynamics of the estimated equations (Beck and Katz 1995b).

Turning to the counterfactual estimates for the components of government spending, it is evident that the substantive effects of globalization and left-labor power were more muted. Nonetheless, it would be very difficult to construe these results as supporting the conventional view about the effects of market integration on economic policy. It is true that in the trade boxes for civilian consumption expenditures and capital spending were not highest in the lower-right cells. But the spending gap between low and high levels of left-labor power was always larger in the high market integration cells than for the left-hand columns. Furthermore, the capital mobility counterfactuals for the two largest components of government spending that are the most important from the standpoint of partisan politics – income transfers and civilian consumption – conformed perfectly with the patterns for total spending. Government spending on income transfers and civilian consumption programs was highest when countries were dominated by left parties and encompassing labor market institutions and when there were no restrictions on cross-border capital flows.

In sum, the evidence presented in this section is considerably more supportive of my argument than of the notion that globalization led the industrial democracies to converge around smaller public sectors. Irrespective of the complexity of the empirical tests, two things stand out about government spending in the period 1966–1990. First, the greater the combined power of the left and organized labor, the higher public expenditures were. Second, the partisan distinctiveness of government spending increased with the greater integration of national economies into global markets.

4.2 TAXATION

This section begins by replicating for government revenues from taxation the battery of statistical techniques used to analyze the political economy of public expenditures. Relying solely on data from the size of revenues to assess the interactive effects of partisan politics and market integration on taxation, however, may conceal important relationships pertaining to the structure of tax systems. For example, total tax revenues could be the same in two countries even if in one case all economic activity was taxed at a single rate (a completely "flat tax" regime), whereas in the other the rate of income tax increased with earnings. The latter "progressive" structure is typically associated with the left; the former, with the right. The conventional wisdom about globalization is that national

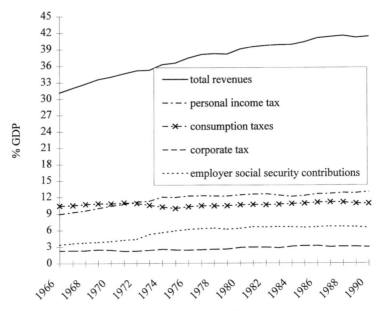

Source: OECD, Revenue Statistics (various). 14-country averages.

Figure 4.3. Tax revenues

Figure 4.3 *Tax revenues*

systems have converged around much flatter tax regimes as a result of market integration (Lee and McKenzie 1989; Steinmo 1993). There are great difficulties inherent in gathering comprehensive cross-national and time-varying data on the structure of taxation. Given the importance of this issue, however, I present rudimentary analyses of the available information on the structure of personal and corporate income taxation.

Figure 4.3 plots changes over time in the average level of total government revenues and the four major types of taxation.[7] Total revenues grew very steadily from 1966 to 1990, but there were substantial variations among specific tax programs. Personal income taxes replaced consumption taxes (on the purchase of goods and services) as the major source of government revenue in the early 1970s and continued to grow throughout the period. Average consumption tax revenues remained at more or less the same level relative to GDP from 1966 to 1990. Revenues from direct taxes on corporate income were also very stable. However, the effective tax burden falling on corporations did increase from the late 1960s to 1990, in the form of growing employer contributions to social security funds.

This picture is quite different from the conventional wisdom about growing constraints on taxation in the global economy. Overall tax revenues increased

Table 4.3. *Left-Labor Power and Tax Revenues*

	Total revenues	Personal income tax	Consumption taxes	Corporate taxes	Employer social security contributions
1966–1973	0.48	0.53	0.54	-0.63	-0.16
1974–1979	0.51	0.55	0.62	-0.74	-0.03
1980–1984	0.51	0.43	0.64	-0.39	0.25
1985–1990	0.54	0.38	0.51	-0.31	0.28

Figures are correlations between the left-labor power index and tax revenues (as % of GDP) in each of the periods.

steadily. This growth was largely the product of increasing revenues from personal income taxation (typically a relatively progressive program). Furthermore, although revenues from taxes on corporate profits were stable, firms' contributions did increase substantially through higher payments for their employees' social security benefits.

Let us now consider cross-national variations in taxation. Changes over time in the relationship between left-labor power and government revenues are reported in Table 4.3 (see Appendixes 4.1 and 4.2 for raw data on revenues for the benchmark period and the era of global markets). The first thing to note about these relationships is that the positive correlation between left-labor power and total taxation revenues increased across the four periods. This supports my general argument about the impact of partisan politics on domestic responses to market integration. The picture was more complex, however, for the different components of tax revenues.

Although revenues from personal income taxation grew steadily from 1966 to 1990, cross-national partisan differences for this form of taxation declined, suggesting somewhat of a "citizen revolt" in countries with histories of high personal income taxation. Of course, as the preceding section showed, this did not mean that voters in these countries wanted governments to cut the public provision of welfare and other services.[8]

The correlation between left-labor power and consumption taxes was very strong, stronger indeed than that for total tax revenues (except for the 1985–1990 period). Combined with the declining correlation between left-labor power and income tax revenues, this suggests that the left shifted some of the tax burden away from income taxation and toward consumption taxes. One might think that this is a clear indication of a globalization constraint on taxing high income earners, because consumption taxes are usually considered to be regressive (on the assumption that the poor spend disproportionate amounts of their income on items subject to sales tax). However, the regressivity of consumption taxes depends on the range of goods and services to which they are applied (e.g., luxuries versus necessities), and there is some evidence that left-labor regimes tend to deploy less regressive systems (e.g., by not taxing the purchase of food and clothing). Thus, there are reasons to question the identification of rising consumption taxes with the triumph of global markets over leftist domestic politics. I develop this argument in Chapter 6.

Consider now the portion of the tax burden falling on corporations. This can be broken down into two components: revenues collected from corporate profits and those in the form of employer contributions to social security programs. In the first two periods under analysis, left-labor power was correlated with lower corporate tax revenues and had very little relationship to employer social security contributions (see Table 4.3). This is obviously very different from the prevalent view that, in the past, the left has imposed the most onerous tax burdens on corporations.[9] The negative relationship between left-labor power and corporate tax revenues, however, decreased substantially in the 1980s. Furthermore, the magnitude of social security contributions paid by employers became positively correlated with greater left-labor power. These results thus suggest that the propensity of governments in strong left-labor cases to tax corporations (either directly or indirectly) increased from the 1970s to the 1980s.

As in the case of spending, however, it would be imprudent to base conclusions about the effects of globalization and left-labor power on tax revenues simply on these bivariate correlations. Accordingly, I estimated a series of equations that regressed total tax revenues and their components on the same battery of control variables and the left-labor power–market integration interactions, and using the same procedures and diagnostics as I did for government spending.

The panel regression equations for government revenues are reported in Table 4.4. The estimation procedure generated well specified and robust estimates of the determinants of tax revenues. For present purposes, however, the most important observation to be drawn from these equations is that the market integration–left-labor power interaction specifications had considerably less impact on revenues than was the case for government expenditures.

In contrast with the total spending equation, trade and capital mobility did not significantly affect total tax revenues, whereas the left-labor power parameter estimate was positive and statistically significant. Furthermore, the interaction terms were of different signs and neither was statistically significant – in contrast with the positive and significant coefficients in the spending equations. This pattern of relationships was replicated in the income tax revenues equation. The estimates for the other components of taxation were generally inconclusive. In two cases, for trade in the consumption tax equation and for capital mobility in the social security contributions, there was some evidence that the independent effect of market integration was to reduce revenues. But in both instances, this was mitigated by positive coefficients for the market integration–left labor power interaction terms.

Taken together, these equations imply that although there were very powerful pressures on governments to increase spending to compensate losers from the process of market integration, the incentives to balance these with increased taxes were much weaker. I discuss the effects of this disjuncture in the next section with respect to public sector deficits and interest rates. I then return in Chapter 6 to the problem of funding large welfare states into the future. With respect to market integration, the revenue results yield no support for the argument that globalization powerfully constrains the ability of governments to tax. What about the overall effects of left-labor power and market integration?

One consequence of the weakness of the revenue equations is that the bulk of the left-labor power–market integration interactions were not jointly significant. The only exception was the total revenues equation with respect to trade. For this equation, I estimated counterfactual levels of tax revenues under different mixes of market integration and left-labor power, based on the 20th and 80th percentile scores in the data set for the relevant variables. The results are reported in Figure 4.4.

As was the case for spending, estimated revenues were highest in the lower-right cell (i.e., where both left-labor power and trade were high) and lowest in the upper-right cell. The revenue gap between cases of high and low left-labor power, however, was smaller at the higher level of trade (0.5 percentage points of GDP, compared with 1.2 points at low levels of trade). Moreover, all of these effects were smaller relative to GDP than was the case for total spending – on average only around half the size. Whereas spending grew rapidly in strong left-labor regimes in response to globalization, revenues did not increase at the same rate.

It should be remembered at this point, however, that the preceding analyses do not examine the structure of taxation. Fine-grained, time-varying cross-national data on tax systems are virtually impossible to come by. Nonetheless, I present below rudimentary analyses of data on two important aspects of the structure of national tax systems – the progressivity of personal income taxes and the effective marginal rates of taxation on corporate income.

Tables 4.5 and 4.6 present simple measures of the progressivity of income taxation for twelve of the fourteen countries in this study in the mid 1970s and the late 1980s. The notion of progressivity refers to the extent to which higher income earners pay more of their gross incomes in taxes. All else being equal, one would expect tax systems to be more progressive: the higher the top marginal rate of taxation, the greater the gap between the top and bottom marginal rates, and the larger the number of tax rates in the income tax structure.

The most surprising thing about income taxation in the mid 1970s is that taxes were not clearly more progressive (on these measures at least) in countries with powerful left parties and strong labor market institutions (Table 4.5). There

Table 4.4. *The Determinants of Tax Revenues, 1966–1990*

Independent variables	Total revenues	Personal income taxes	Consumption taxes	Corporate income taxes	Employer social security contributions
Lagged dependent variable	.78***	.88***	.72***	.84***	.88***
	(.03)	(.03)	(.04)	(.06)	(.05)
GDP growth	-.125***	-.066***	.019*	.015	-.029
	(.030)	(.019)	(.011)	(.012)	(.018)
Unemployment	-.080*	-.100***	.026	-.015	-.026
	(.043)	(.023)	(.018)	(.015)	(.026)
Old age population	.280**	.073	.050	.008	.095
	(.111)	(.069)	(.042)	(.037)	(.072)
Capital mobility	-.18	.13	-.08	.04	-.25*
	(.30)	(.18)	(.12)	(.13)	(.14)
Trade	.0280	.0250**	-.0155*	-.0044	.0123
	(.020)	(.0125)	(.0088)	(.0089)	(.0092)
Left-labor power	.410**	.199**	-.039	-.046	.053
	(.181)	(.100)	(.079)	(.078)	(.069)
Capital mobility*left-labor power	.061	-.024	.009	.001	.045
	(.058)	(.036)	(.023)	(.002)	(.027)
Trade*left-labor power	-.0027	-.0032	.0014	.0002	-.0005
	(.0031)	(.0019)	(.0014)	(.0015)	(.0012)
Period dummy variables					
1966–1973	-.56	-.14	-.05	-.34*	.31
	(.46)	(.28)	(.19)	(.18)	(.29)
1974–1979	-.58*	-.21	-.20	-.21	.24
	(.33)	(.19)	(.14)	(.13)	(.21)
1980–1984	-.41	-.26	-.03	-.03	.16
	(.29)	(.17)	(.12)	(.12)	(.18)
1986–1990	-.19	-.05	-.07	-.19	.05
	(.29)	(.17)	(.12)	(.12)	(.17)
Country dummy variables					
Austria	2.43	-1.00	3.37***	.91	-1.44
	(2.24)	(1.42)	(1.12)	(.81)	(1.40)
Belgium	3.38	-.05	3.27***	1.25	-1.43
	(2.41)	(1.51)	(1.14)	(.90)	(1.45)
Canada	4.26**	.80	2.49***	1.01**	-1.08
	(1.67)	(1.01)	(.0.80)	(.66)	(1.00)
Denmark	4.43**	1.48	4.11***	.95	-2.08
	(2.22)	(1.39)	(1.14)	(.81)	(1.42)
Finland	3.25	.51	3.53***	.96	-1.34
	(1.90)	(1.18)	(1.02)	(.71)	(1.17)

was a weak positive correlation between left-labor power and the highest marginal rate of income tax, but the gap between the highest and lowest rates decreased with left-labor power. Furthermore, there was a small negative correlation between left-labor power and the number of steps in the income tax scale. This suggests that although strong left-labor regimes used government spending to generate substantial redistribution of wealth and social risk, they were happy to

Table 4.4. *The Determinants of Tax Revenues, 1966–1990 (coninued)*

Independent variables	Total revenues	Personal income taxes	Consumption taxes	Corporate income taxes	Employer social security contributions
Country dummy variables					
France	4.70**	-.46	3.14***	.76	-.40
	(1.98)	(1.24)	(0.96)	(.75)	(1.26)
Germany	2.19	-.40	2.43**	.84	-1.25
	(2.18)	(1.36)	(1.00)	(.83)	(1.36)
Italy	2.63	-.11	2.19**	1.10	-.56
	(1.98)	(1.24)	(0.92)	(0.75)	(1.31)
Japan	2.93**	.02	.85	1.28**	-.81
	(1.47)	(.90)	(.64)	(0.62)	(.87)
Netherlands	4.43**	-.48	3.24***	1.25	-1.43
	(2.21)	(1.36)	(1.05)	(.84)	(1.27)
Norway	3.93*	-.53	4.62***	1.32	-1.42
	(2.33)	(1.43)	(1.25)	(0.87)	(1.38)
Sweden	4.29***	.30	3.10***	.92	-.68
	(2.35)	(1.43)	(1.12)	(.86)	(1.45)
United Kingdom	2.61	-.18	2.48***	1.13	-1.63
	(2.14)	(1.33)	(0.92)	(0.82)	(1.37)
United States	3.15**	.70	0.83	.75	-.70
	(1.55)	(.95)	(0.66)	(.59)	(1.03)
Observations	350	350	350	350	350
Adjusted R-squared	.979	.984	.984	.893	.965
Wald's test for the joint significance of the left-labor power-capital mobility interaction	.171	.106	.781	.480	.105
Wald's test for the joint significance of the left-labor power-trade interaction	.018	.194	.164	.498	.599

OLS estimates using panel corrected standard errors; intercept suppressed; *** p<.01; ** .01<p<.05;
* .05<p<.10

offer high income earners a relatively light tax burden. In contrast, some countries
– perhaps most notably the United States – with weak left parties and trade
unions and small public economies seem to have had very progressive systems of
income taxation.

Things were quite different in the late 1980s (Table 4.6). There was an
across-the-board decline in the progressivity of personal income tax schemes from
the mid 1970s to the late 1980s. The average highest marginal tax rate fell by
thirteen percentage points, the gap between the top and bottom rates dropped
by nineteen points, and the average number of bands in tax systems halved. It is
also clear, however, that the move to less progressive income tax schemes was

Trade

		Low	High
Left-labor power	Low	36.4	37.6
	High	37.6	38.1

The counterfactuals are calculated on the basis of the total taxation regression equation reported in Table 4.6. The only interaction specification that was jointly significant at the .05 level or better was that for left-labor power and trade in the total taxation equation.

Figure 4.4 *Counterfactual estimates of tax revenues (% GDP)*

much stronger in countries where the left and organized labor were weaker. Left-labor power was strongly associated both with higher marginal rates at the top end of the scale and with larger gaps between the highest and lowest income tax bands. Thus, the impact of partisan politics on progressivity was far more apparent in the late 1980s than it had been a decade earlier.

Turning to the structure of corporate tax systems, Table 4.7 presents data for 1981 and 1990 for twelve of the countries in this study with respect to the highest marginal rates of corporate taxation, minus statutory reductions in this rate for profits that were reinvested in the national economy. As one might expect, there was a strong positive correlation between left-labor power and higher effective rates of corporate taxation in 1981 (but given that corporate tax revenues were lower in these regimes, it is clear that there were numerous other tax breaks built into these systems). Because the 1980s was a decade in which the pace of market integration was rapid, however, one might have anticipated growing pressures to cut corporate taxation – particularly in cases where the left and organized labor were strong. Indeed, a commonly hypothesized effect of globalization is convergence in corporate taxation at ever lower levels (Lee and McKenzie 1989). The evidence, however, is very different from this prediction. Comparing the two columns of Table 4.7, the most striking feature of corporate taxation in the 1980s is the stability in the highest effective rates in most countries. Moreover, cross-national variations increased somewhat, as did the positive correlation between left-labor power and higher rates of taxation.

Table 4.5. *Left-Labor Power and Tax Progressivity in the mid-1970s*

Country	Highest marginal rate	Gap between highest and lowest marginal rates	Number of tax rates
Austria	66	45	11
Sweden	85	53	11
Denmark	73	23	3
Norway	41	36	8
Germany	56	34	4
Italy	72	62	32
Belgium	60	43	21
Netherlands	72	52	10
United Kingdom	83	48	10
Canada	47	38	13
United States	70	56	25
France	60	55	13
Average	65	45	13
Correlation with left-labor power	0.16	-0.31	-0.24

Presented in rank order on the left-labor power index, 1966–1973. Data are from Heidenheimer, Heclo and Adams [1990: 211–12] and OECD, *The Tax/Benefit Position of Production Workers* (various).

Taken as a whole, the data on the structure of national tax systems presented in Tables 4.5 through 4.7 belie the notion that the left was forced by globalization to move away from more progressive forms of taxation toward flatter systems. Indeed, the evidence points in the other direction. What can one conclude more generally about the effects of globalization on tax policy? Two features stand out. On the one hand, there is good evidence that the relationship between left-labor power and larger and more progressive systems of taxation strengthened with globalization. This is completely consistent with the overall thrust of my argument and reinforces the results from the previous section with respect to government spending. But on the other hand, taxes were considerably more sticky than government spending. It was not possible for governments in countries with strong left parties and powerful organized labor movements to increase taxes to keep pace with the rapid growth in public expenditures. The next section explores the implications of the stickiness of taxation for the interactive effects of globalization and partisan politics on the size of public sector deficits and on the interest rates charged on government debt.

Table 4.6. *Left-Labor Power and Tax Progressivity in the late 1980s*

Country	Highest marginal rate	Gap between highest and lowest marginal rates	Number of tax rates
Austria	62	41	10
Sweden	55	50	2
Italy	50	40	7
Norway	29	19	3
Belgium	70	46	13
Denmark	73	23	3
Germany	56	34	4
Netherlands	72	56	9
United Kingdom	40	25	3
France	56	51	13
United States	31	16	3
Canada	29	12	3
Average	52	34	6
Correlation with left-labor power	0.44	0.44	0.09

Presented in rank order on the left-labor power index, 1966–1973. Data are from Heidenheimer, Heclo and Adams [1990: 211–212] and OECD, *The Tax/Benefit Position of Production Workers* (various).

4.3 MACROECONOMIC POLICY

The conventional wisdom about the political economy of macroeconomic policy comprises two basic propositions. First, budget deficits and accommodating monetary policy are viewed as the quintessential policy instruments of social democratic corporatism in the halcyon days of the mixed economy in the 1960s and early 1970s. Second, the subsequent pace of globalization is considered to have rendered expansionary macroeconomic policies far less feasible, eroding the policy distinctiveness of countries with powerful left-wing parties and labor market institutions.

The analysis of government spending and tax revenues in the previous section implies that the conventional wisdom is inaccurate with respect to public sector deficits. The combination in countries with strong left parties and organized labor movements of rapid increases in spending in response to globalization and sticky taxes resulted in the increasing partisan distinctiveness of fiscal policies. This

Table 4.7. *Corporate Taxation in 1981 and 1990*

Country	Highest effective rate[a]	
	1981	1990
Sweden	48	40
Norway	50.8	50.8
Denmark	40	40
Germany	56	50
Italy	36.3	46.4
United Kingdom	52	34
Belgium	43	45
Netherlands	36	35
Canada	41.3	39.1
Japan	42	37.5
United States	36	34
France	40	37
Average	43	41
Correlation with left-labor power	0.50[b]	0.58[c]

[a]Highest marginal rate less investment incentives
[b]Left-labor power, 1974–1979
[c]Left-labor power, 1985–1990

Presented in rank order on the left-labor power index, 1974–1979. Data from Cummuns, Hassett and Hubbard [1995: tables 1 and 2].

section demonstrates this relationship directly and then analyzes the consequences of budget deficits for monetary policy in the global economy. It shows that one important consequence of the increasing relationship between left-labor power and deficits was that interest rates on government bonds also rose with left-labor power, particularly under conditions of high capital mobility. I do not discuss here the effects of globalization on exchange rate policy – arguably the most important facet of macroeconomic policy in the global economy. Rather, I take up this issue in Chapter 6 with respect to the tumultuous events of the early 1990s in Europe's exchange rate markets.

Let us begin the analysis of macroeconomic policy with simple trends over time in average budget deficits and real (i.e., inflation-adjusted) interest rates on one year government bonds (see Figure 4.5).[10] The data can be broken down into

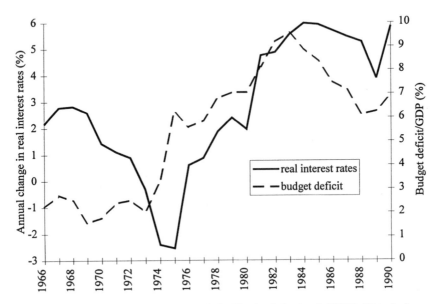

Sources: IMF, International Financial Statistics Yearbook (various); OECD, Historical Statistics (various). 14 (13)-country averages for budget deficits (real interest rates)

Figure 4.5 *Macroeconomic policy*

three periods. Up until about 1976, real interest rates and budget deficits moved together. Increases in budget deficits (reflecting looser fiscal policy) were accompanied by lower real interest rates (looser monetary policy). Macroeconomic policy took on a classically Keynesian guise. This is, fiscal and monetary policy were both countercyclical, as evidenced by the distinct loosening of macroeconomic policy during the recession precipitated by the first OPEC oil shock in October 1973.

In the period between 1976 and 1983, deficits and real interest rates both increased rapidly. The growth in deficits can largely be attributed to the countercyclical stabilizers in place during the most severe downturn in the international business cycle since the 1930s. Across the industrial democracies, spending increased with growing unemployment but revenues stagnated as a result of low or negative growth rates. What is more noticeable about this period, however, is that real interest rates increased dramatically after 1975 in response to very high rates of inflation. Thus, the unique combination of both supply shocks and demand shocks in this period – stagflation – resulted in macroeconomic policy that worked at cross-purposes. Fiscal expansion was offset by monetary contraction.

Deficits declined after 1983 as the growth in public spending slowed, but real interest rates remained at very high levels. Macroeconomic policies were

Table 4.8. *Left-Labor Power and Macroeconomic Policy*

Period	Real interest rates	Budget deficit/GDP (%)
1966–1973	0.17	-0.25
1974–1979	0.27	0.11
1980–1984	-0.28	0.18
1985–1990	-0.14	0.07

Figures are correlations between the left-labor power index and the policy indicators in each of the periods.

highly contractionary across the industrial democracies in the late 1980s. This outcome is the type of evidence cited by those who claim that global markets are incompatible with expansionary macroeconomic policies. Let us now consider whether this contention is correct by analyzing the interactive effects of market integration and partisan politics on public sector deficits and interest rates.

Recall that the conventional wisdom is that strong leftist parties and organized labor movements were associated with more expansionary macroeconomic policies in the period of relatively closed national economies (1966–1973 in this study), but that this relationship was eroded by market integration. By the era of global markets (1985–1990), the relationship should have all but evaporated.

Table 4.8 provides an initial test of this argument based on time-varying correlations between left-labor power and macroeconomic policies (country-by-country breakdowns are provided for the first and last periods in Appendixes 4.1 and 4.2). None of these correlations is strong (reflecting the predominance of economic factors in the determination of macroeconomic policy), but the trends in the data lend little support to the conventional wisdom. In the benchmark period, 1966–1973, left-labor power was associated with lower deficits and with somewhat higher real interest rates. This is exactly the opposite of the view that the historical policy distinctiveness of social democratic corporatism was manifest primarily in a commitment to countercyclical Keynesianism. In the 1980s, the fiscal policy relationship was reversed. It was only in the period of more integrated markets that left-labor power became associated with somewhat looser fiscal policies, but this was mitigated by even higher interest rates.

Given the likelihood that the business cycle was a far more important determinant of macroeconomic policy than partisan politics or globalization were, the panel regression methodology used in Sections 4.1 and 4.2 is critical to isolating the effects of the variables of primary interest in this book. Accordingly, I regressed budget deficits and interest rates on a range of control variables, country dummies, and the same interaction specifications between left-labor power and market integration that were used in the spending and taxation equations. The interest rate equation included several additional control variables. I used nominal interest rates as the dependent variable with inflation as a regressor to isolate interest rate movements that were independent of fluctuations in the growth of prices. U.S. interest rates were controlled on the assumption that U.S. money markets significantly influenced developments in other countries. This meant that the United States had to be excluded from the interest rate equation. Finally, a measure of central bank independence was used to take into account the possibility that interest rates would always be higher in countries where monetary authority was taken out of the hands of politicians and given to more economically conservative central bankers (Cukierman 1992; Persson and Tabellini 1994).

The budget deficit equation is reported in the left column of Table 4.9. Although fiscal deficits were quite sticky over time, they were also clearly responsive to movements in the business cycle. Deficits increased with slower growth and higher inflation. Only two of the country dummy variables were significant; none of the period dummies was. This suggests that the factors affecting budget deficits were more or less invariant across countries and periods.

The coefficients for the interaction specification between left-labor power and market integration are at first blush confusing. Ceteris paribus, the greater was the combined power of the political left and organized labor, the lower was the deficit. This contradicts the vast literature assuming that the running of deficits is the sine qua non of social democratic economic policy. The independent effects of trade and capital mobility were exactly as anticipated by proponents of the globalization thesis – market integration was associated with smaller public sector deficits. Most importantly, however, the interactive effect of left-labor power and market integration was to increase the deficit – as my argument predicts.

In order to determine the relative magnitude of these effects, I generated a series of counterfactual estimations of the size of budget deficits under different combinations of left-labor power, trade, and capital mobility, holding all other variables at their means. Again, the 20th and 80th percentile scores in the data set were used for the variables of interest so as not to exaggerate their impact on deficits.

The counterfactual estimates of budget deficits at low and high levels of left-labor power and market integration are presented in the top panel of Figure 4.6. These results are diametrically opposed to the conventional wisdom about fiscal policy. Instead, they track closely the relationships outlined in Section 4.2 with respect to government spending. At low levels of trade and capital mobility, deficits were actually smaller at low levels of left-labor power than at high levels. But although increasing trade and capital mobility cut deficits in cases of low left-labor power, public sector deficits increased with globalization in cases where

	Trade				Capital mobility	

A. *Budget deficits*
(%GDP)

		Low	High		Low	High
Left-labor power	Low	6.3	4.1		5.5	5.0
	High	5.5	6.0		5.1	6.2

B. *Interest rates*

		Low	High		Low	High
Left-labor power	Low	9.4	9.4		9.8	9.1
	High	10.6	9.4		10.1	9.9

The counterfactuals are calculated on the basis of the budget deficit and interest rate regression equations reported in Table 4.8. All the interaction specifications were jointly significant at the .05 level or better. Low (high) levels of trade and capital mobility refer to the 20th (80th) percentile scores in the sample. Low (high) levels of left-labor power refer to the 20th (80th) percentile scores on left-labor power index. All other variables are set at their means.

Figure 4.6 *Counterfactual estimates of macroeconomic policy*

left parties and labor market institutions were much stronger. Indeed, the highest deficits were recorded in the high market integration–high left-labor cells.

The size of these partisan and globalization effects was smaller than for public spending because with increasing globalization countries with strong left parties and organized labor movements were able partially to offset increased spending with higher taxes. Nonetheless, moving from the 20th to the 80th percentile in the left-labor distribution is estimated to have increased the deficit by 1.9 percentage points of GDP at high levels of trade and by 1.2 points at high levels of capital mobility. Given the responsiveness of deficits to movements in the business cycle, these effects were far from trivial.

Let us now examine interest rates. The right column of Table 4.10 shows that the business cycle, domestic inflation U.S. interest rates, and central bank independence all exerted powerful influences on interest rates on the price of government bonds. Furthermore, country fixed effects were also clearly evident.

Table 4.9. *The Determinants of Macroeconomic Policy, 1966–1990*

Independent variables	Budget deficits (% GDP)	Interest rates[a]
Lagged dependent variable	.74***	.61***
	(.04)	(.04)
GDP growth	-.264***	.067***
	(.036)	(.025)
Unemployment	.200***	-.130***
	(.06)	(.040)
Old age population	. 041	
	(.128)	
Inflation		.205***
		(.021)
US interest rates		.485***
		(.062)
Central bank independence[b]		6.46***
		(2.21)
Capital mobility	-.83**	-.53**
	(.39)	(.25)
Trade	-.0723***	.0143**
	(.0281)	(.0170)
Left-labor power	-.361	.475***
	(.249)	(.178)
Capital mobility*left-labor power	.200***	.058
	(.072)	(.046)
Trade*left-labor power	.0116***	-.0051*
	(.0430)	(.0027)
Period dummy variables		
1966–1973	.08	.24
	(.58)	(.42)
1974–1979	.63	.03
	(.42)	(.32)
1980–1984	.37	-.29
	(.37)	(.29)
1986–1990	-.31	1.24***
	(.38)	(.028)
Country dummy variables		
Austria	3.65	-8.04***
	(2.88)	(1.94)
Belgium	3.39	-3.58***
	(3.18)	(1.45)

Controlling for all the other factors in the equation, interest rates increased significantly in the 1985–1990 period. Given that trade, capital mobility, and left-labor power are also in the equation, this period effect cannot be attributed to globalization nor to its impact on the balance of political power. Rather, it more

Table 4.9. *The Determinants of Macroeconomic Policy, 1966–1990 (continued)*

Independent variables	Budget deficits (% GDP)	Interest rates[a]
Country dummy variables		
Canada	3.81*	-5.47***
	(2.15)	(1.60)
Denmark	3.15	-5.54***
	(2.79)	(1.73)
Finland	3.62	
	(2.46)	
France	2.36	-5.06***
	(2.48)	(1.32)
Germany	3.42	-7.88***
	(2.83)	(2.03)
Italy	4.11	-4.94***
	(2.54)	(1.37)
Japan	3.12	-5.74***
	(1.89)	(1.12)
Netherlands	4.88*	-5.76***
	(2.89)	(1.74)
Norway	3.56	-4.83***
	(3.00)	(1.33)
Sweden	4.08	-5.88***
	(2.99)	(1.43)
United Kingdom	2.97	-5.33***
	(2.76)	(1.47)
United States	2.21	
	(1.96)	
Observations	350	300
Adjusted R-squared	.888	.926
Wald's test for the joint significance of the left-labor power-capital mobility interaction	.0001	.005
Wald's test for the joint significance of the left-labor power-trade interaction	.009	.012

OLS estimates using panel corrected standard errors; intercept suppressed;
*** $p<.01$; ** $.01<p<.05$; * $.05<p<.10$
[a]12 countries (Finland and the US not included)
[b]Cukierman's (1992: 381) legal autonomy index

likely captures a secular shift in policy ideas toward more contractionary monetary policies in the latter 1980s.

Turning to the partisan politics and globalization terms, it is apparent that the pattern of coefficients was quite different than that for fiscal policy. First, the independent effect of left-labor power was to increase interest rates, rather than cut them. Does this imply that governments in strong left-labor regimes chose on their own to counterbalance fiscal expansions with monetary contractions? Probably not. A more sensible interpretation is that the capital markets charged these governments higher interest rates on their borrowing, in the expectation that governments would attempt to "pay" for their debts with higher inflation in the future. All else being equal, trade was associated with higher interest rates, whereas capital mobility lowered rates (reflecting the greater liquidity of global financial markets). Finally, the left-labor power–globalization interaction terms were much weaker.

The bottom panel of Figure 4.6 presents counterfactual estimates for interest rates under different combinations of partisan politics and globalization. There is only one interesting feature of the trade box. Interest rates were 1.2 percentage points higher in the high left-labor–low trade cell than in any other case (a finding that requires more investigation). The left-labor power–capital mobility estimates were more intuitive. At low levels of capital mobility, the financial markets charged a small (0.3 percentage points) interest rate premium on high levels of left-labor power. Under conditions of more global financial markets, whereas interest rates were cut across the board, the premium on left-labor power more than doubled to 0.8 points. Given the markets' inherent skepticism that the left would choose to inflate away deficits, the fact that deficits increased substantially with globalization in strong-left labor regimes, and that capital flight is easy in a world of global financial markets, this increasing interest rate premium is not surprising. Indeed, perhaps it is more striking – given the increasing partisan distinctiveness of fiscal policy in the global economy – that this interest rate premium was nonetheless quite small, less than a full percentage point.

CONCLUSION

This chapter has analyzed the interactive effects of globalization and the combined strength of the political left and labor market institutions on economic policy from the mid 1960s to 1990. There are two parts to the story. First, the evidence on patterns of government spending is wholly supportive of my hypothesis that the policy distinctiveness of social democratic corporatism (powerful left-wing parties combined with encompassing labor market institutions) has increased with market integration. Globalization increases the political payoffs for governments in these systems to compensate those whose economic insecurity increased with greater competition in international markets. Given that the welfare state, broadly construed, has long been at the core of social democratic corporatism, the results of the public expenditures analysis stand in marked contrast to prophesies of doom about the future of government efforts to redistribute wealth and social risk in favor of market losers.

Second, the heightened partisan distinctiveness of government spending policies was not perfectly matched on the tax side. Government revenues increased faster – and systems of taxation became increasingly more progressive – in strong left-labor regimes than in countries where the right was stronger and labor market institutions were weaker. This is consistent with my general argument about the salience of partisan politics in the global economy. But the growth of taxation in strong left-labor regimes did not keep pace with the mushrooming of public spending in response to market integration. This mismatch between spending and taxation in the global economy was manifest in higher public sector deficits. In turn, global financial markets demanded that governments in strong left-labor countries pay higher interest rates on the bonds issued to pay for public spending.

How one evaluates this balance sheet is surely a matter of personal taste. Proponents of the globalization thesis would highlight larger deficits and higher interest rates as signs of the ultimate futility of big government in the global economy. On the other hand, I would argue that the increasing partisan distinctiveness of spending and taxation is testament to the enduring importance of the balance of political and organization power on the allocation of wealth and risk in the industrial democracies. Certainly, the left and organized labor had to pay a price for redistributive big government in the global economy, but it was clearly one they were willing to bear.

One crucial question, however, remains to be explored. In the end, the evidence I have adduced about the growing policy distinctiveness of social democratic corporatism in the global economy would amount to little if there were substantial macroeconomic costs to this strategy. Chapter 2 suggested reasons why this might not be the case, even in a world of highly integrated international markets. The next chapter presents empirical tests to determine the impact of globalization, the balance of political power, and the structure of labor market institutions on economic performance.

Appendix 4.1. Economic policy, 1966–1973

Country	Macroeconomic policy		Government spending					Taxation				
	Real interest rates	Budget deficit	Total	Income transfers	Civilian consumption	Subsidies to industry	Capital spending	Total	Personal income	Consumption taxes	Corporate income	Employer contributions to social security
Austria	2.6	-0.4	35.8	13.0	13.7	1.9	5.0	36.1	7.6	13.0	1.5	4.5
Sweden	1.5	2.5	43.1	12.4	17.8	1.3	5.7	40.4	18.8	11.9	1.8	4.8
Finland	-	-0.2	31.8	8.6	13.5	2.8	4.4	32.1	13.3	13.1	1.8	3.1
Denmark	1.9	-1.2	37.9	11.1	17.5	3.0	2.2	39.1	18.9	14.5	1.1	0.4
Norway	-0.7	1.0	41.6	13.7	13.8	5.0	3.5	40.7	15.0	16.1	1.2	5.9
Germany	2.7	4.2	37.9	13.5	12.8	1.4	4.7	33.7	9.3	9.8	2.0	5.3
Italy	1.7	5.8	34.0	13.7	12.1	1.6	1.5	28.1	3.2	9.8	2.0	1.2
Belgium	2.4	1.9	37.9	14.4	10.9	1.4	4.4	35.9	8.9	11.9	2.4	6.9
Netherlands	0.5	4.8	43.0	18.0	12.2	1.1	4.9	38.4	10.6	9.8	2.7	6.3
United Kingdom	2.4	3.8	38.1	9.5	12.7	1.9	4.8	34.4	10.8	9.2	2.6	2.6
Canada	2.4	2.8	34.9	8.2	15.8	0.9	3.8	32.0	9.8	9.4	3.8	1.3
Japan	0.6	-0.6	19.6	4.3	6.9	1.1	5.7	20.5	4.7	4.3	3.8	1.9
United States	1.5	4.8	32.6	7.1	11.0	0.5	3.6	27.7	9.3	4.7	3.7	3.1
France	1.6	2.1	37.6	17.4	9.0	2.0	2.8	35.5	4.1	13.0	1.9	9.4

Presented in rank order on left–labor power index. The data on real interest rates are average annual increases. The remaining data are presented as percentages of GDP.

Appendix 4.2. Economic policy, 1985–1990

Country	Macroeconomic policy		Government spending					Taxation				
	Real interest rates	Budget deficit	Total	Income transfers	Civilian consumption	Subsidies to industry	Capital spending	Total	Personal income	Consumption taxes	Corporate income	Employer contributions to social security
Austria	4.7	7.2	49.3	20.3	17.4	2.9	3.4	42.1	9.3	12.8	1.4	6.7
Sweden	4.5	7.3	61.7	20.4	24.3	4.7	2.6	54.4	20.5	13.1	2.2	13.2
Italy	3.5	13.0	50.3	18.2	14.6	2.5	3.5	37.4	10.0	9.3	3.7	8.8
Finland	-	4.4	41.9	12.3	19.0	3.0	3.7	37.5	17.5	13.8	1.6	3.1
Belgium	5.5	7.6	53.2	22.0	13.5	1.8	1.6	45.4	14.6	10.4	3.0	9.5
Norway	8.0	5.5	53.0	17.7	17.3	5.7	3.8	47.5	12.1	17.0	4.5	7.6
Denmark	7.6	7.9	58.0	17.4	23.0	3.2	1.9	50.1	25.5	16.2	2.3	0.6
Germany	4.2	7.1	45.4	16.3	16.3	2.1	2.5	38.4	10.9	9.5	2.1	7.2
Netherlands	5.9	9.6	56.0	28.2	12.6	2.1	2.3	46.3	10.1	11.0	3.4	7.0
Japan	3.8	1.8	32.4	8.4	8.4	1.0	5.8	30.6	7.7	3.5	6.9	4.5
United Kingdom	4.2	5.2	42.5	13.8	16.0	1.4	2.3	37.3	10.2	11.0	4.2	3.5
France	5.7	6.5	50.7	23.1	14.9	2.0	3.3	44.2	5.5	12.3	2.3	12.1
United States	4.9	7.8	37.0	11.1	12.1	0.6	1.7	29.2	10.4	4.3	2.3	5.0
Canada	6.6	10.5	46.0	12.6	17.6	2.1	2.5	35.5	13.6	9.0	2.8	3.1

Presented in rank order on left–labor power index. The data on real interest rates are average annual increases. The remaining data are presented as percentages of GDP.

ECONOMIC PERFORMANCE

This chapter examines the consequences for macroeconomic performance – measured in terms of annual rates of real GDP growth, inflation, and unemployment – of interactions among the balance of political power, labor market institutions, and the integration of national economies into international markets over the period 1966–1990. My primary objective is to determine the impact of globalization on economic performance in social democratic corporatist regimes (characterized by powerful left-wing parties and encompassing labor movements). Most analysts would assert that the macroeconomic consequences of social democratic corporatism deteriorated markedly with the integration of national economies into global markets – citing the perceived competitiveness costs of larger government expenditures, bigger budget deficits, and increased costs of borrowing (see Chapter 4).

In contrast, I hypothesized in Chapter 2 that the social democratic alternative to free market capitalism should be associated with a buoyant macroeconomy where governments are dominated by left parties that are allied with encompassing labor market institutions – even in the global economy. The reason for this is that labor leaders in these cases can be expected to use their market power to regulate overall levels of wage growth in ways that promote the competitiveness of the exposed sector of the economy, in exchange for beneficial government policies. Moreover, this "virtuous circle" (Castles 1978) between government and labor can be expected to generate economic, political, and social stability that is attractive to mobile asset holders.

The evidence presented in this chapter yields two distinct insights into the political economy of macroeconomic performance. On the one hand, my thesis is strongly supported with respect to economic growth and unemployment. Performance with respect to real aggregates in globalized markets, and particularly under conditions of high capital mobility, was better under social democratic

corporatism than for any other combinations of the balance of political power
and the strength of labor market institutions. Where dominant left-wing parties
were allied with encompassing labor movements and there were no government
restrictions on cross-border capital flows, economic growth was faster and unemployment was lower not only than in "incoherent" regimes (strong left-weak
labor and weak left-strong labor cases), but also under "market liberalism" (where
the balance of political power was tilted strongly to the right and where labor
market institutions were very weak).

On the other hand, however, encompassing labor market institutions were
always associated with higher rates of inflation, and this effect was marginally
stronger in cases where left-wing parties were also powerful. The inflation biases of left-labor power, however, were no stronger in countries that were heavily integrated into the global economy than in more closed economies The
relative importance of real aggregates versus inflation – and hence the economic viability of different types of political economic regimes – could be
debated endlessly. For present purposes, however, the most important point
to be taken from the analysis in this chapter is that the macroeconomic consequences of social democratic corporatism in global markets were not uni-
versally negative – far from it. Thus, the redistribution of wealth and social
risk generated by the economic policies of social democratic corporatism in response to globalization was not achieved at the expense of overall macroeconomic performance. This should be heartening to people who support the
goals of interventionist and redistributive government.

The chapter is divided into four sections that mirror the methodological
progression of the last chapter. Section 5.1 describes over-time trends in average
growth, inflation, and unemployment for the countries in this study. Section 5.2
presents a rudimentary test of the effects of globalization on the politics–economic
performance relationship using time-varying bivariate correlations. Section 5.3
deploys more sophisticated panel regressions to isolate the macroeconomic effects
of the interactions among market integration, the balance of political power, and
labor market institutions. Section 5.4 analyses the substantive implications of
these results using counterfactual estimates of economic performance under different constellations of these three variables.

5.1   ECONOMIC PERFORMANCE IN THE
INDUSTRIAL DEMOCRACIES

Figure 5.1 plots annual average rates of real economic growth, inflation and
unemployment for the fourteen countries in this study over the period 1966–
1990. The figure can be broken down into four discrete epochs. First, in the
period up until the first OPEC oil shock in 1973, economic performance was
very good. Annual growth rates were between 4 and 6 percent. Even though

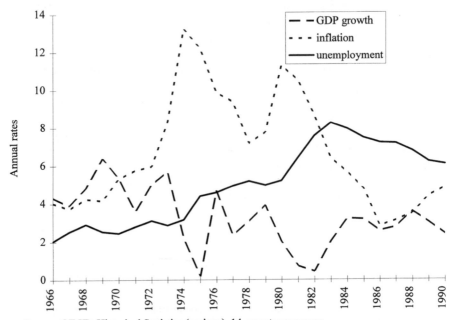

Figure 5.1 *Economic performance*

inflation had begun to rise, it was still very low by the standards of the next decade. Average unemployment was under 3 percent. These clearly were halcyon days for the industrial democracies.

Things changed abruptly after the first oil shock in October 1973, ushering in the second period that lasted until 1979. Inflation skyrocketed while unemployment increased and growth slowed. As I showed in the last chapter, however, fiscal and monetary policies were both loosened in response to the first OPEC shock. Thus, the declines in growth and unemployment performance were not precipitous, but this was at the expense of very high inflation rates.

The third period lasted from the onset of the second oil shock in 1979 until 1984, when unemployment peaked. Governments in the industrial democracies reacted to rising oil prices in the late 1970s with severe monetary contractions. The result was that the inflation spike in 1980 was not as high as the one in 1974, but the ensuing recession was longer and deeper. Most notably, unemployment rates almost doubled between 1979 and 1984.

Macroeconomic outcomes then stabilized in the industrial democracies. Comparing the 1985–1990 period with 1966–1973, however, it is clear that the new performance equilibrium was quite different. Growth rates were much lower and unemployment was much higher in the late 1980s than before the first oil crisis. But inflation rates were somewhat lower. One simple interpretation of these data is that the costs of taming inflation were very high in terms of economic activity and unemployment. Of course, it might also be argued that the deterioration in macroeconomic aggregates was more a function of technological innovation and increasing competitiveness of less-developed countries in low-wage, low-skill products. I return to this issue in Chapter 6.

The primary purpose of this chapter, however, is to determine the impact of market integration and domestic political conditions on the economic performance of individual countries. Let us now turn to that analysis.

5.2 CORRELATIONS BETWEEN DOMESTIC POLITICS AND ECONOMIC PERFORMANCE

My fundamental concern is to identify the interactive effects on economic performance of the globalization of markets and domestic political conditions. Because exposure to trade and capital mobility increased in more or less secular fashion across all the countries in this study from the late 1960s to 1990, time-varying bivariate correlations between domestic political conditions and growth, inflation and unemployment provide a useful starting point for this analysis.

In the case of economic performance, however, my argument cannot be tested simply by correlating the combined power of left parties and labor market institutions with outcomes (as was the case for economic policy). This is because my working hypothesis is that performance should have been better at either end of the left-labor power distribution (reflecting how closely countries approximated the ideal types of social democratic corporatism and market liberalism, respectively) than in the middle of the distribution (more incoherent regimes). A simple way to estimate regime "coherence" is to standardize scores on the left-labor power index in each period with a mean of zero and then to square these scores. Thus, values both at the top and the bottom of the resulting distribution (i.e., more coherent regimes) will be larger than those in the middle.

The time-varying correlations between this measure of regime coherence and economic performance are reported in Table 5.1 (these data are broken down by country for the 1966–1973 and 1985–1990 periods in Appendixes 5.1 and 5.2). In the benchmark period, regime coherence was weakly associated with higher growth and lower inflation, but somewhat more strongly correlated with lower unemployment (and thus with the "misery index" combining the inflation and unemployment rates).[1] Nonetheless, it would be difficult to argue that regime coherence had a strong positive impact on economic performance in the 1966–1973 period.

The beneficial consequences of regime coherence were much clearer in the next two periods following the OPEC oil shocks. In both periods, coherence was correlated with faster rates of economic growth and lower rates of unemployment

Table 5.1. *Regime Coherence and Economic Performance*

	Economic growth	Inflation	Unemployment	Misery index
1966–1973	0.11	-0.10	-0.31	-0.37
1974–1979	0.38	-0.24	-0.28	-0.32
1980–1984	0.30	-0.23	-0.40	-0.42
1985–1990	0.07	0.20	-0.27	-0.14

Figures are correlations between the square of left-labor power (with mean zero) and economic performance in each of the periods. Thus, countries at the top and bottom of the left-labor power index are scored similarly on this measure, to reflect greater coherence between the balance of political power and labor market institutions.

and inflation. These relationships subsequently weakened in the final period, 1985–1990. Although the correlation coefficients were still in the expected direction for growth, unemployment, and the misery index, they were even smaller than in the benchmark period, 1966–1973. Furthermore, greater regime coherence was associated with higher inflation in the 1985–1990 period.

This pattern of coefficients is apparently consistent with the view that globalization decreased the economic efficacy of social democratic corporatism. However, there are three reasons why it would be imprudent to come to such a conclusion on the basis of the bivariate correlations. First, the correlations treat cases at either end of the left power and labor market institutions distributions as equivalent. We thus need to develop tests that distinguish between the macroeconomic effects of social democratic corporatism and market liberalism. Second, as Chapter 3 showed, using periods of time as an approximation of trends in globalization masks considerable cross-national variations in the extent to which economies are integrated into global markets. Third, the dynamics of growth, inflation, and unemployment are very complex, and I would not want to suggest that changes in performance were primarily a function of domestic political and economic conditions. Accordingly, let us now move to a panel regression framework in which the limitations of the bivariate correlations can be rectified.

5.3   THE PANEL REGRESSIONS

This section builds a series of panel regression estimates of unemployment, economic growth, and inflation performance to delineate the macroeconomic effects of market integration, the balance of political power, and the encompassment of labor market institutions. I begin by presenting results for the political power–

labor market institutions interaction, without taking into account the effects of globalization. This is a replication of the methodology Michael Alvarez, Peter Lange and I used in earlier research that demonstrated that social democratic corporatism had beneficial macroeconomic consequences in the period up until 1984 (Alvarez, Garrett, and Lange 1991). These results are then used as a baseline for assessing the impact of globalization on this relationship.

METHODOLOGY

The basic structure of the panel regressions is similar to that used in Chapter 4 with respect to economic policy. The observations in the analysis are country-years. The estimates are based on fixed effects (including both period and country dummy variables) OLS regression equations including lagged dependent variables to control for serial correlation and using Beck and Katz's (1995a) correction for heteroskedasticity. The baseline model for the macroeconomic performance estimations is:

$$PERF_{it} = b_1 PERF_{it-1} + b_2 LEFT_{it} + b_3 LMI_{it} + b_4 LEFT.LMI_{it} + \Sigma(b_j PERIOD_{jt}) + \Sigma(b_k COUNTRY_{ki}) + \Sigma(b_l X_{lit}) + \mu_{it} \tag{1}$$

In this equation, the b's are parameter estimates. PERF represents annual rates of real GDP growth, inflation, or unemployment. The subscripts $_i$ and $_t$ denote, respectively, the country and year of the observations. LEFT and LMI are, respectively, the left power and the labor market institutions indices discussed in Chapter 3. "." is a multiplication dot. The $_j$ period dummy variables (1966–1973, 1974–1979, 1980–1984, 1986–1990) are designated by PERIOD (1985 is the excluded reference year). The $_k$ (fourteen) country dummy variables are denoted by COUNTRY (thus, the intercept is suppressed). The $_l$ control variables (X) that take into account the impact on different countries of changes in international economic conditions are OECD demand (annual OECD growth weighted by a country's exposure to trade) (Alvarez, Garrett, and Lange 1991) and oil dependence (the price of oil in U.S. dollars weighted by a country's dependence on imported oil) (Garrett and Lange 1986).[2]

Following Alvarez, Garrett, and Lange (1991), the best way to test my argument about the beneficial macroeconomic effects of regime coherence – left (right) power will have better macroeconomic effects where labor market institutions are more encompassing (weaker) – is to add a multiplicative interaction term between them to the parameters estimating their independent effects (i.e., LEFT, LMI, and LEFT.LMI). The pattern of parameter estimates that is consistent with my argument for unemployment and inflation is positive coefficients for LEFT and LMI, but a negative parameter estimate for the LEFT.LMI interaction term. This set of estimates would imply that whereas the independent effects of left power and labor market institutions were to increase unemployment and inflation, their combined impact was to reduce jobless rates and price rises. Conversely, the expected constellation of coefficients in the growth equations is the exact opposite of the growth model (because higher growth denotes better performance).

In order to analyze the effects of globalization on these relationships, it is necessary to add four variables to Equation 1 – the market integration term itself (GLOBAL, representing either trade or capital mobility) and its multiplicative interaction with each of the three regime coherence terms (LEFT, LMI, and LEFT.LMI). Thus, the full interaction specification for the globalization–balance of political power–labor market institutions interaction requires seven parameters to be estimated:

$$PERF_{it} = b_1 PERF_{it-1} + b_2 GLOBAL_{it} + b_3 LEFT_{it} + b_4 LMI_{it} +$$
$$b_5 LEFT.LMI_{it} + b_6 GLOBAL.LEFT_{it} + b_7 GLOBAL.LMI_{it} + \quad (2)$$
$$b_8 GLOBAL.LEFT.LMI_{it} + \Sigma(b_j PERIOD_{jt}) + \Sigma(b_k COUNTRY_{ki}) + \Sigma(b_l X_{lit})$$
$$+ \mu_{it}$$

Given that this three-way interaction specification on its own generates high levels of multicollinearity, I estimated the equations for trade and capital mobility separately (unlike Chapter 4 where it was easier to examine the effects of these two facets of globalization in the same equations).[3] I also chose not to complicate the analysis even more by directly testing the theoretical distinction made in Chapter 2 concerning different types of incoherent regimes (see Figures 2.1 and 2.2).[4] To the extent that my hypotheses are correct, however, the estimated equations should understate the positive impact of regime coherence in the estimated equations. This is because these equations assume that performance decreases (or increases) monotonically with incoherence, whereas I hypothesized that performance should begin to improve again in extremely incoherent regimes – where partisan governments have no choice but quickly and decisively to abandon partisan policies.

Equation 2 would support my argument that the beneficial effects of regime coherence (and social democratic corporatism in particular) were not undermined by globalization if the parameter estimates in the inflation and unemployment models took the following form (N.B., the signs should be reversed for economic growth): GLOBAL.LEFT (+), GLOBAL.LMI (+), and GLOBAL.LEFT.LMI (−).

UNEMPLOYMENT

The results of the unemployment equations are reported in Table 5.2. In all three equations, the coefficient on the lagged dependent variable was large and highly significant, whereas higher levels of OECD demand cut the unemployment rate. Oil dependence did not have a significant impact on unemployment rates. Controlling for all the other variables in the equation, there was a secular increase in the unemployment rate across the fourteen countries in this study in the period after the second oil shock, 1980–1984, when monetary policies tended to be very restrictive. Although unemployment was very sticky in all countries, there is scant evidence of any country-specific effects. Diagnostics reveal that the regressions were highly robust to the sequential elimination of individual countries from the analysis and that the estimation procedure dealt successfully with serial correlation and heteroskedasticity among the error terms.[5] Combined with the very high adjusted R-squares for the unemployment models, all of this should increase our confidence in the estimated effects of market integration, left power, and labor market institutions.

In the baseline unemployment equation, the pattern of parameter estimates was as I expected, although the results are not as strong as those reported in Alvarez, Garrett, and Lange (1991).[6] The coefficients for left political power and stronger labor market institutions on their own were positive, whereas their interaction had a negative parameter estimate. This suggests that unemployment would have been lower in both coherent combinations of political power and labor market institutions (i.e., left-encompassing and right-weak) than in more coherent cases, as is demonstrated in the next section.

Consistent with my argument about partisan politics in the global economy, this pattern of parameter estimates was strengthened by the inclusion of the market integration terms. The evidence was clearer for the capital mobility model. The signs for the LEFT, LMI, and LEFT.LMI coefficients were the same as in the baseline model, but their size and significance were considerably greater. Moreover, this pattern was repeated for the CM.LEFT, CM.LMI and CM.LEFT.LMI terms. Given the very high level of collinearity that is built into these three-way interactions, perhaps the most important statistic in the final column is the Wald's test for the joint significance of the three-way interaction among capital mobility, left power, and labor market institutions. This shows that capital mobility had a significant impact on the effects of left power and labor market institutions, and the pattern of coefficients suggests that this effect was to magnify – not dampen – the beneficial consequences of regime coherence.

The coefficients were somewhat less supportive of my argument in the trade equation. Whereas the trade–political power–labor market interaction was jointly significant, the pattern of parameter estimates made it very difficult to discern the combined effects of the three variables without further analysis. Nonetheless, the only coefficient that was significant on its own was that for TRADE.LEFT.LMI, which was negative. The next section uses counterfactual estimates to determine whether this resulted in lower levels of unemployment in countries that were highly exposed to trade with strong left parties and encompassing labor market institutions.

ECONOMIC GROWTH

The economic growth equations are presented in Table 5.3. Lagged growth rates were a significant determinant of economic activity in the next year, but the

Table 5.2. *The Determinants of Unemployment, 1966–1990*

Independent variables	Baseline	Trade	Capital mobility
Lagged dependent variable	.88***	.85***	.85***
	(.03)	(.03)	(.03)
OECD demand[a]	-.002***	-.002***	-.002***
	(.000)	(.000)	(.000)
Oil dependence[b]	-.2	1.2	.6
	(2.4)	(2.5)	(2.3)
Left political power	.27*	-.53	.74***
	(.14)	(.48)	(.25)
Labor market institutions (LMI)	.19	.12	.45
	(.26)	(.45)	(.27)
Left*LMI	-.09	.26	-.29***
	(.06)	(.17)	(.09)
Trade		.0202	
		(.0274)	
Trade*left		.0144	
		(.0111)	
Trade*LMI		-.0008	
		(.0086)	
Trade*left*LMI		-.0059*	
		(.0033)	
Capital mobility			-1.05**
			(.43)
Capital mobility*LMI			.45***
			(.17)
Capital mobility*left			.52**
			(.22)
Capital mobility*left*LMI			-.20***
			(.07)

magnitude of these coefficients was far lower than in the case of unemployment. Again, OECD demand had the expected effect on national growth rates. The oil dependence coefficients were in the anticipated direction, but not statistically significant. Turning to the fixed effects parameters, secular differences in growth rates were apparent among periods and for some countries (especially when capital mobility was not included in the equation). Controlling for all the other factors in the equations, growth was faster in the 1966–1973 era than in any of the subsequent periods. As is well known, Japan's growth rates in the past three decades have been exceptionally high by OECD standards, but the equations also suggest that additional factors not included in the equations also had beneficial growth effects in Canada, France, and the United States.

The pattern of the parameter estimates for the political power–labor mar-

Table 5.2. *The Determinants of Unemployment, 1966–1990 (continued)*

Independent variables	Baseline	Trade	Capital mobility
Period dummy variables			
1966–1973	-.05	-.08	-.16
	(.19)	(.26)	(.26)
1974–1979	.25	.20	.21
	(.18)	(.23)	(.23)
1980–1984	.69***	.67***	.67***
	(.19)	(.22)	(.22)
1986–1990	.03	.06	.02
	(.16)	(.20)	(.20)
Observations	350	350	350
Adjusted R-square	.946	.947	.947
Wald's test for joint significance of the market integration-left-LMI interaction		.013	.020

OLS estimates using panel corrected standard errors. *** $p<.001$; ** $.001<p<.05$; * $.05<p<.10$. The parameter estimates for the fourteen country dummy variables are not reported because none is statistically significant.

[a]OECD GDP growth weighted by national exposure to trade
[b]The price of oil in \$US weighted by dependence on imported oil (as a portion of all energy requirements)

ket institutions in the baseline growth equation was very similar to those in Alvarez, Garrett, and Lange (1991). The LEFT and LMI terms were negative whereas the LEFT.LMI interaction parameter estimate was significant and positive. This pattern was replicated in the trade equation, although none of these coefficients was statistically significant. Each of the parameter estimates for the domestic variables interacted with trade was positive, but none was statistically significant. Furthermore, the Wald's test shows that adding trade to the equation had no significant impact on growth. Thus, although the relationships between political power and labor market institutions fit the expected pattern, these were unaffected by the extent to which national economies were exposed to trade.

Things were different in the capital mobility equation. Each of the terms interacted with capital mobility was statistically significant, and their signs were the opposite of those my argument would suggest. However, the magnitude of these coefficients is very interesting. The positive parameter estimates for

Table 5.3. *The Determinants of GDP Growth, 1966–1990*

Independent variables	Baseline	Trade	Capital mobility
Lagged dependent variable	.13***	.12**	.11**
	(.05)	(.05)	(.05)
OECD demand[a]	.006***	.007***	.007***
	(.001)	(.001)	(.001))
Oil dependence[b]	-6.6	-7.0	-5.8
	(5.9)	(6.5)	(5.8)
Left political power	-.68**	-.85	.29
	(.30)	(1.17)	(.56)
Labor market institutions (LMI)	-.13	-.35	.13
	(.57)	(1.07)	(.63)
Left*LMI	.23*	.08	.07
	(.13)	(.42)	(.19)
Trade		-.0625	
		(.0583)	
Trade*left		.0098	
		(.019)	
Trade*LMI		.0095	
		(.0261)	
Trade*left*LMI		.0003	
		(.0083)	
Capital mobility			-2.77**
			(1.08)
Capital mobility*left			1.48***
			(.53)
Capital mobility*LMI			.63*
			(.38)
Capital mobility*left*LMI			-.29*
			(.15)
Period dummy variables			
1966–1973	1.42***	1.18*	1.58**
	(0.37)	(0.64)	(0.56)

CM.LEFT and CM.LMI were much larger than the negative coefficient for CM.LEFT.LMI. Given that the range on the LEFT and LMI variables is between 0 and about 5, it is likely that even at the high ends of both distributions, the combined impact of left power and encompassing labor market institutions would have been to stimulate – not retard – growth under conditions of high capital mobility. The counterfactual estimates in the next section confirm this speculation.

Table 5.3. *The Determinants of GDP Growth, 1966–1990 (continued)*

Independent variables	Baseline	Trade	Capital mobility
1974–1979	.04	-.07	-.02
	(.39)	(.58)	(.54)
1980–1984	-.54	-.58	-.51
	(.39)	(.56)	(.55)
1986–1990	-.14	-.25	-.10
	(.33)	(.54)	(.53)
Country dummy variables[c]			
Canada	2.35*	5.02*	1.10
	(1.20)	(2.99)	(1.45)
France	2.69***	4.92**	.93
	(0.76)	(2.46)	(1.19)
Japan	4.85***	6.74***	3.21**
	(1.29)	(2.73)	(1.59)
United States	2.39*	3.87	1.37
	(1.24)	(2.47)	(1.41)
Observations	350	350	350
Adjusted R-square	.401	.400	.418
Wald's test for joint significance of the market integration-left-LMI interaction		.185	.001

OLS estimates using panel corrected standard errors. *** $p<.001$; **$.001<p<.05$; *$.05<p<.10$

[a]OECD GDP growth weighted by national exposure to trade

[b]The price of oil in \$US weighted by dependence on imported oil (as a portion of all energy requirements)

[c]Equations contain all fourteen country dummy variables, but only those with statistically significant parameter estimates are reported.

INFLATION

The inflation results presented in Table 5.4 present a radically different picture of the effects of political power, labor market institutions, and market integration than was the case for either economic growth or unemployment. The strength of labor market institutions was consistently associated with higher rates of inflation, whereas the effects of the balance of political power and the extent of market integration were considerably weaker. The effects of the control variables in all of the inflation models was predictable. Lagged inflation rates had a powerful impact on current inflation; more buoyant demand conditions in the OECD

Table 5.4. *The Determinants of Inflation, 1966–1990*

Independent variables	Baseline	Trade	Capital mobility
Lagged dependent variable	.57***	.56***	.52***
	(.06)	(.06)	(.06)
OECD demand[a]	-.006***	-.006***	-.006***
	(.001)	(.001)	(.001)
Oil dependence[b]	6.0	7.2	5.9
	(7.3)	(8.6)	(7.6)
Left political power	.06	-1.42	.37
	(.35)	(1.47)	(.66)
Labor market institutions (LMI)	1.23*	1.24	1.49*
	(.64)	(1.49)	(.85)
Left*LMI	.003	.28	-.09
	(.155)	(.55)	(.22)
Trade		-.0202	
		(.0756)	
Trade*left		.0348	
		(.0320)	
Trade*LMI		.0012	
		(.0241)	
Trade*left*LMI		-.0075	
		(.0103)	
Capital mobility			-2.60
			(1.62)
Capital mobility*left			.71
			(.72)
Capital mobility*LMI			.58
			(.51)
Capital mobility*left*LMI			-.21
			(.19))

promoted price stability, and oil dependence was associated (but not significantly) with higher inflation. There was a secular increase in inflation across the countries in this study in the five years following the first OPEC crisis, whereas inflation tended to be lowest in the final 1985–1990 period. None of the country dummy variables was significant.

The pattern of parameter estimates in the baseline model for the left power–labor market institutions interaction is very different from that reported in Alvarez, Garrett, and Lange (1991). In that paper, we found that although the independent effects of left power and the strength of organized labor was to increase inflation, their combined impact was to reduce the pace of price increases. The baseline model in Table 5.4, in contrast, shows that the strength of labor market institutions was significantly associated with higher rates of inflation, whereas the power of left parties both alone and interacted with labor market institutions had no impact on prices.

Table 5.4. *The Determinants of Inflation, 1966–1990 (continued)*

Independent variables	Baseline	Trade	Capital mobility
Period dummy variables			
1966–1973	.97***	.99	.31
	(.32)	(.78)	(.68)
1974–1979	2.01***	2.04***	1.88***
	(.42)	(0.73)	(0.67)
1980–1984	1.02**	1.04	1.06
	(.41)	(.70)	(.68)
1986–1990	-.02	-.10	-.16
	(.29)	(.66)	(.65)
Observations	350	350	350
Adjusted R-square	.678	.675	.682
Wald's test for joint significance of the market integration-left-LMI interaction		.500	.020

OLS estimates using panel corrected standard errors. *** p<.001; **.001<p<.05; *.05<p<.10. The parameter estimates for the fourteen country dummy variables are not reported because none is statistically significant.
[a]OECD GDP growth weighted by national exposure to trade
[b]The price of oil in $US weighted by dependence on imported oil (as a portion of all energy requirements)

How can one explain the radical difference between these two sets of inflation results? There are numerous possible reasons for this disjuncture, but the most likely is that the data on labor market institutions used in this book are considerably more sophisticated than those in Alvarez, Garrett and Lange (1991).[7] In the earlier work, we (along with most other researchers) relied on qualitative codings of the structural attributes of labor movements based on one-time assessments from the early 1970s. At minimum, these codings likely concealed important inter-temporal variations. They also were potentially biased: Labor movements that produced more price stability were more likely to be coded as encompassing. In contrast, the data used here are derived from recent efforts to quantify time-varying attributes of national labor market institutions. I am thus more confident in the results reported in this book. I discuss in the next section why more encompassing labor organizations may be associated with higher rates of inflation.

The second and third columns of Table 5.4 report the effects of adding globalization terms to the inflation equations. Exposure to trade had no impact on the results of the baseline model. Things were somewhat different, however, with respect to capital mobility. In this equation, although the significant positive coefficient on LMI remained, the LEFT.LMI term was negative (but not significant). Moreover, the pattern of parameter estimates for the capital mobility interaction terms was consistent with the Alvarez, Garrett and Lange (1991) results. The CM.LEFT and CM.LMI coefficients were positive whereas the CM.LEFT.LMI parameter estimate was negative. None of these coefficients was significant at traditional levels, but their t-statistics were around unity and the interaction specification as a whole was significant (the Wald's statistic was .02). Thus, at higher levels of capital mobility, the left-labor interaction more closely approximated the regime coherence hypothesis (most notably, lower rates of inflation in cases of strong left parties and encompassing labor market institutions). Nonetheless, the size of the uninteracted LMI coefficient was much larger than any of these other effects. It is thus unlikely that even at high levels of capital mobility, social democratic corporatism led to good inflation performance.

5.4 THE MACROECONOMIC EFFECTS OF MARKET INTEGRATION, LEFT POWER, AND LABOR MARKET INSTITUTIONS

This section generates counterfactual estimates of economic performance under different combinations of market integration, left power, and labor market institutions on the basis of the regression equations presented in Tables 5.2 through 5.4. Was it the case, as I contend, that economic performance in the global economy was at least as good under social democratic corporatism as under any other constellation of political power and labor movement structures? Or did greater left power and stronger labor market institutions increasingly harm macroeconomic outcomes as countries became more integrated into global markets? This would be the expectation of the conventional wisdom about the effects of globalization, given the results from Chapter 4 that the relationship between left-labor power and interventionist economic policies increased with market integration. If these policies were manifestly inefficient, this should have precipitated a significant deterioration in economic performance in countries with powerful left-wing parties and strong labor market institutions.

It is extremely difficult to answer these questions simply by looking at the parameter estimates discussed in the preceding section because of the complicated interaction specifications deployed in those models. Instead, I present counterfactual estimates of macroeconomic outcomes under different constellations of left power and labor market institutions, taking into account the effects of market integration. The methodology used to construct the counterfactuals is similar to that deployed for economic policies in the last chapter. First, all other variables in the regression equations were set to their mean levels and then multiplied by their corresponding coefficients. Second, the trade and capital mobility variables were set at the 80th percentile scores and multiplied by their regression coefficients. Finally, combinations of left power and labor market institutions (again, multiplying these by their regression coefficients) were added to generate counterfactual estimates of economic performance under different domestic conditions. Counterfactuals were only reported for the full left power–labor market institutions interaction equations when this specification was jointly significant at the .05 level (thus, the equations estimating growth and inflation at different levels of trade were excluded).

In order not to exaggerate the macroeconomic effects of market integration and domestic politics, the counterfactuals were not estimated at the tails of the distributions in the data set. Rather, I only examined the interactive effects of the balance of political power and labor market institutions at the 80th percentile of the trade (85.7 percent for Norway in 1980) and capital mobility (no restrictions on cross-border capital flows, which characterized half the countries in the late 1980s) distributions. In turn, combinations of the 20th and 80th percentile scores were used on the domestic variables. The 20th percentile in the left power distribution was 1.92 (for France in 1976), whereas the 80th percentile was 4.14 (Austria in 1990). The corresponding figures for the labor market institutions index were 0.86 (Canada in 1982) and 4.15 (Austria in 1983).

Let us begin with counterfactual estimates for the baseline models that do not take into account the effects of market integration. These are presented in Figure 5.2. The unemployment estimates accord perfectly with my theoretical expectations about the beneficial consequences of regime coherence. Unemployment was estimated to have been 0.2 percentage points lower in the "left-encompassing" (denoting social democratic corporatism) and "right-weak" (market liberalism) cells than in either incoherent combination. The relatively small magnitude of these effects is not surprising given the great stickiness in national unemployment rates over time.

The other two sets of baseline performance estimates, however, did not follow this pattern as closely. With respect to economic growth, tilting the balance of political power to the left increased growth by half a percentage point or more irrespective of the strength of labor market institutions. Moreover, growth rates were estimated to have been lowest in the cell approximating the market liberalism regime type. The estimated inflation rates were the mirror image of those for growth. Moving from the weak to the encompassing case for labor market institutions increased the inflation rate by more than two percentage points, and inflation was estimated to be highest of all in the left-encompassing cell representing social democratic corporatism.

These counterfactual estimates reinforce the impression gained from the regression equations on which they are based: The interactive effects of the balance of power and the strength of labor market institutions were a mixed bag. Unemployment performance was exactly in keeping with the regime coherence the-

Figure 5.2. Counterfactual estimates of economic performance

Balance of political power

		Left	Right
		Unemployment: 5.3%	5.5%
	Encompassing	*GDP growth*: 2.5%	2.0%
Labor market institutions		*Inflation*: 9.2%	9.0%
		Unemployment: 5.5%	5.3%
	Weak	*GDP growth*: 2.6%	1.7%
		Inflation: 6.8%	6.7%

Counterfactual estimates calculated on the basis of the baseline unemployment, GDP growth and inflation equations reported in the first column of Tables 5.2–5.4 for the left power–labor market institutions interaction (without trade or capital mobility). Low (high) levels of left power refer to the 20th (80th) percentile scores on left power index. Encompassing (weak) refer to the 80th (20th) percentile scores on the labor market institutions index. All other variables were set at their means.

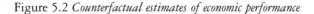

Figure 5.2 *Counterfactual estimates of economic performance*

sis. Left power was associated with stronger economic growth. Inflation was higher where labor market institutions were more encompassing.

How were these relationships affected by globalization? Figure 5.3 presents the estimates for unemployment, economic growth, and inflation at high levels of capital mobility. Recall that my argument is that the macroeconomic effects of social democratic corporatism should have been no worse in the global economy than they were in relatively more closed economies. This stands in marked contrast to the conventional view that the macroeconomic costs of social democratic corporatism increased with market integration.

The counterfactual estimates in Figure 5.3 support my argument over the conventional view. Consider first the unemployment case. At high levels of capital

Balance of political power

Labor market institutions		Left	Right
	Encompassing	*Unemployment*: 4.9%	5.7%
		GDP growth: 3.3%	2.1%
		Inflation: 8.6%	8.6%
	Weak	*Unemployment*: 5.7%	5.4%
		GDP growth: 2.6%	1.7%
		Inflation: 6.2%	5.9%

Counterfactual estimates calculated on the basis of the unemployment, GDP growth and inflation equations reported in the third column of Table 5.2–5.4 for the capital mobility–left power–labor market institutions interactions, which were all jointly significant at the .05 level or better. The counterfactuals are estimates for the 80th percentile in the capital mobility distribution. Low (high) levels of left power refer to the 20th (80th) percentile scores on left power index. Encompassing (weak) refer to the 80th (20th) percentile scores on the labor market institutions index. All other variables were set at their means.

Figure 5.3 *Counterfactual estimates of economic performance at high levels of capital mobility*

mobility, estimated unemployment was 0.5 percentage points lower in the social democratic corporatism cell than in the weak-right case (whereas the rates were the same in the baseline estimates). With respect to rates of joblessness, the relative performance of social democratic corporatism was better at high levels of capital mobility than under conditions of more closed financial markets.

The estimates for economic growth at high levels of capital mobility are even more flattering for social democratic corporatism. Left power was still good for growth, but in the high capital mobility case, the combination of left power and encompassing labor market institutions was particularly beneficial to output.

Balance of political power

		Left	Right
Encompassing		4.9%	5.6%
Weak		5.3%	6.4%

Labor market institutions

Counterfactual estimates calculated on the basis of the unemployment equation reported in the second column of Table 5.4 for the
trade–left power–labor market institutions interaction, which was
jointly significant at the .05 level. The counterfactuals are
estimates for the 80th percentile in the trade distribution. Low
(high) levels of left power refer to the 20th (80th) percentile scores
on left power index. Encompassing (weak) refer to the 80th (20th)
percentile scores on the labor market institutions index. All other
variables were set at their means.

Figure 5.4 *Counterfactual estimates of unemployment rates at high
levels of trade*

Moreover, the gap between the growth performance in the left-encompassing and
right-weak cases was fully twice as large as it was in the baseline case (where
market integration was not taken into account).

Thus, the growth and unemployment estimates at high levels of capital
mobility clearly demonstrate that the combination of strong left-wing parties
and encompassing labor market institutions was the best for real economic aggregates over the 1966–1990 period. Moreover, the unemployment estimates at
high levels of trade reinforced this pattern (see Figure 5.4). The only difference
here was that the estimated rate of unemployment in the right-weak cell was the
highest in the figure, and fully 1.5 percentage points higher than in the left-
encompassing cell. Thus, the evidence on real aggregates strongly supports my
argument that globalization did not undermine the economic performance foundations of social democratic corporatism. Indeed, all the evidence points in the
opposite direction.

The situation was very different, however, with respect to inflation. Figure
5.3 shows that inflation was considerably higher under conditions of high capital
mobility where labor market institutions were encompassing. Furthermore, the
inflation gap between the left-encompassing and right-weak cells was marginally
higher in the high capital mobility case (2.7 percentage points) than it was for
the baseline estimates (2.5 points). As was apparent in Table 5.4, my inflation
analysis stands in marked contrast to the results on real aggregates and delineates
a consistent cost with respect to price increases of social democratic corporatism.

What explains the marked divergence between the growth and unemployment results, on the one hand, and those for inflation, on the other? It is tempting to offer a simple Phillips curve explanation. The left and organized labor were prepared to tradeoff higher inflation for faster growth and lower unemployment, whereas the right (especially where unions were weak) was much more averse to inflation. On this view, inflation was the price that had to be paid in social democratic corporatism for responding to market integration with ever-higher levels of government spending and larger public sector deficits.

There is certainly something to this argument. However, it is also likely that the dynamics of the wage-setting process in countries with encompassing labor market institutions were also very important. Recall from Chapter 2 my argument about social democratic corporatism that in return for government policies redistributing wealth and social risk, the leaders of encompassing labor market institutions would choose to regulate economywide wage growth in ways that would stimulate overall economic performance. I assumed that one manifestation of this would be low rates of inflation – generated by wage restraint.

It has recently been argued, reviving an old argument by James Tobin (1972), that moderate nominal wage increases (and, in turn, matching price increases) may be very helpful to the generation of real wage restraint. The simplest rendering of this argument extends James Buchanan and Richard Wagner's (1977) notion of "fiscal illusion" to wage setting. Workers are more likely to accept no growth or real cuts in their real incomes if the amount of paper money in their pay packets is going up (Akerlof, Dickens, and Perry 1996).

Observers of wage setting in Scandinavia have made a more specific argument pertaining to the strategy of the leaders of encompassing labor market institutions (Calmfors 1993; Iversen 1996b).[8] In addition to being concerned about the externalities of wage growth for the economy as a whole (the conventional argument), there are powerful incentives for the leaders of encompassing labor movements to reduce inequalities among groups of workers. Because all centralized wage bargains will ultimately be eroded to some extent by "wage drift" in profitable and productive sectors (i.e., wage increases above the central agreement), the best way for the leaders of encompassing labor movements to further simultaneously their interests in real wage restraint and income equality is to build "high" nominal increases into national wage bargains.

Of course, the size of these nominal increases is ultimately constrained by their impact on national productivity and competitiveness. Nonetheless, this line of thinking offers a very plausible explanation for the coincidence of high growth, low unemployment and high inflation in countries with encompassing labor market institutions.

CONCLUSION

This chapter has explored the macroeconomic consequences of the balance of political power and labor market institutions in the global economy. It represents the final piece of the central empirical puzzle in this book – the impact of globalization on the political and economic viability of social democratic corporatism in the period up until 1990. Chapter 4 showed that the distinctiveness of social democratic corporatism with respect to fiscal policy increased as international markets became more integrated. This result was subject to an obvious objection, fueled by the evidence that left-labor power was associated with larger public sector deficits and higher interest rates. Surely, social democratic corporatism had dire consequences for the macroeconomy in the era of global markets.

The evidence presented in this chapter cleaved in two directions. On the one hand, growth and unemployment performance were exceptionally good in countries that were highly integrated into global markets and had powerful left parties and encompassing labor market institutions. But on the other hand, inflation increased with greater left power, and especially with stronger labor market institutions. I speculated that this pattern of performance might have to do with the fact that it is easier for the leaders of encompassing labor movements to generate real – rather than nominal – wage restraint. Nominal inflation increases thus might grease the wheel, allowing real levels of wage restraint that promote growth and unemployment.

Thus, the performance results reveal the type of political Phillips curve relationship between inflation and real aggregates that has fallen out of favor since the rational expectations revolution in macroeconomics. Whether one considers social democratic corporatism on balance a good or a bad thing for the economy depends on one's views of the relative importance of inflation versus economic growth and unemployment. Either way, however, this chapter refutes the simplistic notion that globalization has rendered left power and strong labor market institutions unambiguous economic "bads."

The only remaining tasks are to update the analysis into the 1990s (when economic performance in northern Europe deteriorated markedly) and to speculate about the future of social democratic corporatism. Both of these objectives require considerable attention. I devote the final chapter to addressing them.

Appendix 5.1. *Economic Performance, 1966–1973*

Country	Economic growth	Inflation	Unemployment	Misery index[a]
Social democratic corporatism[b]				
Austria	5.3	4.6	1.5	6.1
Denmark	3.9	6.7	3.5	10.2
Finland	5.5	6.3	2.6	8.9
Norway	5.1	6.1	1.1	7.2
Sweden	3.7	5.1	1.8	6.9
Average	4.7	5.8	2.1	7.9
Incoherent[c]				
Belgium	5.1	4.3	3.5	7.8
Germany	4.5	3.9	1.2	5.1
Italy	5.3	4.9	5.8	10.7
Netherlands	4.3	5.9	1.9	7.8
Average	4.8	3.8	3.1	6.9
Market liberalism[d]				
Canada	5.2	4 4	5.4	9.8
France	5.5	5.4	1.5	6.9
Japan	9.5	6.4	1.2	7.6
United Kingdom	3.2	6.4	2.8	9.2
United States	3.4	4.6	4.6	9.2
Average	5.4	5.4	3.1	8.5

[a]Sum of inflation and unemployment rates
[b]Countries that ranked in the top five on the left-labor power index for the period 1985–1990
[c]Countries that ranked in the middle four on the left-labor power index for the period 1985–1990
[d]Countries that ranked in the bottom five on the left-labor power index for the period 1985–1990

Appendix 5.2. *Economic Performance, 1985–1990*

Country	Economic growth	Inflation	Unemployment	Misery index[a]
Social democratic corporatism[b]				
Austria	3.1	2.4	3.4	5.8
Finland	3.4	5.1	4.5	9.6
Italy	2.8	6.3	11.3	17.6
Norway	2.7	6.2	3.3	9.5
Sweden	2.1	6.4	1.8	8.2
Average	2.8	5.3	4.9	10.2
Incoherent[c]				
Belgium	2.7	2.6	10.4	13.0
Denmark	1.6	4.1	7.2	11.3
Germany	3.0	1.5	8.2	9.7
Netherlands	2.7	1.0	9.4	10.4
Average	2.5	2.3	8.8	11.1
Market liberalism[d]				
Canada	3.4	4.4	8.7	13.1
France	2.6	3.6	9.9	13.5
Japan	4.5	1.4	2.5	3.9
United Kingdom	3.2	6.0	8.7	14.7
United States	3.1	3.9	6.1	10.0
Average	3.4	3.9	7.2	11.0

[a]Sum of inflation and unemployment rates
[b]Countries that ranked in the top five on the left-labor power index for the period 1985–1990.
[c]Countries that ranked in the middle four on the left-labor power index for the period 1985–1990.
[d]Countries that ranked in the bottom five on the left-labor power index for the period 1985–1990.

6

THE 1990s AND BEYOND

It is ironic that although the last decade has witnessed an appropriately lauded wave of transitions to capitalist democracy, the advanced industrial countries that stand as the presumed exemplars of the synergies between capitalism and democracy are in deep trouble. The era of noninflationary economic growth and full employment in the OECD ended abruptly in 1973, and whether it will ever return must be in serious doubt. The policy legacy from the golden age of capitalist democracy is under siege in this new straitened economic climate. Just twenty-five years ago, the mixed economy in which governments redistributed wealth and social risk without harming the macroeconomy was considered by many to be the greatest achievement of the postwar industrial democracies. Today, most government interventions in the economy are viewed with skepticism and many pundits contend that redistributive objectives must be sacrificed at the altar of efficiency. The driving force behind this perceived transformation of capitalist democracy is thought to be the globalization of markets and the attendant ease with which production and capital can be moved around the world in search of higher rates of return.

The standard line on globalization is that markets now dominate politics as social forces and there is nothing that governments can do about it. For anyone interested in substantive equality or indeed the vitality of the democratic process, this is a distressing conclusion. Markets generate winners and losers (in the short term at least), but it is commonly assumed today that it is impossible to help losers without inciting socially damaging behavior by winners. The range of visions for governing from which citizens can choose is, on this account, very limited. In effect, the threat of "exit" by mobile asset holders has supplanted the "voice" of citizens as the primary determinant of public policy in the era of globalized markets. In turn, policy convergence by mainstream political parties around less interventionist policies could prompt more radical and destabilizing backlashes – in the form of ever greater support for parties and policies based on appeals to xenophobic nationalism and other populist issues that are not conducive to economic efficiency.

Many social democrats believe that the only plausible way to avoid these odious outcomes is to increase the scope of politics to match more closely that of markets. To take the clearest example, moving both fiscal and monetary authority to Brussels is frequently advocated as the best way to revive social democracy in Europe.[1] But given the tiny size of the current EU budget and the precipitous drop in popular support for "more Europe" after Maastricht, the emergence of a full-blown European federation in the foreseeable future is very unlikely.[2]

This book has offered a very different perspective on the relationship between capitalism and democracy in the era of increasingly global markets in goods, services, and capital. I have argued that there remains a distinctive leftist alternative to free market capitalism at the national level that is not only politically desirable in terms of winning elections, but also consistent with strong macroeconomic performance. To be sure, social democratic corporatism is not the only way to succeed economically and politically under globalization. Nevertheless, it remains a viable option that should receive more consideration in policy debates.

Successful social democratic corporatism comprises four elements. First, leftist governments enact economic policies that redistribute wealth and risk in ways that favor the increasingly large segments of the population that are vulnerable to the vicissitudes of global markets. Second, some of these policies are directly conducive to better economic performance because they promote collective goods that are undersupplied by the market (e.g., investments in human capital and infrastructure). Third, the leaders of encompassing labor market institutions ensure that workers do not take advantage of market-cushioning policies to act in ways that harm the macroeconomy – most importantly, by gearing economywide wage developments to the competitiveness of the sector of the economy exposed to global markets. Finally, the political, economic, and social stability characteristics of social democratic corporatism – coupled with the high productivity of labor – provide an attractive home for investors in the uncertain and volatile international economy. (risk averse)

In this final chapter, I consider three further issues raised by the rest of the book. The first and most important is to extend the analysis into the 1990s. This is crucial because the historical bastions of social democratic corporatism have been shaken by rising unemployment, greater public debt, and welfare cuts. Since residual capital controls were removed in the early 1990s in these countries, it is tempting to conclude that these events are causally linked. But are they final proof that social democratic corporatism is poorly adapted to the era of global markets?

I argue against this interpretation of events in the 1990s. On the one hand, many of the issues that today create problems for the social democratic corporatist regimes also plague countries in which the left and organized labor are much weaker. For example, I show that burgeoning public health and social security costs are a more serious public policy problem in Japan than they are in Sweden, whereas Finland's accumulated public debt-to-GDP ratio is considerably smaller than Canada's. If these problems can be attributed to globalization, it is clear that its effects are not isolated to northern Europe.

On the other hand, problems that do seem more clearly identifiable with social democratic corporatist countries in the 1990s, most notably rising unemployment, were far more the product of the transition to the post–Cold War political economy in Europe than of biting globalization constraints. I argue that the European recession of the early 1990s was largely caused by the demise of the Soviet bloc and, more proximately, by the negative economic externalities of the rapid reunification of Germany. The recession hit the Nordic countries hardest because of their decisions to prepare for joining the European Union by pegging their exchange rates to the Deutsche Mark at precisely the wrong time.

Furthermore, even if rising unemployment in corporatist northern Europe cannot be attributed to the effects of capital mobility, it may nonetheless be time to reassess the utility of concentrating on the headline rate of joblessness as our metric for determining the success of countries in improving the material well-being of people at the lower end of the income distribution. In this vein, one might ask if it is really so much better to be employed in a low-wage job in the United States than it is to be unemployed in social democratic corporatist countries? The answer to this question is not necessarily flattering to the U.S. model.

The second objective of this chapter is to identify the central challenges facing social democratic corporatism as the new millennium approaches. I argue that the leftist alternative to the free market does face significant challenges in the contemporary period, even if they have little to do with globalization. The most important of these problems are stubbornly high unemployment rates (especially among the long-term unemployed), the increasing ratio of populations dependent on the state (especially the aged) to those working and paying taxes, and the strength of public sector unions, which makes economywide wage restraint harder to achieve. I briefly speculate about possible solutions to these problems that do not compromise the broader goals of social democracy. These include further investments in active labor market policies, using floating exchange rates to regain macroeconomic autonomy, reducing welfare benefits to wealthy retirees, and increasing the institutional linkages between public sector unions and those in the exposed sector of the economy.

The final part of the chapter asks how policy makers in countries with strong left-wing parties might try to institutionalize social democratic corporatism in countries with little or no history of it. Building the requisite encompassing labor market institutions is a difficult task, but it is not impossible. Tying the distribution of unemployment benefits to union membership, for example, is a proven method for increasing trade union density. The coverage of collective bargaining can be expanded to nonunion members through legislation. Furthermore, there are numerous examples in recent years – from Australia to the Czech Republic to Greece – of efforts to increase the centralization of authority within labor movements and to coordinate economic policy and wage setting at the national level. Although these attempts to build corporatism have not yet been, and may never be, as successful as they have been in northern Europe, they nonetheless testify to the enduring appeal and importance of alternatives to Chicago school political economy in democratic countries.

The tenor of this chapter, and indeed that of the whole book, is thus optimistic. But I do not think it is unrealistic. Conflict over the economic role of government and its resolution through public discourse and the ballot box have been pivotal facets of democracy since at least the rise of parliamentarism in seventeenth-century England. With the advent of political parties speaking for organized labor at the turn of the twentieth century, debates over the appropriate extent and nature of political control over the economy became even more important. But today many people think that democratic politics is "either uninteresting or irrelevant" given the power of global markets (to quote from Roger Cohen's recent column in *The New York Times* excerpted at the beginning of this book). My goal has been to demonstrate that such simplistic views about globalization do great injustice to the political appeal and economic efficacy of social democratic alternatives to the free market.

6.1   GLOBALIZATION, POLITICS, POLICIES AND PERFORMANCE, 1966-1990

The previous chapters of this book have generated four central propositions about the 1966–1990 period:

- The integration of the industrial democracies into the global economy with respect to both trade and capital mobility increased substantially throughout the period. Notwithstanding this general trend, however, there were important cross-national variations in market integration. The small countries of northern Europe were always more dependent on trade, but controls on cross-border capital flows were removed more slowly in these countries than elsewhere in the OECD. Thus, the manifestations of globalization differed significantly across the capitalist democracies.
- The balance of political power among the industrial democracies as a whole did not move to the right with the globalization of markets, nor did the institutional power of labor deteriorate. Moreover, traditional cross-national differences in left-labor power were largely unaffected by globalization. As a result, there was considerable continuity throughout the 1966–1990 period in the ranks of social democratic corporatist regimes (powerful left-wing

parties allied with encompassing labor market institutions) – Austria, Denmark, Finland, Norway, and Sweden – and of those countries that more closely approximate the ideal type of market liberalism (dominant right-wing parties and much weaker organized labor movements) – Canada, France, Japan, the United Kingdom, and the United States.

- The positive relationship between left-labor power and redistributive big government strengthened with greater exposure to trade and higher capital mobility. This reflected the responsiveness of social democratic corporatist regimes to growing political demands to ameliorate the dislocations and insecurities associated with integration into global markets. Tax revenues in these countries, however, did not increase at the same pace as spending. Thus, the relationship between social democratic corporatism and higher public sector deficits strengthened with market integration. In turn, this led the capital markets to place an interest rate premium on borrowing in corporatist countries.

- The performance of social democratic corporatist regimes in the global economy with respect to real aggregates – economic growth and unemployment – was better than in countries where the balance of political power was tilted more to the right or where labor market institutions were weaker. But the converse was true with respect to price stability. Inflation rates were higher under more encompassing labor market institutions, and this was exacerbated somewhat by the strength of left-wing political parties. Hence, there was a clear trade-off in the industrial countries between real outcomes and price stability, and very different choices were made in social democratic corporatist countries from liberal market regimes.

Taken together, these results call for a substantial scaling back and qualification of arguments about the domestic constraints imposed by globalization. Certainly, the balance sheet was not all positive for social democratic corporatism. Left-labor power was associated with higher public sector deficits, higher interest rates, and higher inflation rates. But these costs must be weighed against the achievements of social democratic corporatism: reduced social risk and inequality coupled with faster growth and lower unemployment. Reasonable people may differ in their evaluations of these outcomes, but their judgments must be based primarily on normative views about the fairness of market allocations.

6.2 GLOBALIZATION, POLITICS, AND POLICIES IN THE 1990s

Having responded to assertions about the demise of social democratic corporatism in the period up until 1990, I suspect that my analysis may only provoke new criticisms. Even if one were willing to accept my results, it could nonetheless be argued that it was only in the 1990s that globalization finally nailed shut the coffin for leftist alternatives to market liberalism. In time, it will be possible to test this claim using the multivariate techniques of Chapters 4 and 5. But all the relevant data currently do not exist. In this section, I rely on available data and more rudimentary methods to analyze developments in the first half of the decade.

MARKET INTEGRATION

The process of globalization continued in the early 1990s. With respect to trade, substantial progress was made on the European Union's internal market program, and other new international liberalization agreements were also signed. The completion of the Uruguay Round of the GATT expanded the scope of the global trading system to include agriculture and services. The Canada–United States Free Trade Agreement was signed in 1989, followed by NAFTA four years later. The consequence of all this activity was considerable growth in OECD trade in the first half of the 1990s, particularly among relatively small traders, such as Canada, Japan, and the United States. Nonetheless, these economies remain quite closed by European standards.

Developments with respect to capital mobility in the 1990s , however, are potentially more important for the arguments made in this book. Four of the five traditional social democratic corporatist regimes retained some restrictions on cross-border financial flows in 1990 – Austria, Finland, Norway and Sweden (see Chapter 3). All of these countries except Norway entered the European Union in 1995, and they removed their remaining capital controls in the run up to accession. Although substantial differences in exposure to trade endure in the OECD today, the playing field is more or less level with respect to capital mobility. This means that the first proposition from the main part of the book requires some modification. But the critical questions concern the effects of increased capital mobility in the 1990s on politics, policy, and performance under social democratic corporatism compared with other industrial democracies.

THE LEFT AND ORGANIZED LABOR

Table 6.1 presents data on the political power of left-wing parties in the 1990s with respect to participation in cabinet governments and seats in the lower houses of national legislatures. There was no clear change from the 1980s in the average strength of left-wing parties, and large cross-national differences remained. The left had substantial cabinet representation in eight of the fourteen countries in this study, including four of the traditional social democratic corporatist regimes – Austria, Denmark, Norway and Sweden (even though the Swedish social democrats were out of office from September 1991 to September 1994). The Finnish social democrats were out of power for almost all the first half of the 1990s, rendering Finland's political economy more "incoherent." It would be wrong,

Table 6.1. *The Political Power of Left-Wing Parties in the 1990s*[a]

| Country[b] | Percentage of cabinet portfolios | | Percentage of legislative seats[c] | |
	Average (1991–1995)	Change (1991–1995) minus (1980–1990)	Average (1991–1995)	Change (1991–1995) minus (1980–1990)
Norway	100	51	49	1
Belgium	52	33	38	5
Austria	50	-24	47	-3
Netherlands	44	36	34	-3
Sweden	40	-35	47	-5
Denmark	38	13	50	4
Italy	32	8	20	-24
France	31	-26	29	-24
Finland	2	-43	38	-3
Japan	2	2	25	-6
Canada	0	0	10	-2
Germany	0	-19	42	-3
United Kingdom	0	0	39	3
United States	0	0	0	0
Average	28	0	33	-4

[a]Definitions of left parties based on Castles and Mair [1984]
[b]Ranked by cabinet portfolios 1991–1995
[c]The lower house in bicameral legislatures
Source: Swank [1995] and *European Journal of Political Research* (Political Data Yearbooks, various).

however, to make too much of these changes, given the historical volatility of cabinet governments (see Chapter 3). Furthermore, it should be remembered that the Swedish social democrats regained control of government in late 1994, and their Finnish counterparts joined a grand coalition a year later.

Moreover, historical differences among countries remained very apparent with respect to legislative representation. Left parties continued to hold more than 40 percent of legislative seats in Austria, Denmark, Germany, Norway and Sweden; Canada and the United States were the only countries in which social democratic parties had little impact on the composition of national legislatures. Only in France and Italy did the balance of power in legislatures change appreciably from the 1980s to the 1990s, and in both cases the swing was to the right.[3] But neither of these countries was a bastion of corporatism in the 1980s.

Assuming that basic cross-national differences in labor market institutions in the 1980s carried over into the next decade, the ranks of the social democratic corporatist and market liberal regimes continued to be quite stable through the mid 1990s.[4] Austria and Norway, and to a lesser extent Sweden, remained exemplars of social democratic corporatism. Denmark became a somewhat marginal case in the 1980s as the result of a significant move to the right in the balance of political power, but this trend was reversed with the electoral victory of the social democrats in 1993. The Finnish social democrats were out of power for most of the first half of the 1990s, making its placement in the corporatist category more debatable. Nonetheless, political and organizational conditions in all five of these traditional bastions of social democratic corporatism remained very different from those squarely in the ranks of market liberalism in the 1990s: Canada, France, Japan, the United Kingdom, and the United States.

ECONOMIC POLICY

Summary data on economic policy in the 1990s are presented in Table 6.2. There was a strong correlation between accumulated left-labor power and government spending in the 1990s.[5] On this simple indicator, the association between social democratic corporatism and big government was more pronounced in the 1990s than it had ever been. Turning to public sector deficits, left-labor power had virtually no impact on deficits in the 1990s, nor on changes from the 1980s.[6] Public sector deficits increased substantially in three social democratic corporatist regimes in the 1990s – Finland, Norway, and Sweden. But deficits were stable and small in Austria and Denmark. Among the market liberalism regimes, annual increases in public sector debt were rapid in Canada, France, and the United Kingdom, whereas only Japan was able to run more or less balanced budgets. In sum, the fiscal policy data suggest that big government was still a distinctive feature of social democratic corporatism in the 1990s and that this was not associated with deficits were out of step with those in other industrial countries.

In recent years, however, attention has been focused more on accumulated levels of public debt rather than on annual deficits as indicators of fiscal responsibility. It is often assumed that profligate social democratic corporatist regimes have been prime culprits in terms of mounting debt. The data on accumulated public debt by 1995, however, show no relationship between larger debt burdens and left-labor power (see Table 6.3). Consider first the countries at the top of the left-labor power distribution. Norway's exceptionally low debt burden is largely attributable to the wealth of state-owned oil companies. But in only two of the other four corporatist countries – Denmark and Sweden – was public debt above average, and in both cases only marginally so. At the other end of the spectrum, Canada's debt was far higher than in any corporatist country; Japanese public debt was virtually identical to Sweden's. As is well known, Belgium and Italy have serious debt problems, but neither has traditionally been considered a social democratic corporatist regime.

Table 6.2. *Fiscal Policy in the 1990s*

Country[a]	Government spending (%GDP)[b] 1991– 1995	Δ^f	Budget deficit (%GDP)[c] 1991– 1995	Δ	Gap between highest and lowest rates of income taxation[d] early 1990s	Δ^g	Effective highest marginal rate of corporate taxation[e] 1992	Δ^h
Austria	51.5	1.5	3.8	0.9	40	-3		.
Sweden	67.3	6.2	8.0	6.9	20	-31.5	30	-19.6
Denmark	61.8	2.7	3.0	0.3	18	-5	38	-7
Norway	49.6	4.9	1.0	5.5	17	-5.5	28	-22.8
Finland	58.0	15.5	5.4	8.6	.	.	.	.
Germany	48.9	1.9	3.0	0.9	34	0	51.9	-3.5
Belgium	56.2	-4.0	6.0	-3.0	30	-14.5	39	-0.4
Italy	54.1	5.0	9.1	-1.9	40	-11	55.2	10.8
Netherlands	53.8	-3.3	3.3	-1.8	30	-24	35	1
United Kingdom	42.5	0.3	5.6	3.6	15	-21.5	33	-8.5
France	53.2	4.1	4.6	3.6	51	-2	34	-9.3
Japan	34.3	2.2	0.9	-0.2	.	.	38.4	-3.4
Canada	48.5	5.0	6.2	1.8	12	-13	39.1	-0.9
United States	34.1	4.1	2.9	3.4	16	-20	34	-2.8
Average	50.9	3.4	4.5	2.1	26	-13	38	-6
Correlation with left-labor power	0.70	0.12	0.10	0.18	0.20	0.18	-0.02	-0.46

[a]Rank order based on average scores for the left-labor power index, 1980–1995
[b]Total government spending (total outlays), OECD [1996: A31]
[c]Budget deficit (total outlays minus current receipts), OECD [1996: A32]
[d]Heclo, Heidenheimer and Adams [1990: 211–212] and OECD, *The Tax/Benefit Position of Production Workers* (various)
[e]The highest rate of corporate taxation less investment incentives. Cummins, Hassett and Hubbard [1995: tables 1 and 2]
[f]1991–1995 minus 1980–1990
[g]Early 1990s minus 1980s
[h]1992 minus 1981–1990

Using accumulated public debt in 1995 as an overall indicator of fiscal performance, it is clear that although governments in strong left-labor regimes have been big spenders, they have been no more irresponsible than other governments in increasing tax revenues to finance public sector expansion. In turn, this implies that over time the interest rate premiums attached to social democratic corporatism will come down.

Let us now turn to how the revenues used to fund government spending were collected (see the right-hand half of Table 6.2). The gap between the highest

Table 6.3. *Accumulated Public Debt in 1995*

Country[a]	Public debt[b]
Austria	69.4
Sweden	81.8
Denmark	78.3
Norway	36.5
Finland	63.0
Germany	61.6
Belgium	131.1
Italy	123.0
Netherlands	79.1
United Kingdom	57.6
France	57.9
Japan	81.3
Canada	99.1
United States	64.3
Average	77.4
Correlation with left-labor power	-0.10

[a]Presented in rank order on the left-labor power
index, 1980–1995
[b]Gross financial liabilities of general government,
OECD [1996: 13]

and lowest bands of personal income taxation in the early 1990s was still somewhat higher in the social democratic corporatist regimes than in other countries,
even though the Danish, Norwegian, and Swedish systems became much "flatter." In contrast, there was a marked convergence in the highest rates of corporate
taxation. Left-labor power had previously been strongly associated with higher
marginal rates, but by 1992 this relationship had vanished – largely as a result
of substantial cuts in corporate tax rates around the turn of the decade in both
Norway and Sweden.

The erosion of the relationship between social democratic corporatism and
higher rates of corporate taxation is the only piece of evidence in Table 6.2 that
is consistent with the view that globalization constraints on redistributive big
government began to bite in the 1990s. One should be reticent, however, to rely
too heavily on this piece of evidence. Recall from Chapter 4 that social democratic
corporatist regimes historically generated less revenue from corporate income
taxes than did other countries. High marginal rates were offset with very generous

investment incentives and depreciation schedules (Garrett and Lange 1991). Governments in strong left-labor regimes seem to have moved away from this type of tax structure in the 1990s. But it seems that they did so because investment incentives proved susceptible to abuse by firms. Indeed, the flattening of the corporate tax structure in the early 1990s was associated with increased revenues from this form of taxation (Swank 1996).

In sum, the evidence in this subsection highlights the stability of the relationships between combined left-labor power and economic policy in the first half of the 1990s. This policy stability would be for naught, however, if the performance consequences of social democratic corporatism deteriorated with increasing capital mobility in the 1990s. As I have already indicated, there is a prima facie case in favor of this proposition. The following section argues, however, that the causal connection between capital mobility and rising unemployment in northern Europe is hard to sustain.

6.3   UNEMPLOYMENT IN THE 1990s

Summary data on macroeconomic performance in the 1990s are reported by regime type in Table 6.4. The OECD went into a recession in the early 1990s. The political upheavals associated with the end of the Cold War followed uncomfortably closely on the heels of the 1987 stock market crash. The 1991 Gulf War added further instability and uncertainty to global markets. It is thus not surprising that there was a slowdown in economic activity throughout the OECD in the early 1990s, nor that the slowdown was more marked in Europe where the economic effects of instability in eastern Europe and the former Soviet Union were most immediately felt.

For the purposes of this book, however, the most important facet of Table 6.4 is the poor unemployment performance of the social democratic corporatist countries in the first half of the 1990s. All these countries had among the lowest unemployment rates in the OECD in the 1980s. In marked contrast to the stability in the other two regime types, average unemployment in the corporatist systems almost doubled between the 1980s and early 1990s. To be sure, these averages conceal important variations within categories. After Japan, corporatist Austria and Norway had the lowest unemployment rates in the OECD in the 1990s. Furthermore, unemployment remained considerably higher in Canada, France, and the United Kingdom than in Sweden.

Nonetheless, the benefits of social democratic corporatism with respect to unemployment that were so evident in the 1970s and 1980s were far less apparent in the first half of the 1990s. Two cases stand out.[7] Sweden went from having the lowest unemployment rate in the OECD to being only an average performer in the 1990s, and this figure conceals the considerable "hidden" unemployment embodied in rapid expansion of retraining programs. Finnish unemployment

Table 6.4. *Economic Performance in the 1990s*

	Economic growth		Unemployment[a]		Inflation	
	1991–1995	Change[b]	1991–1995	Change	1991–1995	Change
Social democratic corporatism[c]						
Austria	2.0	-0.4	5.7	2.5	3.2	-0.3
Denmark	2.1	-1.0	11.3	3.0	2.0	-4.5
Finland	-0.7	-4.0	14.7	9.9	2.6	-4.9
Norway	3.7	1.0	5.5	2.5	2.4	-5.6
Sweden	0.2	-1.7	7.1	5.3	4.5	-3.7
Average	1.5	-1.2	8.9	4.6	2.9	-3.8
Incoherent[d]						
Belgium	1.3	-0.7	8.5	-2.4	2.5	-2.3
Germany[e]	2.2	0.1	6.7	-0.9	3.5	0.6
Italy	1.2	-0.9	10.8	0.5	5.1	-5.7
Netherlands	1.9	0.3	6.4	-3.2	2.7	-0.2
Average	1.7	-0.2	8.1	-1.5	3.5	-1.9
Market liberalism[f]						
Canada	1.6	-1.0	10.5	1.3	2.3	-4.1
France	1.1	-0.8	11.1	2.1	2.2	-4.8
Japan	1.3	-2.9	2.6	0.1	1.4	-1.1
United Kingdom	1.2	-0.8	9.5	0.0	3.4	-4.2
United States	1.9	-0.6	6.5	-0.2	3.1	-2.3
Average	1.4	-1.2	8.0	0.7	2.5	-3.3

[a]OECD standardized definition, except for Austria and Denmark
[b]Average (1991–1995) minus average (1980–1990)
[c]Countries that ranked in the top five on the left-labor power index for the period 1980–1995
[d]Countries that ranked in the middle four on the left-labor power index for the period 1980–1995
[e]Western Germany
[f]Countries that ranked in the bottom five on the left-labor power index for the period 1980–1995
Source: Data from OECD [1996]

averaged almost 15 percent in the period 1991–1995, second highest for the whole OECD behind only Spain (where the official figures do not take into account extensive employment in the gray economy).

There is a globalization-based explanation for the rapid increases in unemployment in the 1990s under social democratic corporatism, and in Finland and Sweden in particular. Corporatism has always been an inefficient regime that could only maintain high levels of employment because of constraints on cross-border capital flows. The removal of capital controls in the early 1990s precipitated capital flight, which, in turn, made it impossible for social democratic corporatism to sustain full employment.

This is a simple and superficially appealing explanation for rising unemployment in some corporatist countries, but it is not persuasive. The direction of causality is wrong. Capital outflows from the social democratic corporatist countries in the 1990s were certainly made easier by the removal of capital controls. But the large-scale capital flight that ensued was not the root cause of rising unemployment. Rather, capital flight and unemployment were both the result of deeper macroeconomic problems in Finland and Sweden. Put simply, overheated domestic economies were hit hard by the decline in economic activity associated with the end of the Cold War. The resulting recession was exacerbated by futile attempts to move to a fixed exchange rate with Germany at precisely the worst time to do this, namely, when German monetary policy was extremely poorly suited to the needs of the Finnish and Swedish economies.

Table 6.5 presents data on net international capital flows (inflows minus outflows) of both foreign direct investment and international portfolio investment (equities and bonds) for the 1991–1994 period, and correlations between these flows and left-labor power and unemployment. The first thing to note about the table is that outflows of direct investment were not higher the stronger the left and organized labor were. Why did foreign direct investors not flee the corporatist countries in the 1990s once restrictions on capital flows were removed? One answer that is consistent with my argument in this book is that these countries remained attractive to asset holders with (or contemplating) lasting economic stakes in them.

The picture was different, however, with respect to net outflows of portfolio investment, which were correlated with more left-labor power and more strongly with higher unemployment. There is no gainsaying that the sale of bonds held by foreigners and the desire of local capital to invest offshore led the Finnish and Swedish governments to raise interest rates to stem capital outflows – putting a brake on domestic economic activity. This capital flight, however, had very little to do with the structural attributes of social democratic corporatism. Rather, the magnitude of capital outflows is better explained by an extremely undesirable set of conjunctures that befell these economies and poor short-term policy choices made by governments in response to them.

Analysts agree on the causes of the Nordic recessions in the early 1990s (from which Norway was largely insulated by its oil wealth).[8] These economies boomed in the second half of the 1980s as a result of the deregulation of domestic credit markets. When the boom turned to bust around the end of the decade, domestic consumption declined precipitously as households increased savings in efforts to repay debts accrued during the expansion. Banking crises ensued, putting a heavy drag on domestic economic activity.

The timing of these Nordic recessions was most inopportune because they coincided with the broader European economic downturn of the early 1990s that

Table 6.5. *International Capital Flows in the 1990s*

	Net foreign direct investment (%GDP)[b]		Net foreign portfolio investment (%GDP)[c]	
Country[a]	1991–1994	Change	1991–1994	Change
Austria	-0.4	-0.4	-1.7	-0.3
Sweden	0.3	2.4	-0.7	-0.4
Denmark	-0.3	0.0	-5.5	-4.9
Norway	-0.2	0.2	0.2	2.4
Finland	-1.1	-0.3	-7.1	-5.2
Germany	-0.9	-0.2	-2.1	-2.2
Belgium	1.6	0.9		
Italy	-0.3	-0.3		
Netherlands	-2.1	-0.4	1.3	1.8
United Kingdom	-0.8	0.1	2.5	1.0
France	-0.4	-0.1	-1.2	-0.1
Japan	-0.5	0.2	0.4	-0.9
Canada	-0.1	0.0	.	.
United States	-0.3	-0.7	-0.2	0.4
Average	-0.4	0.1	-1.3	-0.8
Correlation with left-labor power, 1980–1995	.13	.39	-.43	-.29
Correlation with unemployment, 1991–1995	-.02	-.10	-.67	-.61

[a]Rank order based on left-labor power index, 1980–1995
[b]Inflows minus outflows. Investments in foreign entities that represent a "lasting interest"
[c]Assets minus liabilities. Debt and equity issues (does not include currency transactions).
[d]1991–1994 minus 1980–1990
Source: Data from IMF, *Balance of Payments Statistics Yearbook*, various

was precipitated by the end of the Cold War. The instability and uncertainty associated with the biggest political and economic upheavals in the world since the rise of communism were bound to dampen European economic activity in the short run. But these effects were exacerbated by the economic consequences of German reunification in 1990.[9]

The Bundesbank reacted to what it considered irresponsible economic decisions by Chancellor Helmut Kohl – first the one-for-one conversion of ostmarks into DMs (the market rate was somewhere between four and seven to one) and subsequently massive fiscal transfers to the East (approximately 8 percent of West German GDP) – by substantially raising German interest rates. Indeed, the official German discount rate on lending to banks reached a postwar high of 8.75 percent in 1992. These interest rate hikes were then passed on to the other members of the European Monetary System, exacerbating the recessions these countries were already experiencing. This damaging transmission mechanism ultimately resulted in the effective dismantling of the ERM, but not before considerable damage had been done to most European economies.

How does this story affect our understanding of increasing unemployment in Finland and Sweden in the first half of the 1990s? Both countries had long histories of coupling cheap domestic credit and currency depreciation as tools of macroeconomic management. In virtue of their neutrality, neither country had sought membership in the European Union. With the end of the Cold War, however, both the Finnish and Swedish governments decided to pin their hopes for the future on joining Europe. There may have been numerous good reasons for this, ranging from security concerns to reaping the full benefits of the EU's internal market. There was, however, at least one great cost.

The Finnish and Swedish governments both believed in the early 1990s that participation in Europe's projected monetary union was essential to proving their status as "good Europeans." This seemed a reasonable assumption in 1991 and early 1992 because of the apparent successes of the EMS and the widespread enthusiasm for monetary union in the period around the signing of the Maastricht treaty. As a result, Finland and Sweden decided to peg to the DM, as a precursor to joining the EU, and eventually EMU. The combination of this choice with their domestic recessions was disastrous, with speculative attacks against the krona and the markka and large capital outflows. Nonetheless, both governments clung to their "hard money" commitments until short-term interests rates became astronomical and their foreign currency reserves were exhausted.

The final sad element in the 1990s Nordic tale was the dire effect the demise of the Soviet Union had on the Finnish economy. Finland's exports declined by 13 percent in 1991 alone. More than half of this was directly attributable to lost demand from the Soviet Union (OECD 1992: 13). Thus, on top of everything else, the Finnish economy had to deal with one of its most important export markets drying up overnight.

Whether the poor performance of the Finnish and Swedish economies in the early 1990s was due to bad luck or bad management could be debated endlessly. The commitment to hard money was no doubt very poorly timed. But it is understandable in the turmoil of the early 1990s that both countries placed their faith in the EU and its extant hard money regime, especially because the governments in both countries were bourgeois, not social democratic, when the critical decisions were made. Furthermore, it is doubtful that Finland and Sweden could have maintained their historical employment levels even if they had floated their exchange rates – the broader European recession would still have hurt their exports. Nonetheless, there are good reasons to believe that the increases in unemployment would have been smaller. Certainly, the Finnish and Swedish economies both rebounded strongly after their governments abandoned the commitment to fixed rates.

The simple fact remains, however, that unemployment rose dramatically in these social democratic corporatist regimes in the early 1990s, and it has yet to decline. If unemployment rates are now lower in liberal market economies, most notably the United States, isn't this the ultimate indictment of leftist alternatives to the free market? Let me make two responses. First, this line of argument overlooks persistently high unemployment in other liberal market economies – Canada and the United Kingdom, as well as France – and the fact that low unemployment in Japan has been maintained through life-time employment guarantees and the like, rather than free labor markets.

Second, the relatively good unemployment performance of the United States has been attained at the expense of growing income inequality and cutting back already small welfare benefits (Freeman 1994). Table 6.6 presents the latest available data on the internationally accepted definition of poverty – the percentage of households whose disposable income (i.e., market income plus the net effects of taxes paid and transfers received) is less than 50 percent of the median. The clear message of these data is that (with or without the United States) the stronger left parties and organized labor are, the lower poverty rates are. Consider the polar cases of Finland and the United States. Even though the average unemployment rate in Finland was 14.7 percent in the first half of the 1990s, the portion of population living in poverty was 5.0 percent. Average unemployment in the United States in the early 1990s was 6.5 percent, but the poverty rate was 18.4 percent.[10] Replacing employment with the alleviation of poverty as an indicator of the performance of social democratic corporatism would thus dramatically change our assessments of the 1990s.

6.4 THE CHALLENGES FACING SOCIAL DEMOCRATIC CORPORATISM

The previous two sections have updated the book's analysis through the mid 1990s. Two observations stand out. First, the policy distinctiveness of social democratic corporatism was unaffected by the removal of residual capital controls in northern Europe. In fact, big government became even more strongly associated with left-labor power in the 1990s, without generating deficit and debt problems that were larger than in other countries. Second, although unemployment rates increased markedly in some corporatist regimes in the 1990s, this cannot be attributed to the effects of market integration. Thus, we should be wary about using the first half of the 1990s as evidence of the declining fortunes of social democratic corporatism.

Table 6.6. *Poverty Rates in the late 1980s*

Country[a]	Adults with disposable incomes less than 50% of median[b]
Austria[c]	6.7
Sweden	7.6
Norway	7.3
Finland	5.0
Germany	6.5
Belgium	4.7
Italy	10.5
United Kingdom	9.1
France	7.5
Canada	12.2
United States	18.4
Average	8.4
Correlation with left-labor power (excluding US)	-.62 (-.49)

[a]Ranked by the left-labor power index, 1980–1995
[b]OECD [1995: 42]. Disposable income is money income plus welfare transfers minus taxes paid, based on survey data from the Luxembourg Income Study
[c]Excludes income from self-employment

This is not to overlook the very real challenges that do face contemporary social democratic corporatism. But it must be stressed that these have little to do with claims about the lack of fit between this alternative to the free market and globalization. This section outlines the challenges confronting social democratic corporatism and briefly sketches some potential responses to them.

SUPPLY- AND DEMAND SIDE-RESPONSES TO UNEMPLOYMENT

The specter of continuing high rates of unemployment is a serious problem for social democratic corporatism (and for Europe more generally) even if the two are not causally connected. Potential paths to lowering unemployment rates can usefully be divided into supply- and demand-side responses. Beginning with the supply-side, most analysts agree that the rapid pace of technological change in the past decade has resulted in a significant skills mismatch in labor markets in the industrial democracies. Many people who used to work on assembly lines have found new jobs at similar incomes hard to come by in the service sector or in manufacturing occupations that have become ever-more dependent on computers. The result has been increasing skill-based wage premiums in the United States and higher unemployment rates among less-skilled workers in Europe. Potential solutions to this problem can be divided into those that concentrate on reducing "rigidities" in labor markets and those that propose greater government efforts to increase skill levels in the labor force.[11]

The OECD's (1994) *Jobs Study* came out strongly in favor of reducing labor market rigidities through policies such as lowering the minimum wage, cutting unemployment benefits, and reducing regulations on working conditions. This approach is premised on the seemingly superior employment performance of the U.S. economy relative to Europe in the past decade. Richard Freeman (1995) among others, however, claims that the successes of the U.S. model must be significantly qualified. In addition to the poverty problems highlighted in Table 6.6, Freeman (1995: 63–4) argues that "the reduction in the pay of less-skilled Americans did not increase their employment or time worked. Despite large pay-cut-induced movements down the demand curve for the less-skilled, demand shifts dominated changes in employment, so that falling wages were associated with falling work." He also estimates that long-term unemployment rates (on which most attention has been focused) in the United States would be no lower than those in Europe if the large portion of the U.S. population in prison in the early 1990s (1.9 percent of the labor force) were added to conventional measures.

Governments in social democratic corporatist regimes are unlikely to embrace the policy prescriptions of the *Jobs Study* (even those that have been picked up by the European Commission). Rather, the corporatist countries can be expected to rely more on the supply-side strategy they have used so successfully in the past – active labor market policies combined with economywide wage restraint orchestrated by encompassing labor movements. In the contemporary period, the goals of active labor market policies are to give workers the skills they need to find jobs in those portions of the economy that benefit most from high technology and to provide incentives for employers to hire and train workers with lower skill levels (Nickell and Bell 1995).

All the attention to the supply-side of the economy has tended to conceal the potential of demand-side measures to alleviate Europe's unemployment problems. For the heavily trade-dependent social democratic corporatist countries, demand outside national boundaries is clearly critical to future employment growth. When the costs of unification in Germany decline, if the Japanese economy rebounds from the banking and political crises of the early 1990s, or if the Chinese economy becomes a voracious consumer of Western exports, this would clearly lead to cuts in the unemployment rolls of most European countries.

But this does not mean that governments in small countries can do nothing on their own to increase the demand for jobs. With respect to the social democratic corporatist regimes, currency depreciations that are not matched in the short term by higher domestic inflation (i.e., that lower real exchange rates) have long been an important tool for increasing competitiveness, growth, and employment opportunities. It is often assumed, however, that this option is no longer viable (Moses 1994). Countries that float their exchange rates are said to open themselves to damaging speculative attacks in the currency markets. The logic underpinning the notion that global financial markets make fixed exchange rates a virtual necessity has two components. The first is that countries that do not commit themselves to a fixed exchange rate will lose inflation-fighting "credibility." According to this view, countries that choose to float the exchange rate will have to pay hefty interest rate penalties because the financial markets will assume that this is a signal that the governments are soft on inflation.

The recent evidence in Europe, however, suggests that any such credibility penalties are very small. The speculative attacks against national currencies in the 1990s were against countries that tried to maintain fixed exchange rates that were manifestly unsustainable, not only in Finland and Sweden, but also in Britain, Italy, and Spain. Once these countries were forced to float their currencies, the mayhem stopped. The currencies depreciated until they reached more sustainable levels and then stabilized (OECD 1996: 30). More importantly, there is no indication that the European countries that might have been expected to lose market credibility as a result of being forced to abandon fixed exchange rates subsequently had to pay higher real interest rates on their borrowing. To take the most telling counterexample, the interest rate differential between Finland and Germany was actually smaller in 1995 than it was during the period when the markka was pegged to the DM (Dornbusch 1996: 38).

Thus, the appropriate conclusion to draw from monetary politics in Europe in the early 1990s is that floating the exchange rate is still an effective macroeconomic strategy; irrational commitments to fixed rates are not.[12] This does not mean that none of the social democratic corporatist countries should try to enter Europe's would-be monetary union (irrevocably fixing their exchange rates). Participating in EMU makes good sense for national economies that are part of Europe's "optimum currency area" – most importantly, whose business cycles are highly correlated with those of Germany – and for whom intra-European is very important. Among the corporatist regimes, Austria certainly belongs in EMU. So, too, may Denmark.[13] But the economic case for Finland or Sweden to join Europe's monetary union is much weaker (Garrett 1997).

Moreover, it is simply not true that by joining EMU, countries such as Austria and Denmark would lose all macroeconomic autonomy. Certainly, they would have no choice but to adopt the union's monetary policy (over which they would nevertheless have some say in the European Central Bank). But members' room for maneuver in fiscal policy arguably would not be greatly affected. This is because the rules laid down at Maastricht on "excessive deficits" are vague, because countries may be tempted to run large deficits in response to idiosyncratic shocks, and because big debtors will likely believe that they would ultimately be bailed out by other members of the union (Buiter, Corsetti, and Roubini 1993; Garrett 1993b; Kletzer 1996). German Finance Minister Theo Waigel's strident calls for a "stability pact" imposing severe penalties on relatively small deficits (greater than 3 percent of GDP) underline his country's concerns about the potential for national fiscal autonomy under EMU.

THE POWER OF PUBLIC SECTOR UNIONS

Just because governments in corporatist countries will likely be able to use expansionary macroeconomic policies well into the next century – inside or outside EMU – does not necessarily mean that these will be effective. Their effectiveness is contingent upon domestic expansions not being undermined by higher inflation. For much of the postwar period, the social democratic corporatist regimes were clearly able to achieve this. Some scholars have argued that this became much harder in the 1980s, in Denmark and Sweden in particular, because labor market institutions lost the ability to tailor wage developments to external competitiveness constraints (Iversen 1996a; Pontusson and Swenson 1996). In this subsection, I argue that public sector union strength has become a significant obstacle to optimal wage setting in Scandinavia, but that the experiences of Austria offer potential solutions to this problem.

Public sector union strength poses problems for corporatist systems because wage setting is not subject to a direct competitiveness constraint (Garrett and Way 1995). The proximate determinant of employment is not productivity but rather the willingness of governments to provide public sector jobs. Especially during downturns in the rest of the economy, governments have strong incentives to prop up public sector employment. Knowing this, their employees can bid up their wages without having the same unemployment fears as their private sector counterparts. Workers in the exposed sector of the economy, however, will be hurt by public sector wage push. Bigger deficits and higher inflation rates (to pay for larger public sector wage bills) increase interest rates and the exchange rate, decreasing the competitiveness of national products in international markets.

Table 6.7 shows that the potential for damaging public sector wage push is considerable in social democratic corporatist regimes, particularly in Scandinavia, that are characterized by high levels of government employment and high levels of public sector unionization. Governments in these countries have long used public sector jobs as a way of increasing female labor force participation, and they have actively promoted unionization among these employees (Huber and Stephens 1996; Swenson 1991a). Moreover, explicit commitments to maintaining total employment levels through public sector expansion and reducing wage differentials across occupations ("wage solidarity") that favor less productive public sector workers have been a central element of the Scandinavian model.

There is, however, one clear example of a social democratic corporatist regime

Table 6.7. *The Power of Public Sector Unions in 1990*

Country[a]	Public employment/total employment (%)	Unionized public sector employees (%)
Austria	23.8	57
Sweden	39.3	81
Finland	27.7	86
Denmark	36.2	70
Italy	16.9	54
Norway	34.9	75
Germany	21.7	45
Netherlands	20.8	49
United Kingdom	23.0	55
France	23.0	26
Japan	7.9	56
United States	14.8	37
Canada	19.7	60
Average	23.8	58
Correlation with left-labor power	0.65	0.61

[a]Presented in rank order on the left-labor power index, 1980–1990.
Source: Public sector employment data from OECD, *Historical Statistics*, 1960–1992. Public sector unionization data from Visser [1991]

that has not suffered from public sector wage push. Austria's public sector is only of average size and union density, and the clout of public sector workers has been further limited by legal restrictions on their bargaining rights (Traxler 1994). In turn, the Austrian labor movement has not pushed nearly as hard for wage leveling as their counterparts have in Scandinavia (Pontusson 1996).[14] Nonetheless, the tax-transfer system in Austria is sufficiently effective that inequalities in disposable income are very similar to those in Scandinavia (see Table 6.6). It is thus not surprising that economic performance in the past decade has been better in Austria than in Scandinavia (see Table 6.4).

Looking to the future, the Scandinavian countries could try to reduce public sector employment and public sector unionization to Austrian levels. But this is implausible (and probably undesirable) given current unemployment rates. The OECD (1987) advocates increasing competition in the provision of public sector services. Some contend that Scandinavian governments should try to earn repu-

tations for not acceding to public sector wage demands, for example, by joining
EMU (Iversen 1996b). As I have already argued, however, the constraints imposed
by hard money on fiscal policy are not very binding.

A more feasible strategy for reorienting wage setting in Scandinavia to external competitiveness constraints is to weaken the commitment to wage solidarity. This has already happened in the private sector, largely at the insistence
of employers (Pontusson and Swenson 1996). Public sector unionists also need
to take the broader economic consequences of their wage demands into account,
especially because the redistributive effects of Austria's tax-transfer system demonstrate that wage solidarity is not essential to material equality. There is a
heritage for such a strategy dating back to Sweden's "Basic Agreement" of the
1930s, which was designed to constrain wage growth in non-tradables to that in
the exposed sector (Swenson 1991a). This idea was updated in the Aukrust and
EFO models that were influential in Scandinavia thirty years later (Martin 1984).
If these ideas can be rekindled in Scandinavia, this would make an important
contribution to maintaining the macroeconomic effectiveness of social democratic
corporatism in the future.

DEMOGRAPHIC DEMONS

The previous two subsections have dealt with issues pertaining to the macroeconomic consequences of social democratic corporatism. Let us now turn to the
other facet of this regime that is under siege in the contemporary period – the
welfare state. There is no doubt that government budgets throughout the industrial democracies will be put under increasing stress in the coming decades.
But globalization is not the source of these pressures. Rather, the root causes of
the looming welfare state crisis are, in the context of stable working-age populations, significant increases in steady state rates of unemployment and, more
importantly, the growing ranks of the aged populations entitled to state pensions
and health benefits.

Table 6.8 presents cross-national data on the generosity of unemployment
benefits in 1990. The correlation between left-labor power and the size of benefits
received by each unemployed person is positive but not particularly strong.[15]
Nonetheless, increasing unemployment in the 1980s and 1990s has put upward
pressure on welfare budgets in the social democratic corporatist countries, as well
as in other countries. Because most of these programs were built long ago on the
assumption of more or less full employment, it is not surprising that governments
in recent years have been forced to try to cut the size and scope of unemployment
and related welfare benefits. But the magnitude of these cuts in the corporatist
countries should not be overstated. Current provisions in Scandinavia, for example, are still extremely generous by comparative standards (Huber and Stephens 1995). As for the future, it is clear that the longer unemployment rates
remain high in countries with ambitious programs for maintaining workers' stan-

Table 6.8. *The Generosity of Unemployment Benefits in 1990*

Country[a]	Unemployment benefits (per person unemployed, $1980)
Austria	4090
Sweden	6731
Finland	2268
Denmark	7150
Norway	3805
Italy	789
Germany	4096
Netherlands	6503
United Kingdom	2059
Japan	2132
Canada	5418
United States	1095
France	3195
Average	3795
Correlation with left-labor power	0.32

[a]Presented in rank order on the left-labor power index, 1966-1990
Source: Data from Garrett and Mitchell [1996]

dards of living irrespective of their employment status, the harder the choices governments will face between cutting benefits and raising taxes. But this just returns us to the previously discussed issue of how to alleviate today's unemployment problems.

The graying of populations in the industrial democracies poses a much greater threat to the future of the welfare state than unemployment does. The aging problem is more significant for two reasons. First, the benefits old people receive from public health care and pensions are considerably more generous than those for the unemployed. Second, the number of recipients is greater and rising all the time. Indeed, it is estimated that for the OECD as a whole, the average portion of the population over sixty-five will double to almost 40 percent of total population by 2030 (OECD 1995b: 58). Even if unemployment rates fall considerably, dealing with aging societies will be a fundamental challenge for all the industrial democracies in the next century.

Table 6.9 shows the OECD's projections for increases by 2030 in government spending on pensions and health care as a result of aging, based on the assumption

Table 6.9. *The Projected Impact of Aging on Government Spending by 2030*

Country[a]	Projected increase in government spending on health and pensions (%GDP)[b]
Sweden	5.5
Denmark	6.1
Norway	7.9
Finland	11.1
Germany	5.8
Belgium	6.4
Italy	9.4
Netherlands	10.2
United Kingdom	2.1
France	5.6
Japan	7.5
Canada	7.1
United States	4.3
Average	6.8
Correlation with left-labor power	0.20

[a]Presented in rank order on the left-labor power index, 1980–1995
[b]Based on current policies and projected demographic change, minus spending based on no change in the respective expenditure to GDP ratios after the year 2000
Source: OECD [1996: 25]

that countries do not alter their current policies. The average projected increase for the countries in this study is enormous – 6.8 percent of GDP. Although the costs of aging are not strongly correlated with left-labor power, there is no gain-saying that demographic change will increasingly strain the public purse in all countries, including the ranks of social democratic corporatism. Few would dis-agree with the OECD that the essential goal of welfare reform must be "to reduce social benefits in those areas where they are no longer required (e.g., to subsidize the retirement income of the comfortably off) and to increase them in areas of real need (for example, the long-term unemployed)" (OECD 1987: 337). The obstacles to this type of reform are considerable, however, because of the political power of the aged and the broad-based popular support for retirement programs.[16]

The path chosen by Bill Clinton and the U.S. Congress "to end welfare as we know it" – drastically cutting government support for the unemployed and the young poor while steadfastly opposing cuts to Social Security and medical care for the aged - will no doubt come back to haunt the U.S. The government has simply chosen to put off the tough decisions that must be made concerning the welfare of retirees. Governments in Europe must take a much stronger stand if they do not wish to break their historical commitments to the poor and the unemployed. Many policy makers suggest that privatizing pensions is the best strategy, but this necessarily entails forgoing the redistributive effects of most current social security systems.

Combining higher eligibility ages for retirement benefits with means-testing benefits is a more desirable pension reform strategy from a social democratic perspective. As the riots in France in the winter of 1995–1996 vividly showed, however, any reforms of social security programs are likely to meet with stern popular resistance. But it is certainly not unrealistic to expect that the wheels of reform might be better greased in the social democratic corporatist countries, where appeals to long-run collective goods over short-sighted behavior have historically been successful.

FUNDING THE WELFARE STATE

Even if it is possible to mitigate the consequences of the impending demographic crisis by reducing the growth of welfare state expenditures, many assume that current spending levels may not be sustainable into the future because globalization has precipitated an effective tax revolt by mobile actors – both corporations and high-income individuals (Rodrik 1997; Steinmo 1993). As was documented earlier in this chapter, the past decade has witnessed significant cuts in marginal rates of corporate taxation, particularly in social democratic corporatist countries. Moreover, it is clear that in most countries the scope for increasing personal income taxes is very limited. Thus, there seems to be a strong tax-based constraint on the future of the welfare state.

Can large public economies in social democratic corporatist regimes continue to be funded if the global economy puts downward pressure on both corporate and personal income taxes? Table 6.10 may offer the key to an affirmative answer. The table demonstrates that the relationship between consumption taxes and left-labor power has been extremely strong in recent years, irrespective of whether one measures consumption tax rates on their own or relative to taxes on individual and corporate income. The conventional view of these data is that they attest to the dire straits in which big-spending corporatist countries find themselves. Governments in these countries have only been able to feed their appetites for public sector expansion by relying on what is normally considered the most regressive form of taxation. Thus, so goes the argument, the redistributive effects of gov-

Table 6.10. *Consumption Taxes in the 1990s*

Country[a]	Consumption tax rate		Consumption tax rate/labor tax rate		Consumption tax rate/capital tax rate	
	1991	Change[b]	1991	Change	1991	Change
Austria	20.4	-1.0	0.51	-0.03	0.91	-0.05
Sweden	25.7	2.7	0.53	0.07	0.39	-0.03
Denmark	33.6	-0.9	0.76	-0.06	1.08	0.09
Norway	33.4	-3.3	0.81	-0.13	0.93	0.03
Finland	29.1	0.5	0.87	-0.02	0.51	-0.25
Germany	18.6	3.3	0.41	0.02	0.66	0.14
Belgium	16.6	0.0	0.36	0.00	0.47	0.03
Italy	15.4	2.6	0.36	0.03	0.49	0.00
United Kingdom	17.1	0.7	0.70	0.08	0.33	0.07
Netherlands	18.2	0.5	0.35	0.00	0.55	-0.05
France	15.4	-5.6	0.33	-0.15	0.58	-0.19
Japan	6.2	1.1	0.22	0.02	0.12	0.01
Canada	10.4	-2.3	0.33	-0.15	0.21	-0.11
United States	4.6	-0.7	0.16	-0.03	0.11	-0.02
Average	18.9	-0.2	0.48	0.0	0.52	0.0
Correlation with left-labor power	0.79	0.23	0.65	0.26	0.73	0.17

[a]Rank order based on average scores for the left-labor power index, 1980–1995
[b]1991–(1980–1990)
Source and methods: Mendoza, Milesi-Feretti and Asea [1996]. The consumption tax rate is the percentage difference between the post-tax consumer price of a good and the pre-tax price at which firms supply the good. The labor tax rate is the reduction in total individual income associated with the difference in a representative agent's pre- and post-tax income (i.e. income taxes and social security taxes). The capital tax rate is the reduction in the operating surplus of the economy associated with all taxes on capital assets (capital gains, corporate income, property, financial transactions).

ernment spending will be increasingly offset by regressive taxation in the global economy.

There are good reasons, however, to question this interpretation of the growing reliance of social democratic corporatist countries on consumption taxes. Consumption taxes are only regressive to the extent that they fall disproportionately on poor people. In practice, most governments exempt numerous consumer staples – such as food and clothing – from consumption taxes, and this trend is evident in countries with histories of strong left-wing parties and labor market institutions.[17] Thus, consumption taxes in practice are unlikely to be as regressive as is often assumed. Moreover, rapid increases in self-employment among high-income earners and the proliferation of complex multinational production regimes in recent years have significantly reduced the portion of national income that can be effectively subjected to pay-as-you-earn taxation. Put simply, income-based tax evasion is a significant problem in the global economy because it is hard for governments to identify much individual and corporate income (Giovannini 1989; Lassard and Williamson 1987).

Thus, governments in corporatist countries can piggyback on neoclassical economics' advocacy of consumption taxes (Stiglitz 1986). Such taxes may minimize "distortions" in investment decisions, but they are also an effective way of increasing the tax take in the global economy. A system that taxes the corporate consumption (i.e., purchases of goods and services rather than profits) represents perhaps the best response to globalization for countries with large spending commitments. The data suggest that governments in strong left-labor regimes have known this for a long time.

6.5   EXPORTING SOCIAL DEMOCRATIC CORPORATISM

The fundamental argument of this book is that the globalization of markets has not lessened the viability of social democratic corporatism. The previous section extended my argument by addressing other challenges facing social democratic alternatives to the free market. In this section, however, I want to address a final question: "So what" if my argument is correct? If the appropriate structural conditions for social democratic corporatism – strong left-wing parties allied with encompassing labor market institutions – have only ever been met by the small countries of northern Europe, lessons from these political economies would not seem be particularly instructive or important for the rest of the world. Certainly, this seems to be the view of the international agencies that are in the business of exporting political economic regimes, such as the IMF and the World Bank. Their templates for political economic development are built on small market-friendly government and assume there is little room for organized labor to play a constructive role in economic policy formulation or macroeconomic management.

In contrast, I want to argue for the proposition that social democratic corporatism can, and should, be exported outside northern Europe. It can be exported because left-wing parties are successful in many countries and there are viable strategies available to governments for increasing the ability of labor to act collectively and responsibly. Social democratic corporatism should be exported not only because it benefits the less well-off but also because it provides a stable and profitable home for business that may not be reproduced in many countries through more neoclassical routes.

The political precondition for social democratic corporatism remains the existence of powerful left-of-center parties committed to mitigating the efficiency–welfare trade-off. For the foreseeable future, this rules out countries such as Canada, Japan, and the United States. Time will tell with respect to Britain's "new" Labour party. In the past decade, however, social democratic parties have held dominant positions in countries ranging from Australia to the Mediterranean to Latin America to Eastern Europe.

These countries do not have histories of trade union movements that are sufficiently encompassing to complete the virtuous circle with social democratic governments, combining redistributive economic policies and competitiveness-enhancing national wage setting. However, many governments have sought to complete this circle by involving organized labor in policy making. The "accord" process facilitated a major restructuring of Australia's economy in the 1980s (Castles, Gerritson, and Vowles 1996). Cooperation between government and labor has increased significantly in Greece, Ireland, Portugal, and Italy in the 1990s in Europe (Regini 1996). Furthermore, relations between the government and the trade union movement in the Czech Republic have many distinctive corporatist features.

Given the importance in many peoples' eyes of using "shock therapy" as the benchmark against which to measure the success of transitions to capitalist democracy in Eastern Europe, perhaps the Czech case is the most interesting. David Stark and László Bruszt argue that, despite the neoliberal rhetoric of Vaclav Klaus, the Czech government has actively solicited – and institutionalized – the involvement of the peak federation of labor (along with that of business) in major economic policy decisions. This has led to outcomes that have both facilitated the reform process and protected the interests of workers. This is a far cry from Poland's version of shock, notwithstanding Lech Walesa's Solidarity roots. Stark and Bruszt (1997: 316) characterize corporatism, Czech-style in the following manner: "From the outset, the relationship between the government and organized labor has shown a consistent pattern of mutual restraint. . . . The result has been the conflictual production of social harmony as institutionalized negotiations repeatedly reproduce a three-pillared growth strategy based on low wages, low unemployment, and robust trade union rights."

There are four common threads that tie together the Czech case and the other recent successful experiments with social democratic corporatism. First, governments have sought actively to involve organized labor in economic policy formulation and macroeconomic management. Second, labor leaders have cooperated with government with the explicit goal of improving national economic performance. Third, the leaders of trade union movements have been able to deliver the support of most workers to these agreements. Finally, these agreements apparently have elicited favorable responses from capital; certainly, they have not resulted in capital flight.

Of course, these nascent corporatist bargains must be considered somewhat fragile because labor market institutions in these countries are not as encompassing as those in northern Europe. Union density and collective bargaining coverage are relatively low, and authority in the labor movement is not particularly concentrated. But governments are not powerless to increase the scope and centralization of labor movements.

The time-tested way to increase density is to attach work-related and unemployment benefits to union membership. Legislation can be passed to extend collective bargaining agreements well beyond the ranks of union members. Centralizing authority within labor movements is a more difficult task. Turning Olson (1982) on his head, however, it may be easier to do this in the emerging capitalist democracies of eastern and southern Europe than in countries with more entrenched institutional structures. To use a historical example, it was extremely difficult to create a powerful and centralized Trades Union Congress in the United Kingdom because of the long-standing strength of craft-based production. In northern Europe, in contrast, the birth of organized labor was more coincident with the emergence of industrial capitalism, and this facilitated the development of highly centralized peak labor confederations (Cameron 1978; Katzenstein 1985). If the governments in the countries that have experimented with corporatism in the 1990s can match the institutional achievements of these regimes, the ranks of stable corporatist regimes may in time significantly expand.

CONCLUSION

There is no reason why social democratic corporatism should not be presented as a viable alternative to the neoclassical perspective for developing and prospering in the era of global markets. Redistributive government, powerful labor movements, and vibrant capitalism are mutually reinforcing for three reasons. First, the globalization of markets has increased political demands for government policies that reduce burgeoning inequalities of risk and wealth. Second, where labor movements are sufficiently powerful to adapt labor market developments to the broader national economic context, big government is compatible with strong macroeconomic performance. Finally, although this outcome is very different from that prescribed in neoclassical economics textbooks, it nonetheless is attractive to mobile asset holders who value the stability and productivity these regimes generate.

This book has thus argued that it is still possible to mitigate the efficiency–welfare trade-off in the global economy. Moreover, the range of contexts in which this is feasible may extend well beyond the birthplace of social democratic corporatism in northern Europe. I hope my arguments and analyses encourage more discussion of the contending paths to thriving in the global economy. Democratic politics at the national level is alive and well, and the policy choices citizens face are at least as important as they have ever been. Organized labor is not necessarily a thorn in the side of business. Rather, unions may often produce economically important collective goods. These lessons of social democratic corporatism are no less true today than they were twenty-five years ago, long before talk of globalized markets came to dominate public discourse.

NOTES

1. INTRODUCTION

1 Most people assume that technological change and globalization go hand-in-hand as the stimuli for political and economic change. Although these two forces are clearly linked, in this book I concentrate on the increasing depth and scope of international markets rather than on computerization and information technology. For research that focuses specifically on the effects of technological change for domestic polities, see Lash and Urry (1987) and Pontusson and Swenson (1996).

2 Indeed, international agencies such as the International Monetary Fund (IMF), the Organization for Economic Cooperation and Development (OECD), and the World Bank all champion the notion that effective government requires the exclusive pursuit of market friendly policies. These policies are thought to comprise the provision of basic public goods such as secure property rights and fair enforcement of contracts, coupled with microeconomic deregulation and macroeconomic stabilization. For a clear statement of this perspective, see Summers and Thomas (1993). *The World Development Report* (World Bank 1997) is a welcome broadening of official approaches to development. Nonetheless, it's views of "good government" remain too limited, in my opinion.

3 The ranks of exponents of the globalization thesis grow seemingly on a daily basis. Some examples of academic research in this vein include Andrews (1994), Cerny (1990), Gill and Law (1989), Moses (1994), and Ruggie (1995). For more widely accessible treatments, see Barber (1995), Goldsmith (1994), McKenzie and Lee (1991), and Strange (1986).

4 Trade and capital mobility on some definitions are no greater today than before World War I (McKeown 1991; Taylor 1995; Zevin 1992). Moreover, the process of globalization has not reached many parts of the world – most notably, Africa (Wade 1996).

5 The New Zealand labor party in the late 1980s is the only clear exception to this rule (Castles, Gerritson, and Vowles 1996).

6 For an excellent summary of all the permutations of recent work on economic growth, see Barro and Sala-i-Martin (1995).

7 For less general, but nonetheless similar, arguments, see Alesina and Perotti (1997) and Summers, Gruber, and Vergara (1993).

8 These rigidities, however, may contribute to the persistence of unemployment once rates rise (see Chapter 6).

9 I thus adapt to the context of the global economy my earlier research with Michael Alvarez and Peter Lange on the interactive effects of partisan politics and labor market institutions (Alvarez, Garrett and Lange 1991; Garrett and Lange 1986; Lange and Garrett 1985).

10 Layard, Nickell, and Jackman (1991), for example, argue that unemployment schemes of limited duration that are integrated with worker retraining schemes will increase overall levels of employment.

11 Among political scientists and sociologists, see the collections edited by Berger (1981), Goldthorpe (1984) and Lindberg and Maier (1985). Among economists, similar book-length treatments include Bruno and Sachs (1985) and Flanagan, Soskice, and Ulman (1983).

12 The work of Adam Przeworski and Michael Wallerstein has greatly influenced my thinking on the relationship between capitalism and democracy for more than a decade (Przeworski and Wallerstein 1982, 1988; Wallerstein and Przeworski 1995).

13 Australia, Ireland, and New Zealand were not included because the best data on labor market institutions do not extend to them. Switzerland was excluded because the partisan composition of cabinet governments in Switzerland is not determined by electoral results, and governments are not subject to votes of confidence in the legislature (Laver and Schofield 1990: 242). The southern European countries were left out because of data limitations and because they were not stable democracies throughout the period under analysis.

14 It should be noted that this book follows the convention of labeling the U.S. Democrats as a centrist, rather than a left-wing, party.

15 This is not to deny, however, that there are important differences between the Austrian and Swedish political economies (see Chapter 6).

16 Japan's statist tradition and its system of informal business coordination render its political economy very different from those of Canada, the United Kingdom, and the United States on dimensions other than left-labor power (Pempel 1978, Soskice 1990).

17 The index combines standardized scores for left power (based on the partisan balance of political power in cabinet governments and legislatures) and for labor market institutions (which aggregates standardized scores for union density, the number of unions in the largest labor confederation, the share of total union members in this confederation, and the portion of unionized employees in the public sector).

18 These relationships are not apparent in the types of correlations presented in Table 1.3 because interest rates are largely determined by economic factors that must be controlled to isolate political effects.

19 Jeffrey Frankel (1993) provides an excellent analysis of the issues involved in measuring international capital mobility.

20 The data are from various issues of the International Monetary Fund's *Annual Report on Exchange Arrangements and Exchange Restrictions*. Other studies that use these data as a measure of capital mobility include Banuri and Schor (1992) Eichengreen, Rose and Wyplosz (1995) and Leiderman and Razin (1994). Where there are overlaps with other indicators of financial integration (such as those based on savings–investment relationships and appropriate comparisons of interest rates), these vary closely with the IMF data.

21 As was mentioned in the previous section, these controls were subsequently removed in Austria, Finland, and Sweden as a result of their decisions to join the European Union.

2. POLITICS, POLICY, AND PERFORMANCE

1 The first study to make this point was by Bruno Frey and Friedrich Schneider (1978).

2 Seymour Martin Lipset (1961) was one of the first to make this argument. The most recent systematic cross-national study supporting the basic partisan politics thesis is Klingemann, Hofferbert, and Budge (1994).

3 The literature building on the seminal contributions of Duncan Black and Anthony Downs is voluminous. The collections edited by James Enelow and Melvin Hinich (1984, 1990) are good examples of the spatial approach to elections.

4 The pathbreaking analysis of this phenomenon in the United States was by Gerald Kramer (1971). For more recent cross-national research using both surveys and aggregate election returns, see Lewis-Beck (1988) and Norpoth, Lewis-Beck, and Lafay (1991).

5 The clearest and strongest exposition of this argument is by Paulette Kurzer (1993).

6 This is not true, however, of the best expositions of the globalization thesis. See, for example, Rodrik (1997).

7 The collections edited by Suzanne Berger (1981), John Goldthorpe (1984) and Leon Lindberg and Charles Maier (1985) contain many of the significant contributions to the first generation of corporatism research.

8 For a more elaborate discussion of the argument and evidence, see Calmfors (1993b).

9 For a similar argument, see Scharpf (1988).

10 The willingness of left governments to pursue partisan policies on entering office will likely be enhanced by the economic ideologies of their policy advisers (Hall 1989) and by the legislative "honeymoons" often granted to new governments (Alt 1985).

11 This is not to say, of course, that scholars believe there is no longer any feasible role for "the left." Kitschelt (1994), for example, highlights the fact that left-wing parties may perform extremely well in the electoral arena so long as they reorient their strategies around what he considers a "libertarian" agenda based on issues such as ecology, feminism, and human rights.

12 Indeed, Kitschelt's (1994: 27) own analysis supports this view, although he wishes to divide the public sector in terms of the degree of their attachment to post-materialist values.

13 For a more detailed exposition of this argument and supporting empirical evidence, see Garrett and Way (1995).

14 The Bretton Woods system effectively broke down in 1971 (close to the beginning of my analysis) when the United States closed the gold window. Moreover, capital was not very internationally mobile in the 1960s.

15 I discuss this issue in Chapter 6 with respect to Finland and Sweden. I thus side with Notermans (1993) against Moses (1994) by arguing that pegging to the DM was a bad policy choice, rather than the inevitable consequence of capital mobility.

3. MARKET INTEGRATION AND DOMESTIC POLICIES

1 The process of globalization has not extended to labor, except for highly skilled professionals. This mismatch is central to claims about the political ascendance of mobile asset holders over labor (Rodrik 1997).

2 I have not included the geographic composition of trade in the empirical analyses in Chapters 4 and 5 because other research suggests that the domestic effects of imports from outside the OECD (that is, low wage competition) have not been significantly different from trade competition within the OECD (Garrett and Mitchell 1996).

3 For an excellent discussion of the issues involved in measuring capital mobility, see Frankel (1993).

4 A more elaborate coding of the IMF's data has recently been undertaken by Quinn and Inclan (1997). Their measures of financial openness, however, are highly correlated with the one used in this book.

5 Following Bayoumi (1990), the reported figures are parameter estimates for the impact of private domestic savings on private domestic investment for annual fourteen-country bivariate regressions. It is important to exclude government savings and investment because they are likely to have a large countercyclical component that would bias the estimates against a find of integrated capital markets.

6 Robert Wade (1996) shows that these assumptions are even less appropriate when one considers all the countries outside the OECD.

7 Cameron (1978) remains the seminal analysis of the relationship between trade and left-labor power. For a recent attempt to determine the impact of politics on the removal of capital controls, see Quinn and Inclan (1997).

8 The position of parties in Castles-Mair is very similar to that in most other party scales (Laver and Schofield 1990: 245–266). Furthermore, because this book seeks to determine whether nominal partisan labels such as "labor" or "social democratic" continue to have substantive implications for economic policy and performance in the era of global market, the fact that the Castles-Mair survey was conducted before the globalization process began in earnest (in the early 1980s) makes it an ideal benchmark.

9 There is an alternative data source on partisanship that may not be subject to this criticism: party codings based on content analyses of campaign platforms

(Laver and Budge 1993). These data are not well suited to my analysis, however, precisely because I want to determine where simple party labels have continued to influence public policy as markets have become more global.

10 These data are available on an annual basis. However, I present them here at five-year intervals to make them comparable with the other data on labor market institutions used in this study.

11 The French data are also arguably misleading because collective bargaining agreements are legally extended to cover much of the nonunionized labor force (Traxler 1994).

12 In Canada, France, and Japan, there are numerous peak associations of labor that compete for members. In the United Kingdom and the United States, although most unionists belong to a single confederation, the sheer number of unions in these confederations creates significant obstacles to collective action (although the number of unions in these countries decreased substantially in the 1980s).

4. ECONOMIC POLICY

1 Military spending and the costs of servicing the public debt are not plotted separately because my arguments about partisan politics do not pertain to them.

2 Given that there are only fourteen observations in these correlations, it is not surprising that most of the correlations are not statistically significant at the .025 level (correlations of .53 or higher). This is not of major concern, however, because I base my conclusions on the panel regressions.

3 The data on capital expenditures were mixed. The correlation with left-labor power increased greatly after the first OPEC oil shock, but subsequently declined to its historically low level.

4 Although similar in direction, the coefficients were less significant statistically in the industrial subsidies and capital spending equations. In the case of subsidies to industry, the independent effect of increasing left-labor power was to reduce government spending.

5 I would like to thank Larry Bartels for suggesting this method of presentation to me.

6 This is a better indication of statistical significance than those based on the standard errors for individual coefficients because the use of multiplicative interaction terms necessarily introduces considerable collinearity with the market integration and left-labor power parameter estimates.

7 Property taxes and social security contributions from employees were not included because they are very small sources of government revenue.

8 The next section shows that the result of this ambivalence among the public was rising public sector deficits in strong left-labor countries in the global economy.

9 The likely reason for this seemingly paradoxical result is that left governments often use the corporate tax system to induce capital to reinvest in the national economy, by providing large tax breaks for profits that are invested rather than consumed (King and Fullerton 1984). I return to this issue later in this chapter with respect to the structure of corporate taxation.

10 There are no data for Finland on interest rates.

5. ECONOMIC PERFORMANCE

1 As was the case in Chapter 4, these coefficients were rarely statistically significant. Again, however, I ultimately rely on regression evidence rather than these correlations.

2 The combination of the lagged dependent variable, OECD demand, and oil dependence is only a very crude reduced form analysis of the economic processed underpinning performance outcomes. Rather than entering the thorny thicket of perspectives in economics about these issues, my strategy is simply to capture some fundamental economic forces affecting growth, inflation, and unemployment in order to isolate the effects of the variables of primary interest to me.

3 As I discussed in Chapter 4, the inclusion of country dummy variables is an effective way to take into account the historical relationships between trade, left-labor power, and capital mobility.

4 To test this argument would have entailed adding an LMI^2 term, and then interacting it with both left power and market integration. Deriving meaningful results from an equation with so many two- and three-way interaction terms – and the degree of collinearity among regressors this generates – would have been extremely difficult.

5 This was also true for the growth and inflation equations reported in Tables 5.3 and 5.4.

6 I discuss potential reasons for this discrepancy below in the context of the inflation equations.

7 There are numerous other minor differences in the specifications, including the periods under analysis, estimation procedures, the use of fixed effects parameters, and the operationalization of the dependent variable.

8 For a sophisticated theoretical and empirical analysis of this argument, see Card and Hyslop (1996).

6. THE 1990s AND BEYOND

1 Fritz Scharpf (1991: 263-9) presented a prescient rendering of this argument. Today, it is standard fare on the European left.

2 Indeed, the most persuasive scenario for the emergence of federalism in Europe assumes that the distributional costs of monetary union will be enormous and that national governments will not be able to respond domestically with expansionary policies (Eichengreen 1996).

3 The balance of power in Italian politics then moved back to the left in 1996 under the government of Romano Prodi.

4 Unfortunately, there are no comparative data on developments in the structural attributes of labor market institutions in the 1990s. Given historical patterns, however, it is unlikely that major changes have occurred.

5 Whereas the left-labor power index uses political data gathered for the whole period (1980-1995), the labor market institutions measures were only for the period up until 1990. See Chapter 3 for an explanation of the construction of the index.

6 These data are not strictly comparable with those in the rest of the study because the spending definition is narrower whereas the revenues definition is broader. The only case in which this affected cross-national rankings was Denmark, where the deficits reported in this chapter are relatively small. The reason for the data inconsistencies is that the most recent OECD data from the *Economic Outlook* series do not include the spending and taxation aggregates from the OECD *Historical Statistics* and *Revenue Statistics* publications relied on in the rest of the book.

7 Among the other corporatist countries, Denmark suffered along with other members of the EMS. So, too, did Austria in virtue of its stable bilateral peg to the DM. Norway, in contrast, was relatively insulated because it did not seek to maintain a fixed exchange rate, although declining demand in the rest of Europe was clearly harmful to its exports.

8 See, for example, Calmfors (1993), Huber and Stephens (1995), Moene and Wallerstein (1995) and OECD (1992).

9 For a detailed analysis of the macroeconomic consequences of the end of the Cold War and German unification, see Eichengreen and Wyplosz (1993).

10 Recent estimates by Deborah Mitchell (private communication) using the Luxembourg Income Study data suggest that the poverty figures reported in Table 6.6 for the late 1980s remained very similar in the early 1990s.

11 The economics literature on the unemployment problem is voluminous. For an official survey, see OECD (1994). Other influential studies include Bean (1994), Freeman (1994), Layard, Nickell, and Jackman (1991) and the special issue of *Oxford Review of Economic Policy* 11 (1).

12 There is evidence, however, that once currency crises begin, they mushroom beyond what adjusting to economic fundamentals would require. As a result, some analysts have called for the imposition of a "Tobin tax" on currency transactions to slow down the pace of exchange rate movements (Eichengreen, Rose, and Wyplosz 1995, Eichengreen, Tobin, and Wyplosz 1995).

13 Danish participation in EMU may, of course, be ruled out because of broader concerns about sovereignty.

14 It should be noted that the German system of wage setting is very similar to the Austrian.

15 As others have noted, Christian democratic welfare states tend to be as generous as those in the corporatist countries with respect to income transfer programs, but not to the provision of social services (Esping-Andersen 1990).

16 Some countries in continental Europe have a potential safety valve: increasing female labor force participation. But this is not an option for the Scandinavian countries where most women already work. Only in Austria among the ranks of social democratic corporatism could increasing female labor force participation reduce dependency rations. There are, however, substantial religious and cultural obstacles to doing so (Huber and Stephens 1996).

17 Unfortunately, it is extremely hard to find systematic cross-national data on the coverage of consumption taxes.

REFERENCES

Akerlof, George, William Dickens, and George Perry. 1996. "The Macroeconomics of Low Inflation." *Brookings Papers on Economic Activity* 1: 1–76.

Alesina, Alberto. 1989. "Politics and Business Cycles in Industrial Democracies." *Economic Policy* 8: 55–98.

Alesina, Alberto, and Howard Rosenthal. 1994. *Partisan Politics, Divided Government, and the Economy.* New York: Cambridge University Press.

Alesina, Alberto, Vittorio Grilli and Gian Maria Milesi–Ferretti. 1994 "The Political Economy of Capital Controls." CEPR Discussion Paper No. 793.

Alesina, Alberto, and Roberto Perotti. 1997. "The Welfare State and Competitiveness." *American Economic Review* (forthcoming).

Alesina, Alberto, and Nouriel Roubini. 1992. "Political Cycles in OECD Economies." *Review of Economic Studies* 59: 663–88.

Alvarez, R. Michael, Geoffrey Garrett, and Peter Lange. 1991. "Government Partisanship, Labor Organization and Macroeconomic Performance." *American Political Science Review* 85: 541–556.

Andrews, David M. 1994. "Capital Mobility and State Autonomy." *International Studies Quarterly* 38: 193–218.

Aschauer, David Alan. 1990. *Public Investment and Private Sector Growth.* Washington D.C.: Economic Policy Institute.

Austen–Smith, David and Jeffrey Banks. 1988. "Elections, Coalitions and Legislative Outcomes." *American Political Science Review.* 82: 405–22.

Barber, Benjamin. 1995. *Jihad Versus McWorld.* New York: Times Books.

Baron, David P. 1991. "A Spatial Bargaining Theory of Government Formation in Parliamentary Systems." *American Political Science Review* 85: 137–64.

———. 1994. "Electoral Competition with Informed and Uninformed Voters." *American Political Science Review* 88: 33–47.

Barro, Robert. 1991. "Economic Growth in a Cross Section of Countries." *Quarterly Journal of Economics* 106: 407–33.

———. 1996. "Democracy and Growth." *Journal of Economic Growth* 1: 1–27.

Barro, Robert, and Xavier Sala–i–Martin. 1995. *Economic Growth*. New York: Mc-Graw Hill.

Bayoumi, Tamin. 1990. "Savings–Investment Correlations." *IMF Staff Papers* 37: 360–87.

Bean, Charles. "European Unemployment: A Survey." *Journal of Economic Literature* 32: 573–619.

Beck, Nathaniel, and Jonathan Katz. 1995a. "What to Do (and Not to Do) with Time–Series–Cross–Section Data in Comparative Politics." *American Political Science Review* 89: 634–47.

1995b. "Nuisance Versus Substance: Specifying and Estimating Time–Series–Cross–Section Models." Manuscript, UCSD.

Berger, Suzanne (ed.). 1981. *Organizing Interests in Western Europe*. New York: Cambridge University Press.

Boix, Carles. 1996. "Political Parties and the Supply–Side of the Economy." *American Journal of Political Science* (forthcoming).

Brody, Richard, and Benjamin Page. 1973. "Indifference, Alienation and Rational Decisions." *Public Choice* 15: 1–17.

Bruno, Michael, and Jeffrey Sachs. 1985. *The Economics of World–Wide Stagflation*. Cambridge: Harvard University Press.

Bryant, Ralph. 1987. *International Financial Integration*. Washington, D.C: Brookings.

Buchanan, James, and Gordon Tullock. 1962. *The Calculus of Consent*. Ann Arbor: University of Michigan Press.

Buchanan, James, and Richard Wagner. 1977. *Democracy in Deficit*. New York: Academic Press.

Buiter, Willem, Giancarlo Corsetti, and Nouriel Roubini. 1993. "Maastricht's Fiscal Rules." *Economic Policy* 16: 57–100.

Calmfors, Lars. 1993a. "Lessons from the Macroeconomic Experience of Sweden." *European Journal of Political Economy* 9: 25–72.

1993b. "Centralization of Wage Bargaining and Macroeconomic Performance – A Survey." *OECD Economic Studies* 21: 161–91.

Calmfors, Lars, and John Driffill. 1988. "Bargaining Structure, Corporatism, and Macroeconomic Performance." *Economic Policy* 6: 13–61.

Cameron, David R. 1978. "The Expansion of the Public Economy: A Comparative Analysis." *American Political Science Review* 72 (4): 1243–61.

1984. "Social Democracy, Corporatism, Labor Quiescence, and the Representation of Economic Interest in Advanced Capitalist Society." In Goldthorpe, John H. (ed.), *Order and Conflict in Contemporary Capitalism*. Oxford: Oxford University Press.

Card, David, and Dean Hyslop. 1996. "Does Inflation 'Grease the Wheels' of the Labor Market?" NBER Working Paper 5538.

Castles, Francis. 1978. *The Social Democratic Image of Society*. London: Routledge. (ed.) 1982. *The Impact of Parties*. Newbury Park, Calif.: Sage.

Castles, Francis, Rolf Gerritson, and Jack Vowles (eds.). 1996. *The Great Experiment: Labour Parties and Public Policy Transformation in Australia and New Zealand*. Sydney: Allen & Unwin.

Castles, Francis, and Peter Mair. 1984. "Left–Right Political Scales: Some Expert Judgments." *European Journal of Political Research* 12: 73–88.

Cerny, Philip G. 1990. *The Changing Architecture of Politics*. London: Sage.

Cohen, Benjamin J. 1996. "Phoenix Risen: The Resurrection of Global Finance." *World Politics* 48: 268–96.

Corsetti, Giancarlo, and Nouriel Roubini. 1991. "Fiscal Deficits, Public Debt and Government Insolvency." *Journal of Japanese and International Economies* 5: 354–80.

1995. "Political Biases in Fiscal Policy." In Barry Eichengreen, Jeffry Frieden, and Jürgen von Hagen (eds.), *Monetary and Fiscal Policy in an Integrated Europe*. New York: Springer.

Crouch, Colin. 1985. "Conditions for Trade Union Wage Restraint." In Leon N. Lindberg and Charles S. Maier (eds.), *The Politics of Inflation and Economic Stagnation*. Washington, D.C.: Brookings.

Cukierman, Alex. 1992. *Central Bank Strategy, Credibility, and Independence: Theory and Evidence*. Cambridge: MIT Press.

Cummins, Jason G., Kevin A. Hassett, and R. Glenn Hubbard. 1995. "Tax Reforms and Investment: A Cross–Country Comparison." NBER Working Paper Series. No. 5232.

Cushman, David. 1988. "Exchange Rate Uncertainty and Foreign Direct Investment in the United States." *Weltwirtschaftliches Archiv* 124: 322–36.

Dornbusch, Rudiger. 1976. "Expectations and Exchange Rate Dynamics." *Journal of Political Economy* 84: 1161–76.

1996. "The Effectiveness of Exchange Rate Changes." *Oxford Review of Economic Policy* 12 (3): 26–38.

Downs, Anthony. 1957. *An Economic Theory of Democracy*. New York: HarperCollins.

Eichengreen, Barry. 1992. "Should the Maastricht Treaty be Saved?" *Princeton Studies in International Finance*. Princeton N.J.: International Finance Section.

1996. "A More Perfect Union? The Logic of Economic Integration." *Essays in International Finance*. No. 198. Princeton, N.J.: International Finance Section.

Eichengreen, Barry, Andrew Rose, and Charles Wyplosz. 1995. "Exchange Market Mayhem." *Economic Policy* 21: 249–312.

Eichengreen, Barry, James Tobin, and Charles Wyplosz. 1995. "Two Cases for Sand in the Wheels of International Finance." *Economic Journal* 105: 162–75.

Eichengreen, Barry, and Charles Wyplosz. 1993. "The Unstable EMS." *Brookings Papers on Economic Activity* 1: 51–143.

Enelow, James M., and Melvin J. Hinich. 1984. *The Spatial Theory of Voting: An Introduction*. New York: Cambridge University Press.

(eds.) 1990. *Advances in the Spatial Theory of Voting*. New York: Cambridge University Press.

Esping–Andersen, Göta. 1985. *States Against Markets*. Princeton, N.J.: Princeton University Press.

1990. *Three Worlds of Welfare Capitalism*. Cambridge: Polity.

Feldstein, Martin, and Charles Horioka. 1980. "Domestic Savings and International Capital Flows." *The Economic Journal* 90: 314–29.

Flanagan, Robert, David Soskice, and Lloyd Ulman. 1983. *Unionism, Economic Stabilization and Incomes Policies*. Washington D.C.: Brookings Institution.

Flora, Peter. 1989. "From Industrial to Postindustrial Welfare State." *Annals of the*

Institute of Social Science. Tokyo: Institute of Social Science, University of Tokyo.

Frankel, Jeffry. 1993. *On Exchange Rates*. Cambridge: MIT Press.

Freeman, Richard B. 1995. "The Limits of Wage Flexibility in Curing Unemployment." *Oxford Review of Economic Policy* 11 (1): 63–72.

(ed.). 1994. *Working Under Different Rules*. New York: Russell Sage.

Frey, Bruno and Friedrich Schneider. 1978. A Politico–Economic Model of the UK." *Economic Journal* 88: 243–53.

Friedman, Milton. 1968. "The Role of Monetary Policy." *American Economic Review* 58: 1–17.

Fukuyama, Francis. 1992. *The End of History and the Last Man*. New York: Basic.

Garrett, Geoffrey. 1993a. "The Politics of Structural Change: Swedish Social Democracy and Thatcherism in Comparative Perspective." *Comparative Political Studies* 25: 521–47.

1993b. "The Politics of Maastricht." *Economics and Politics* 5: 105–24.

1995. "Trade, Capital Mobility and the Politics of Economic Policy." *International Organization* 49: 657–87.

1997. "The Transition to Economic and Monetary Union." In Barry Eichengreen and Jeffry Frieden (eds.), *The Political Economy of European Integration: The Challenges Ahead*. Ann Arbor: University of Michigan Press.

Garrett, Geoffrey, and Peter Lange. 1986. "Performance in a Hostile World." *World Politics* 38: 517–45.

1991. "Political Responses to Interdependence: What's 'Left' for the Left?" *International Organization* 45: 539–64.

1995. "Internationalization, Institutions and Political Change." *International Organization* 49: 627–55.

Garrett, Geoffrey, and Deborah Mitchell. 1996. "Globalization and the Welfare State." University of Pennsylvania. Manuscript.

Garrett, Geoffrey, and Christopher Way. 1995. "The Sectoral Composition of Trade Unions, Corporatism and Economic Performance." In Barry Eichengreen, Jeffry Frieden and Jürgen von Hagen (eds.), *Monetary and Fiscal Policy in an Integrated Europe*. New York: Springer.

Gill, Stephen R., and David Law. 1989. "Global Hegemony and the Structural Power of Capital." *International Studies Quarterly* 33: 475–99.

Giovannini, Alberto. 1989. "Capital Taxation." *Economic Policy* 9: 345–86.

Golden, Miriam. 1993. "The Dynamics of Trade Unionism and National Economic Performance." *American Political Science Review* 87: 439–54.

Golden, Miriam, and Wallerstein, Michael. 1995. "Unions, Employers, and Collective Bargaining: A Report on Data for 16 Countries from 1950 to 1990." Paper presented at the Annual Meetings of the Midwest Political Science Association, Chicago.

Goldsmith, James. 1994. *The Trap*. New York: Macmillan.

Goldthorpe, John (ed.). 1984. *Order and Conflict in Contemporary Capitalism*. New York: Oxford University Press.

Goodhart, Charles. 1995. "The Political Economy of Monetary Union." In Peter Kenen (ed.), *Understanding Interdependence*. Princeton, N.J.: Princeton University Press.

Goodman, John B., and Louis R. Pauly. 1993. "The Obsolescence of Capital Controls?." *World Politics* 46: 50–82.

Heidenheimer, Arnold J., Hugh Heclo, and Caroyln Teich Adams. 1990. *Comparative Public Policy* (3d ed.). New York: St. Martin's.

Helpman, Elhanan. 1981. "An Exploration in the Theory of Exchange Rate Regimes." *Journal of Political Economy* 89: 865–90.

Herring, Richard J., and Robert E. Litan. 1995. *Financial Regulation in the Global Economy.* Washington, D.C.: Brookings Institution.

Hibbs, Douglas. 1987a. *The American Political Economy.* Cambridge: Harvard University Press.

    The Political Economy of Industrial Democracies. Cambridge: Harvard University Press.

Hicks, Alexander. 1988. Social Democratic Corporatism and Economic Growth." *Journal of Politics* 50: 677–704.

Hicks, Alexander, and Duane Swank. 1992. "Politics, Institutions and Welfare Spending in Industrialized Democracies." *American Political Science Review* 86: 658–74.

Huber, Evelyn, John Ragin, and John Stephens. 1993. "Social Democracy, Constitutional Structure and the Welfare State." *American Journal of Sociology* 99 (3): 711–749.

Huber, Evelyn, and John Stephens. 1995. "The Future of European Social Democracy." *Quo Vadis Europa 2000?* UCLA, March 16–18.

    1996. "Political Power and Gender in the Making of the Social Democratic Service State." Research Committee 19, International Sociological Association, ANU, August 19–23.

International Monetary Fund. Various. *Exchange Arrangements and Exchange Restrictions.* Washington, D.C.: IMF.

Iversen, Torben. 1996a. "Power, Flexibility and the Breakdown of Centralized Wage Bargaining." *Comparative Politics* 28: 399-436.

    1996b. "The Real Effects of Money." Harvard University. Manuscript.

Iversen, Torben, and Anne Wren. 1996. "Equality, Employment and Fiscal Discipline: The Trilemma of the Service Economy." Annual Meeting of the American Political Science Association. San Francisco, August 29–September 1.

Jackman, Robert. 1986. "Elections and the Democratic Class Struggle." *World Politics* 39: 123–46.

Kapstein, Ethan B. 1996. "Workers and the World Economy." *Foreign Affairs* 75: 16–37.

Katzenstein, Peter. 1985. *Small States in World Markets* Ithaca, N.Y.: Cornell University Press.

Keohane, Robert O. and Joseph Nye. 1977. *Power and Interdependence.* Boston: Little, Brown.

King, Mervyn, and Don Fullerton (eds.). 1984. *The Taxation of Income from Capital.* Chicago: University of Chicago Press.

Kitschelt, Herbert. 1994. *The Transformation of European Social Democracy.* New York: Cambridge University Press.

Kletzer, Kenneth. 1996. "The Implications of Monetary Union for Fiscal Policy in

Europe." In Barry Eichengreen and Jeffry Frieden (eds.), *The Political Economy of European Integration: The Challenges Ahead*. Ann Arbor: University of Michigan Press.

Klingemann, Hans–Dieter, Richard I. Hofferbert, and Ian Budge. 1994. *Parties, Policies and Democracy*. Boulder, Colo.: Westview.

Kobrin, Stephen J. 1996. "The Architecture of Globalization." In John Dunning (ed.), *Globalization, Governments and Competitiveness*. New York: Oxford University Press.

Kramer, Gerald. 1971. "Short–Term Fluctuations in US Voting Behavior." *American Political Science Review* 65: 131–43.

Krieger, Joel. 1986. *Reagan, Thatcher and the Politics of Decline*. Cambridge: Polity.

Krugman, Paul. 1994. "Past and Prospective Causes of High Unemployment." In *Reducing Unemployment*. Federal Reserve Bank of Kansas City.

Kurzer, Paulette. 1993. *Business and Banking*. Ithaca, N.Y.: Cornell University Press.

Lange, Peter, and Geoffrey Garrett. 1985. "The Politics of Growth." *Journal of Politics* 47: 792–827.

Lange, Peter, Michael Wallerstein, and Miriam Golden. 1995. "The End of Corporatism? Wage Setting in the Nordic and Germanic Countries." In Sanford Jacoby (ed.), *The Workers of Nations*. New York: Oxford University Press.

Lash, Scott, and John Urry. 1987. *The End of Organized Capitalism*. Madison: University of Wisconsin Press.

Lassard, Donald R., and John Williamson (eds.), *Capital Flight and the Third World*. Washington, D.C.: Institute for International Economics.

Laver, Michael, and Ian Budge (eds.). 1993. *Party Policy and Coalition Government in Western Europe*. London: Macmillan.

Laver, Michael, and Norman Schofield. 1990. *Multiparty Government: The Politics of Coalition in Europe*. New York: Oxford University Press.

Layard, Richard, Stephen Nickell, and Richard Jackman. 1991. *Unemployment: Macroeconomic Performance and the Labor Market*. New York: Oxford University Press.

Leiderman, Leonardo, and Assef Razin (eds.). 1994. *Capital Mobility: The Impact on Consumption, Investment and Growth*. New York: Cambridge University Press.

Lewis–Beck, Michael. 1988. *Economics and Elections*. Ann Arbor: University of Michigan Press.

Lindbeck, Assar, et al. 1994. *Turning Sweden Around*. Cambridge: MIT Press.

Lindberg, Leon, and Charles Maier (eds.). 1985. *The Politics of Inflation and Economic Stagnation*. Washington, D.C.: Brookings Institution.

Lindblom, Charles. 1977. *Politics and Markets*. New York: Basic.

Lipset, Seymour Martin. 1961. *Political Man*. Baltimore: Johns Hopkins University Press.

Lucas, Robert E. 1972. "Expectations and the Neutrality of Money." *Journal of Economic Theory* 4: 103–24.

——— 1988. "On the Mechanics of Economic Development." *Journal of Monetary Economics* 22 (July): 3–42.

Mackie, Thomas, and Richard Rose. 1991. *The International Almanac of Electoral History* (3d ed.). New York: Free Press.

Mankiw, N. Gregory. 1990. "A Quick Refresher Course in Macroeconomics." *Journal of Economic Literature* 28: 1645–60.

Martin, Andrew. 1984. "Trade Unions in Sweden." In Peter Gourevitch et al., *Unions and Economic Crisis*. Boston: Allen & Unwin.

McKenzie, Richard, and Dwight R. Lee. 1991. *Quicksilver Capital: How the Rapid Movement of Wealth Has Changed the World*. New York: Free Press.

McKeown, Timothy. 1991. "A Liberal Trade Order? The Long–Run Pattern of Imports to the Advanced Capitalist States." *International Studies Quarterly* 35: 151–72.

McKinnon, Ronald I. 1988. "Monetary and Exchange Rate Policies for International Financial Stability." *Journal of Economic Perspectives* 2: 83–103.

Mendoza, Enrique, Gian Marie Milesi–Ferreti, and Paul Asea. 1996. "On the Effectiveness of Tax Policy in Altering Long–Run Growth: Harberger's Superneutrality Conjecture." CEPR Discussion Paper No. 1378.

Milner, Helen V., and Robert O. Keohane. 1996. "Internationalization and Domestic Politics: An Introduction." In Robert O. Keohane and Helen V. Milner (eds.), *Internationalization and Domestic Politics*. New York: Cambridge University Press.

Moene, Karl–Ove, and Wallerstein, Michael. 1992. "The Decline of Social Democracy." In Karl Gunnar Persson (ed.), *The Economic Development of Denmark and Norway since 1870*. Gloucester: Edward Elgar.

1995. "How Social Democracy Worked." *Politics and Society* 23: 185–211.

Moses, Jonathan. 1994. "Abdication from National Policy Autonomy: What's Left to Leave?" *Politics and Society* 22: 125–48.

Mundell, Robert. 1962. "A Theory of Optimal Currency Areas." *American Economic Review* 51 657–65.

Nickell, Stephen and Brian Bell. 1995. "The Collapse of Demand for the Unskilled and Unemployment Across the OECD." *Oxford Review of Economic Policy* 11: 40–62.

Norpoth, Helmut, Michael Lewis–Beck, and Jean–Dominique Lafay (eds.). 1991. *Economics and Politics: The Calculus of Support*. Ann Arbor: University of Michigan Press.

OECD. 1987. *Structural Adjustment and Economic Performance*. Paris: OECD.

1992. *Economic Surveys – Finland, 1991/1992*. Paris: OECD.

1993. *Taxation in OECD Countries*. Paris: OECD.

1994. *OECD Jobs Study*. Paris: OECD.

1995a. *Income Distribution in OECD Countries*. Social Policy Studies No. 18. Paris: OECD.

1995b. *Aging Populations, Pension Systems and Government Budgets*. Working Papers No. 68.

1996a. *Economic Outlook 59*. Paris: OECD.

1996b. *Enhancing the Effectiveness of Active Labor Market Policies*. Paris: OECD.

Ohmae, Kenichi. *The End of the Nation State*. New York: Free Press.

Olson, Mancur. 1965. *The Logic of Collective Action*. Cambridge: Harvard University Press.

1982. *The Rise and Decline of Nations*. New Haven: Yale University Press.

Palfrey, Thomas R. 1984. "Spatial Equilibrium with Entry." *Review of Economic Studies* 51: 139–56.

Pauly, Louis. 1995. "Capital Mobility, State Autonomy and Political Legitimacy." *Journal of International Affairs* 48: 369–88.

Pempel, T. J. 1978. "Japanese Foreign Economic Policy." In Peter Katzenstein (ed.), *Between Power and Plenty*. Madison: University of Wisconsin Press.

Perotti, Roberto. 1996. "Growth, Income Distribution and Democracy: What the Data Say." *Journal of Economic Growth* 1: 149–87.

Persson, Torsten, and Guido Tabellini. 1994. "Is Inequality Harmful for Growth?" *American Economic Review* 84: 600–21.

Phelps, Edmund S. 1968. Money–Wage Dynamics and Labor Market Equilibrium." *Journal of Political Economy* 76: 687–711.

1994. *Structural Slumps*. Cambridge: Harvard University Press.

Pierson, Paul. 1994. *Dismantling the Welfare State*. New York: Cambridge University Press.

1996. "The New Politics of the Welfare State." *World Politics* 48: 143–79.

Piven, Frances Fox (ed.). 1991. *Labor Parties in Postindustrial Societies*. New York: Oxford University Press.

Ploug, Niels. 1996. "Welfare State – Consistent Attitudes in a Changing World." The Danish National Institute of Social Research, Center for Welfare State Research.

Polanyi, Karl. 1944. *The Great Transformation*. Boston: Beacon.

Pontusson, Jonas. 1992. "The Political Economy of Class Compromise: Labor and Capital in Sweden." *Politics and Society* 20: 305–32.

1996. "Wage Structure and Labor Market Institutions in Sweden Austria and Other OECD Countries." Institute for European Studies, Cornell University. Manuscript.

Pontusson, Jonas, and Peter Swenson. 1996. "Labor Markets, Production Strategies and Wage–Bargaining Institutions: The Swedish Employers' Offensive in Comparative Perspective." *Comparative Political Studies* 29: 223–50.

Przeworski, Adam, and John Sprague. 1986. *Paper Stones: An History of Electoral Socialism*. Chicago: Chicago University Press.

Przeworski, Adam, and Michael Wallerstein. 1982. "The Structure of Class Conflict in Democratic Capitalist Societies." *American Political Science Review* 76: 215–38.

1988. "Structural Dependence of the State on Capital." *American Political Science Review* 82: 11–30.

Quinn, Dennis P., and Carla Inclan. 1997. "The Origins of Financial Openness." *American Journal of Political Science* (forthcoming).

Regini, Marino. 1996. "Still Engaging in Corporatism? Some Lessons from the Recent Italian Experience of Concertation." Eighth International Conference on Socio-Economics, Geneva, 12–14 July.

Richardson, J. David. 1995. "Income Inequality and Trade: How to Think, What to Conclude." *Journal of Economic Perspectives* 9: 33–55.

Rokrik, Dani. 1996. "Why Do More Open Economies Have Larger Governments?" NBER Working Paper Series. No. 5537.

1997. *Has Globalization Gone Too Far?* Washington, D.C.: Institute for International Economics.

Romer, Paul M. 1990. "Endogenous Technological Change." *Journal of Political Economy* 98: 79–102.

Roubini, Nouriel and Jeffrey Sachs. 1989. "Government Spending and Budget Deficits in the Industrial Countries." *Economic Policy* 8: 100–32.

Rowthorn, Bob. 1992. "Corporatism and Labor Market Performance." In Jukka Pekkarinen, Matti Pohjola, and Bob Rowthorn (eds.), *Social Corporatism: A Superior Economic System?* Oxford: Oxford University Press.

Ruggie, John Gerard. 1983. "International Regimes, Transactions and Change: Embedded Liberalism in the Postwar Economic Order." In Stephen D. Krasner (ed.), *International Regimes* (Ithaca, N.Y.: Cornell University Press).

1995. "At Home Abroad, Abroad at Home." *Millenium: Journal of International Studies* 24: 507–26.

Saint–Paul, Gilles. 1996. "Exploring the Political Economy of Labor Market Institutions." *Economic Policy* 23: 263–316.

Sala–i–Martin, Xavier. 1992. "Transfers." NBER Working Paper Series. No. 4186.

Scharpf, Fritz. 1988. "Game Theoretical Interpretations of Inflation and Unemployment in Western Europe." *Journal of Public Policy* 7: 227–57.

1991. *Crisis and Choice in European Social Democracy*. Ithaca, N.Y.: Cornell University Press.

Schmitter, Philippe C. "Interest Intermediation and Regime Governability in Contemporary Western Europe and North America." In Suzanne D. Berger (ed.), *Organizing Interest in Western Europe*. New York: Cambridge University Press.

Schwartz, Herman. 1994. "Small States in Big Trouble." *World Politics* 46: 527–55.

Shonfield, Andrew. 1965. *Modern Capitalism*. New York: Oxford University Press.

Slemrod, Joel. 1995. "What Do Cross–Country Studies Teach Us About Government Involvement, Prosperity and Economic Growth?" *Brookings Papers on Economic Activity* 2: 373–431.

Soskice, David. 1990. "Wage Determination: The Changing Role of Institutions in Advanced Industrialized Countries." *Oxford Review of Economic Policy* 6: 36–61.

Stark, David and László Bruszt. 1997. *Postsocialist Pathways: Transforming Politics and Property in East Central Europe*. New York: Cambridge University Press (forthcoming).

Steinmo, Sven. 1993. *Taxation and Democracy*. New Haven: Yale University Press.

Stiglitz, Joseph. 1986. *The Economics of the Public Sector*. New York: Norton.

Strange, Susan. 1986. *Casino Capitalism*. New York: Basil Blackwell.

Summers, Lawrence, Jonathan Gruber and Rodrigo Vergara. 1993. "Taxation and the Structure of Labor Markets." *Quarterly Journal of Economics* 108: 385–411.

Summers, Lawrence and Vinod Thomas. 1993. "Recent Lessons of Development." *World Bank Research Observer* 8: 241–54.

Swank, Duane. 1995. "Eighteen Nation Pooled Time Series Data Set, 1955–1992." Marquette University. Manuscript.

1996. "Funding the Welfare Sate, Part I." Presented at the Annual Meetings of the American Political Science Association, San Francisco, August 29–September 1.

Swenson, Peter. 1991a. "Labor and the Limits of the Welfare State." *Comparative Politics* 23: 379–99.

1991b. "Bringing Capital Back in, or Social Democracy Reconsidered." *World Politics* 43: 513–34.

Taylor, Alan M. 1996. International Capital Mobility in History. NBER Working Paper Series. No. 5743.

Thelen, Kathleen. 1993. "European Labor in Transition." *World Politics* 46: 23–49

Tobin, James. 1972. "Inflation and Unemployment." *American Economic Review* 62: 1–18.

Traxler, Franz. 1994. "Collective Bargaining: Levels and Coverage." In *OECD Employment Outlook*. Paris: Organization for Economic Cooperation and Development.

Visser, Jelle. 1991. "Trends in Trade Union Membership." In *OECD Employment Outlook*. Paris: Organization for Economic Cooperation and Development.

Wade, Robert. 1996. "Globalization and Its Limits." In Suzanne Berger and Ronald Dore (eds.), *National Diversity and Global Capitalism*. Ithaca, N.Y.: Cornell University Press.

Wallerstein, Michael. 1995. "The Impact of Economic Integration on European Wage–Setting Institutions." Prepared for the Conference on the Political Economy of European Integration. University of California, Berkeley, April 20–22.

Wallerstein, Michael, and Adam Przeworski. 1995. "Capital Taxation with Open Borders." *Review of International Political Economy* 2: 425–55.

Western, Bruce. 1995. "A Comparative Study of Working Disorganization: Union Decline in Eighteen Advanced Industrial Countries." *American Sociological Review* 60: 179–201.

Williamson, John (ed.). 1994. *The Political Economy of Policy Reform*. Washington, D.C.: Institute for International Economics.

Wood, Adrian. 1994. *North–South Trade, Employment and Inequality*. Oxford: Oxford University Press.

World Bank. 1997. *World Development Report: The State in a Changing World*. New York: Oxford University Press.

Zevin, Robert. 1992. "Are World Financial Markets More Open?" In Tariq Banuri and Juliet Schor (eds.). *Financial Openness and National Autonomy*. New York: Oxford University Press.

INDEX

Page numbers followed by f and t refer to Figures and Tables.